From Many Centuries

From Many Centuries

A COLLECTION OF
HISTORICAL PAPERS

by

Francis S. Betten, S.J.

PROFESSOR OF HISTORY IN MARQUETTE UNIVERSITY

Essay Index Reprint Series

BOOKS FOR LIBRARIES PRESS
FREEPORT, NEW YORK

Imprimi Potest:
PETRUS A. BROOKS, S.J.
Praep. Provinciae Missourianae

Nihil Obstat:
RAPHAEL N. HAMILTON, S.J.
Censor Deputatus

Imprimatur:
✠ SAMUEL ALPHONSUS STRITCH
Archiepiscopus Milwaukiensis

Junii 29, 1938

First Published 1938
Reprinted 1968

LIBRARY OF CONGRESS CATALOG CARD NUMBER:
68-16910
PRINTED IN THE UNITED STATES OF AMERICA

Preface

SOME of these papers are plain presentations of important conditions and happenings, putting them upon a wider background and entering more into detail than ordinary textbooks can do. Others conduct the reader to the original sources of our knowledge and enable him to see for himself in what way historical statements arise from the searching and close examining of the information preserved for us in the documents of the past.

This collection is divided into two Parts. Part One is general, consisting of fifteen articles arranged roughly in chronological order, and concluded by a longer essay on the life of St. Peter Canisius. In Part Two are grouped together several papers, mostly of greater length, that deal with events and conditions of the seventh and eighth centuries.

May this volume be of some service to students of history in and out of schools.

FRANCIS S. BETTEN, S.J.

Marquette University
April 27, 1938
Feast of St. Peter Canisius

Introduction

FEW American scholars have done more for the increase and diffusion of historical knowledge than the venerable author of this collection of essays. As I write these lines in tribute to his contribution to contemporary historiography, Father Betten has just passed his seventy-fifth birthday. His life has been about equally spent in his own native land, Germany, and here in the United States where for almost forty years he has taught the historical sciences in the Jesuit colleges and universities of Buffalo, St. Louis, Cleveland, and Milwaukee.

Out of a surprisingly large number of occasional essays in various periodicals Father Betten has chosen nineteen, most of them in the fields he has made particularly his own: medieval institutions and the Counter Reform. The volume is divided into two sections: the first, containing fifteen essays which range from the Acts of the Apostles to the late Jesuit historian, Hartmann Grisar. The second section contains four essays on subjects which may justly be said to be the special work of a lifetime, namely the period of St. Bede and St. Boniface.

Probably, the one essay many will be delighted to see reprinted is that on St. Peter Canisius (1521-1597) whom a grateful nation rightly calls the "Second Apostle of Germany." The period of the Counter Reform has yet to find a competent historian, and this essay will undoubtedly inspire some of our younger

Catholic scholars to enter this unworked area of research.

Father Betten's best known books are *The Ancient World, Historical Terms and Facts,* and *Ancient and Medieval History.* These textbooks are so widely used today that his name is well known to thousands of high school and college students and teachers. It is not given to every research-scholar to be able to write entertainingly on the subjects of interest to him, and it is not given to every Catholic scholar to approach his subject with an objectiveness that makes for a calm, though positive, interpretation of facts and movements which are under dispute with historians not of his Faith.

These two gifts Father Betten possesses in a remarkable degree.

Many citations might be given from his first essay to show how clearly he grasps the historian's duty in regard to a truthful presentation of the past. In speaking to Catholic historical writers, he says: "When choosing a subject for either article or address we may feel inclined to give preference to these points which are often misrepresented by non-Catholics. These are, indeed, of great importance and should be treated fearlessly. Nor should we fight shy of the dark sides in the life of the Church or her members and ministers. The full truth is always in favor of the Church."

This last sentence might well serve as a sub-title to Father Betten's volume, for its effect is seen in his "Tudor Queens: a Comparison" and in his essay on the pontificate of Clement VIII. It takes courage to write that France in the last decade of the sixteenth century "badly needed a religious reform," and to emphasize the fact as follows: "The material devastations caused by the Huguenot wars were terrible, but not the worst of the evils. Seven of the fourteen archbishoprics and almost forty of the one hundred bishoprics were vacant; and many of the actual bishops had been intruded into their dioceses illegally and were leading the life of secular noblemen. In wide territories the morality of the clergy, secular and regular, was deplorable."

Probably, the most striking evidence in this volume of Father Betten's dispassionate love of the truth can be found in his essay on the part Cardinal Bellarmine had in the case of Galileo, and in his estimate of the work of Father Hartmann Grisar, S.J., wherein he pays a tribute to a scholar of his own native land and trained in the same school: "Inflexible in all points where truth came into question . . . his [Grisar's] objective was simply to represent things as they appear when seen through the medium of honest and unbiased historical research, whether favorable or unfavorable to those who advocate or condemn them."

The full burgeoning of Father Betten's scholarship may be seen in his essay on St. Peter Canisius. Herein the reading of a host of books in all languages has been epitomized, and we see more distinctly than ever the causes and the effects of the religious revolt of the sixteenth century which has split the Christian Church asunder, perhaps forever.

In the second section of this volume we find rich treasures in Father Betten's essay on Bede and in his treatment of the controversy between St. Virgil and St. Boniface. Bede he pictures as the great model of the ecclesiastical historian; and there is a significant message in the following admonition: "A word for us Americans. St. Bede wrote his history of the

Anglo-Saxon Church before it was too late; before all
the documents referring to those times had perished;
before all those had died who could assist him by their
word-of-mouth contributions. We of America are not
much further removed from the beginnings of the
Catholic Church in this country than he was from
those of his. We should now write our history. A good
beginning has been made. But we need more than one
Bede. Our country and our Church offer too great a
variety of facts to be happily consolidated by any one
man. God grant that St. Bede multiply himself in our
midst."

It is naturally a distinct pleasure to the present
writer to call the reader's attention to the fact that the
larger part of this volume appeared in the pages of
the *Catholic Historical Review,* the official organ of
the American Catholic Historical Association, of
which Father Betten was one of the founders in 1919,
and to place on record the more important fact that
for the past nineteen years no one has had a larger
share in the progress of the Association than the
venerable professor of history in Marquette University.

This volume is not a valedictory. It is but another
proof of an ever-increasing interest in the history of
the Catholic Church. It is a harbinger of what needs
to be written to bring her history closer to the knowledge of the members of that Faith.

The Society of Jesus whose training produced a
scholar like Father Betten, the Catholic University
of America which has so largely profited by that erudition through the *Review,* the host of friends Father
Betten has won during these many years of devotion
to his science, the generation of students he has trained
through lectures and seminars, the generous spirit who

has made the publication of this volume a reality, and all who love historical truth will welcome this well-chosen group of essays.

PETER GUILDAY

Catholic University of America

Table of Contents

PART ONE: GENERAL

PART TWO: THE SEVENTH AND EIGHTH CENTURIES

PART ONE

GENERAL

I

THE INCREASE AND THE DIFFUSION OF HISTORICAL KNOWLEDGE [1]

BY its Constitution the American Catholic Historical Association declares its object to be "to promote study and research in the field of Catholic history." Both study and research are to be promoted, and evidently not only among the members of the Association but in wider circles as well. In fact nothing could be more desirable to the Association than to be instrumental in making every American Catholic a genuine student of Catholic history within the limits of his opportunity.

These two terms, research and study, seem to indicate two phases of endeavor: the increase of historical knowledge and its diffusion. *The amount of historical knowledge depends entirely upon research,* and can be augmented by no other means. We can communicate to others just so much concerning the events of the past, secular as well as ecclesiastical, as the sources referring to each individual fact have taught us, and farther we are not allowed to go. The panegyrist may say no more in glorification of his hero than is vouched for by the sources. In defending a Pope against accusations we must rely completely and exclusively upon the result of the labor of those who have investigated the

[1] Paper read at first Annual Meeting of the American Catholic Historical Association, Washington, D. C., December 27, 1920. Reprinted with some changes from *Catholic Historical Review,* Vol. VII (1921-1922), pp. 141-151.

sources. Whatever is beyond that may be material for a novel or a pious romance, but it is not history.

Nor can our historical lore be added to except by the same means: research, investigation, examination, of the sources. Considered in itself, the amount of historical information which is contained in the archives of ecclesiastical and secular offices, the books of the libraries of the world, the inscriptions found on the walls of ancient buildings or in and on sepulchres, the remains of art and handicraft, the oral traditions —this amount is practically boundless. But all the evidence which these witnesses of the past are able to give avails us nothing, unless there are those who listen to them, who take down and sift and combine their testimony, and then communicate to us what they have learned and discovered. So far as this has been done—and it requires much labor, energy, and patience—so far does our actual historical knowledge reach, and no farther. There is no other way of extending its boundaries than the same toilsome method of research, the *investigationis labor et mora,* laborious and enduring investigation, as Pope Leo XIII says in his Brief on Historical Studies.

One of the most instructive instances of such an increase in historical knowledge in consequence of research is the early history of the Hellenic lands. Some fifty years ago we had only hazy notions of the conditions of these islands and coasts and their population prior to the year 1000 B. C., but investigations, continued perseveringly for years, have brought to light the fact that many centuries before that date the shores of the Aegean Sea were alive with the activity of highly cultured races; and although our knowledge is still far from satisfying our curiosity, it is surprising how much we know either with certainty or with a high degree of probability.

Sometimes the increase of historical knowledge consists in the correction of errors. These, says Leo XIII, must be refuted *adeundis rerum fontibus*, "by going directly to the sources." For centuries the French Pope, John XXII (1317-1334), was held up to the desecration of mankind as a miser, a cruel and greedy despot, who by all means fair and foul gathered untold millions chiefly for the benefit of unworthy relatives and left behind an enormous treasury. But when Pope Leo XIII had opened the Papal archives to the students of history, German and French Catholic scholars set to work examining the account books of John XXII, which are still extant, and after years of laborious research their publications forced the accusers of John XXII to retreat.

Instances like this may serve to convince us more fully of the fact that genuine historical knowledge extends just so far as the investigation of the sources has blazed the way, and that therefore research work is the most important function of the science of history. If on the other hand some historical view, say, on the migration of the nations, or on the character of the invaders of Spain, is once accepted by historians of repute, we may indeed be inclined to doubt it, but we have no right to declare it unfounded unless we prove our differing view from sources, *adeundis rerum fontibus*. We must either find sources not utilized by our adversaries, or we must show that the sources used by them have been misunderstood or misinterpreted. Unproven assertions can carry no weight, however brilliantly they may be proposed.

To render this all-important function of research easier, and to make it possible to a larger number of students, great enterprises have been undertaken by individuals, by learned societies, and by the governments of various states. There are the magnificent collections of European sources brought out chiefly by public subsidies: the *Monumenta Germaniae Historica* with its long row of volumes, referring in the first place to the history of Germany and German nations; the *Collection de Textes pour servir a l'Étude de l'Histoire,* published by France. These and numerous other collections, some general, some confined to particular phases or events, as, the Council of Trent, the Avignon Period, the French Revolution, put many scholars in a position to engage in useful research work far away from the place where the documents are preserved. The very latest progress in this line has been made by enlisting the services of the art of photography, thus reproducing not only the words of the documents but the very shape they have in the original.

Historical societies as well as state governments furthermore promote research work by subsidizing able workers or paying for the publication of their books, which often are of such a nature that the sale alone would never reimburse the publisher, much less leave anything over for the author. In some important cities, so-called *Historical Institutes* have been established to serve as headquarters for original work in archives, libraries, and other depositories of historical documents. The City of the Popes, above all, offers the most valuable information concerning the history of the whole world, including countries as far distant as Greenland. From a list printed in 1903 it appears that there were in Rome at that date Historical Institutes maintained by Holland, Belgium, Hungary, Italy, France, Austria, Prussia, and by the Görres Society of the German Catholics.

The fact that many of these Institutes are presumably manned by non-Catholics should not disconcert us too much. Those of the non-Catholic historians of our days who work directly on the sources and from the sources, as a class, honestly and sincerely seek the truth and nothing but the truth. More than one Protestant fable has been forever relegated to the scrapheap by the labor of fair-minded non-Catholics. Indications are that the number of such unbiased investigators is on the increase. It is not the non-Catholic research workers that rehash the oft-refuted slanders against us and our Church, but chiefly the little fry of penny-a-liners who concoct the "historical contributions" for the Sunday editions of the newspapers.

Let us hope, then, that our new American Catholic Historical Association will soon be able to contribute a considerable share to the increase of sound historical knowledge by vigorously promoting historical research. Let us hope that men will be found fitted as well as willing to undertake the toilsome task of gathering and examining sources and throwing the light of the past, the only light which really illumines, upon the events of the past. Let us hope that our Association will be in a position to assist these workers both by competent advice and, if need be, by financial aid, especially by securing a market for the fruits of their patient labor.

We now come to our second point, the *Diffusion of Historical Knowledge*. History is no occult science. Its teachings are not to be the privileged possession of a small initiated caste. It participates in the general character of all good things, the tendency to diffuse itself. *Bonum est diffusivum sui.* If, therefore, we mean to treat history as its nature demands, the promotion of a general study of this noble branch must be part of our program.

We welcome the appearance of books written in a more popular vein. Happily many even of those works, which for the first time disclose the true character of a period or fact directly from the sources, are cast in such a language as to appeal to the average educated reader. This is the case with Janssen's *History of the German People,* especially as re-edited by Pastor, that epoch-making work on the century of the Reformation; with the *Histories of the Popes* both by Pastor and Mann; while the *Life of Luther* by Grisar represents as some think rather "hard reading."

Most popular books do not go directly to the last sources but utilize the results of the labor of others. They may not be so deep, but they are no less useful for the diffusion of actual knowledge in a larger public. Works of this kind have indeed the right of existence. No less a person than Pope Leo XIII refers to them when he says that, after the more ponderous works which are based immediately upon the testimony of documents have once been produced, the next step would be to pick from these the more prominent points and clothe them in an appropriate language for wider circles. Although this is not so difficult, it will, he says, produce no little good, and it is an occupation to which even the most excellent minds may devote their industry.

All these publications will carry the message of Catholic history to a larger public and will rouse and foster a general interest in the events of the Christian past. Let us encourage the writers and publishers of historical works by buying them for ourselves and for our friends—books often make a very appropriate sort of present—or even for those outside the Faith. Let us recommend them in our private conversation, and, perhaps, in public addresses. There was a time when, locally at least, an indulgence could be gained by every effort made to contribute to the spread of good books. The fact that this inducement no longer exists does not make activity of this kind less commendable or useful for the public weal.

Many attempts have been made to secure the acquisition of Catholic books by our public libraries. The articles on this subject contributed to our Catholic press, and the pamphlets published for this purpose, make quite a literature. Although the results were nowhere so satisfactory as was anticipated, we should not overlook the fact that in consequence of this campaigning, thousands of Catholic books are now on the shelves of our public libraries, and are at the disposal of all who want to see the Catholic side of many an historical controversy. Often liberal-minded Catholics or wide-awake societies have presented these works. But while these endeavors are certainly commendable, we should remember the Catholic libraries even more. There are in some cities large Catholic book collections open to general use. There are the libraries of sodalities and other societies. It is incredible how much good these insignificant libraries are apt to do. There are, last not least, the libraries of our Catholic academies, high schools, and colleges. They should indeed not be overlooked. The Apostle exhorts us to show our interest first of all to the *Domestici Fidei,* the members of the household of the

Faith. It is here that above all a sound scientific and historical sentiment must be fostered. Book donations need not necessarily go into the hundreds of dollars. If we think it beneath our dignity to donate a dollar or two, a book costing a dollar or two is always an appropriate gift, provided only it will fit into the collection to which it goes.

On the same line with books or pamphlets are articles for our magazines and newspapers. They must, however, be adapted to the character of each individual publication. Editors of Sunday papers may think that such contributions are not timely enough, and those of illustrated magazines may complain that they have no suitable pictures to go with them. Some editors do not themselves know what history is. Many, however, will gladly give space to historical contributions from time to time. In this way the widest circles can gradually be trained up to a taste for history, which, to use again the words of Leo XIII, possesses so eminent a degree of nobility, *quae tantum habet nobilitatis*. This would also serve to improve the general tone of our Catholic press and to increase its educative power.

Another very powerful means to the same effect would be the giving of addresses and lectures on historical topics. There are indeed many other subjects which may fittingly and usefully be treated in Catholic societies and in public and private assemblies, but the history of the Church certainly belongs to those topics that are most appropriate. Let the officers and members of societies propose such lectures, or ask for them. Even those organizations which do not exist expressly for literary or educative purposes can occasionally put a lecture on the program of their meetings. Illustrations by lantern slides, though not at all indispensable, will certainly be welcome. Half a dozen slides are often enough to enliven a lecture of thirty or forty minutes.

In connection with addresses or talks or lectures, may I be permitted to make an humble suggestion to the Reverend clergy? The history of the Church is after all a sacred subject. It is more. It is elevating, encouraging, inspiring. The Kingdom of Christ is the only organization on earth which has ever been victorious and emerged triumphantly from the most terrible trials. Could not its vicissitudes and successes be made the subject of sermons? No doubt the people would go home with a renewed love for the immortal Church after listening to an account, say, of the Vatican Council; of the spiritual and other achievements of *monasticism;* of the Council of Trent; of the Western Schism and its conclusion; of the silent glories of the Catacombs; of the great missionary enterprises of all ages. Not every subject, however, is equally suitable to every congregation. Nor may the spiritual character of the sermon be sacrificed. A lecture on Church history may be somewhat like a sermon, but a sermon must never become a mere lecture.

Thus both the printed page and the living voice may be made serviceable in the diffusion of historical knowledge. There is one place, however, where both appear combined, and that is the class room of the parochial and high school and the lecture hall of the college. The American Catholic Historical Association harbors the greatest respect for the hundreds of history teachers who have been and are doing excellent work in imparting sound historical doctrine, both secular and ecclesiastical, to the thousands of our young people. We know their ideals fully coincide with ours. Let them continue giving to their charges, many of whom some day, we hope, will be members of our organization, that systematic knowledge of past events which does not lose itself in details. The average student who leaves our schools should possess a bird's-eye view of the matter or period treated, so as to be able to place other matters of which he subsequently hears or reads in their proper position. History moreover participates in the character of philosophy, which is a *Cognitio rerum ex causis,* a knowledge of things from their causes. History is not a succession of disconnected events, but a continuous stream in which under the influence of human liberty, subsequent events are dependent in a great variety of ways and degrees upon those which preceded them.

We cannot come forward with special recommendations to our history teachers, but we can well give them our support. Encouragement is everywhere gratefully received. I know of a gentleman who during a number of years offered a premium for an historical essay in the college which he had himself attended. He allowed the college authorities to designate the subject. As they naturally chose some point which was in close connection with the matter actually treated, the noble donor's act added noticeably to the zest of the students in the daily work of their history classes.

These few words on the activity of the schools lead to a general remark on historical publications, in particular essays, articles, and historical lectures. The author should always try to indicate the historical and chronological whereabouts of his subjects. This is often done without any special effort because the topic imperatively demands it. But it should never be neglected completely. We smile at the custom of some ancient writers, to start from the creation of mankind and hurry in some short passages over long distances of time to arrive at the point where their own subject begins. There is some reason for this quaint practice. It proceeded from the desire of placing the event they wish to narrate in the proper time and surrounding. In our case a few sentences referring to nation or country or contemporary personages would serve the same purpose. If thus the event under discussion appears in its real setting, the reader will derive a double benefit from the perusal of the article. Those brief indications will enable him to acquire a more orderly insight into the things of the past, to see the coherence of historical facts, and to rectify or widen his knowledge of the main streams of the fortunes of a nation or of the Church at large, or of the development or cessation of some important movement.

One more remark in conclusion. When choosing a subject for either article or address we may feel inclined to give preference to those points which are often misrepresented by non-Catholics. These are, indeed, of great importance and should be treated fearlessly. Nor should we fight shy of the dark sides in the life of the Church or of her members and ministers. The full truth is always in favor of the Church. A truthful presentation of such matters will relieve the minds of the Catholics, who have these things thrown up to them in offices and factories. They rejoice to see that the Church was victorious in the end; or that, if overpowered by physical force she is the only party which deserves our sympathy and enthusiasm. But on the other hand we should not forget that the office of history is not principally apologetic. Man's hand is able to wield the sword, but woe to mankind when all hands wield the sword and none are left for other occupations. History, too, must be ready for defence, but its primary and surpassing aim is of a positive nature, the setting forth of those facts which make up the glorious past of the Church, whether they have ever been the object of attacks and misrepresentations or not. I fear we are a little too much under the impression that, unless non-Catholic authors of the intolerant variety have directed our attention to it by slanders or vilifications, an historical event is not worth knowing about. No, the Church would be great and her history fascinating, even if she were not impugned by any malicious writers.

II

"Parthians and Medes and Elamites . . ."[1]

WHEN listening to the Epistle read on the Feast
of Pentecost we receive an official report of the descent
of the Holy Ghost, and of the first wonderful effects
of the new divine power on earth. This selection from
the Book of Books in more than one way rouses our
interest.

And when the days of Pentecost were accomplished, they
were all together in one place. And suddenly there came a sound
from heaven, as of a mighty wind coming. And it filled the
whole house where they were sitting. And there appeared to
them parted tongues as it were of fire, and it sat upon every
one of them. And they were filled with the Holy Ghost. And
they began to speak in diverse tongues according as the Holy
Ghost gave them to speak.

Now there were dwelling at Jerusalem Jews, devout men,
out of every nation under heaven. And when this was noised
abroad, the multitudes came together, and were confounded in
mind, because that every man heard them speak in his own
tongue. And they were all amazed and wondered, saying:

"Behold, are not all these that speak Galileans? How then
have we heard every man our own tongue wherein we were
born—(1) Parthians, and (2) Medes, and (3) Elamites, and
inhabitants of (4) Mesopotamia, (5) Judea, and (6) Cappadocia, of (7) Pontus, and (8) Asia, (9) Phrygia, and (10)
Pamphylia, (11) Egypt, and the parts of Lybia about (12)
Cyrene, and strangers from (13) Rome—Jews also and
proselytes—(14) Cretans and (15) Arabians: we have heard
them speak in our own tongues the wonderful works of God."
—Acts ii, 1-11.

[1] From *The Historical Bulletin,* Vol. VI (1927-1928), pp. 33-37.

This long list of nations and countries and cities, all of which we meet more or less frequently in secular history, rightfully attracts our attention. Such enumerations do not often occur in historical sources.

The author on the whole proceeds from east to west. But several deviations from this direction would seem to introduce an element of disorder. Are these deviations due to carelessness on the part of the author, or were they intentional? What after all did St. Luke have in view when he wrote this long series of geographical names? These and similar questions are deserving of a brief investigation.

The context shows that St. Luke wishes to give to his readers a correct idea of the greatness of the "Miracle of the Tongues," which the Holy Ghost worked in the Apostles. His readers are to realize what he means when he says, there were in Jerusalem "Jews, devout men, from every nation under heaven." We know from other sources, that the larger cities and provinces of the Roman Empire had a more or less considerable number of Jewish inhabitants. These were the "Jews of the Dispersion." The fifteen names embodied in St. Luke's text indeed help us to conceive how vast the area was from which the Pentecost multitudes had come. The territory covered by these names is about three million square miles. It is about three thousand miles long, from Parthia to Rome, with Jerusalem in the center, and about a thousand miles wide. Men from all these parts were in Jerusalem, and listened with astonishment to the message of the Apostles.

But St. Luke has still another object in view, an object much more important than the vastness of the territory from which these multitudes had come. He wishes to show and bring home to his readers the multiplicity of languages spoken in these lands. This aim guided him in the selection of the names, for they in fact indicate so many different languages. Hence many cities and countries which possessed large Jewish colonies, are omitted, for the reason that they did not represent different languages. Before we enter upon this point, however, some words of explanation are necessary concerning several of the names.

The terms, *Jews also and proselytes,* have no geographical meaning. The word "Jews" is here taken in its strictest sense, denoting real physical descendants of Abraham. It is here opposed to the "proselytes," that is, converts from paganism, who either completely submitted to the Mosaic law, or at least worshipped and prayed to the true God and observed His commandments. This class was worth mentioning, not only because it was rather numerous, but also because a large percentage of it belonged to the higher strata of society. These proselytes, too, had their representatives among the astonished crowds which assembled around the Apostles on that memorable Pentecost day. The phrase is put among the geographical names because it belongs to all of them, and probably also because this position helps to give a pleasing variety to the enumeration; possibly the proselytes were noticeably numerous among the "strangers from Rome." The Jews of the Dispersion, as we here learn from the sacred text, spoke the languages of the nations in which they were born, and looked upon these languages as their mother-tongues. "Behold, are not all these that speak Galileans? How then do we, every man, hear our own tongue wherein we were born?" (The more educated among them, however, also knew the

Hebrew of the Old Testament, and perhaps even the Aramaic tongue then spoken by the people of Palestine.)

Asia does not refer to the continent of that name, but to the Roman province of "Asia," which was situated in the west of Asia Minor on the coasts of the Aegean Sea. The city of *Cyrene* harbored a large colony of Jews. We know of Simon of Cyrene, who was forced to assist Our Lord in carrying the cross. *Lybia* was at that time a current name of what we now call Africa.[2] By *Arabians* are probably meant the dwellers in the cities along the coast of the Red Sea rather than the nomadic tribes of the interior of the country.

Since the days of Alexander the Great the Greek language was very common in the Orient. Many of the Jews of the Dispersion, too, spoke Greek. (It was for the benefit of those living in Alexandria that the Bible had been translated into Greek. In Alexandria the Jews occupied a large quarter, and enjoyed almost complete self-government.) But in the provinces and kingdoms of Asia the native languages had by no means disappeared. These languages still dominated in those regions farther removed from the coast of the Mediterranean, which had remained rather free from Greek influence. These regions form the bulk of the countries which St. Luke enumerates in his list. He is very careful to forestall the objection that a considerable part of his cities and nations are Greek-speaking. In "Asia" he has reached the eastern coast of the Aegean Sea, where Greek was the native tongue. From there he at once turns back to the interior, to the country of Phrygia. Pamphylia, which comes next,

[2] See Betten, *Historical Terms and Facts*, Boston, under "Africa."

though on the coast, was only partly hellenized. He does not mention any of the cities, districts, and islands of Greece proper, though there were Jewish settlements all over the Greek world. He does not really include the city of Cyrene, which was entirely Greek, but speaks of "the parts of Lybia about Cyrene," the inland districts, which were inhabited by natives with their own language. He passes by Greek-speaking Alexandria, which he might have introduced as the representative of the land of Egypt, just as he makes Latin Rome the representative of Latin Italy. There were Jews in the land of Egypt, who did not speak Greek but employed the native Egyptian tongue, the forerunner of the present Coptic.[3] Thus St. Luke's roster of fifteen cities and countries stands for the same number of languages. The mentioning of both "Asia" and Crete at first sight seems to be a duplication, since we know Crete as a Greek speaking land. But the caution with which St. Luke in the other parts of his list avoids any such repetition suggests that either the Greek dialect of Crete formed a separate language of its own, or that beside the Greek ancient Cretan was still spoken throughout the island.

Thus the apparent disorder in St. Luke's enumeration, which superficial readers may be tempted to attribute to carelessness or even ignorance, in reality shows St. Luke to have possessed quite an exact knowledge of the countries of which he speaks, and to have made an excellent selection among the lands where

[3] The Jewish historian, Josephus Flavius, clearly distinguishes between the Jews living in Egypt and those of Alexandria. "The Jews have places assigned to them in Egypt, wherein they dwell, over and above what is particularly allotted to them in Alexandria." *Antiquities of the Jews,* Book XIV, Chap. VII, 2. Josephus bases his statement on Strabo, the Greek geographer.

Judaism existed. His contemporaries were in a still better position than we to realize the weight of his demonstration. Besides his well calculated deviations give to his set of names an air of leisure and prevent the impression of pedantry. This latter aim is evidently the purpose of his last move. After reaching Rome, the western boundary of the territory he wishes to cover, he returns with one bold sweep by way of Crete and Arabia, right through the middle of his field, to the neighborhood of Jerusalem.

The interpreters of Holy Scripture tell us that the "Miracle of the Tongues" may have taken place in two ways. The Apostles may have spoken in different languages to crowds of listeners from different countries; or they spoke in one language to crowds consisting of men from different nations, and were understood by each listener in his own tongue. We are at liberty to choose whichever interpretation pleases us best.

Though St. Luke's aim is to demonstrate the greatness of the "Miracle of the Tongues," he also contributes, at least by way of confirmation, towards our knowledge of the Jews of the Dispersion. Two other writers have drawn up similar lists, but with no other purpose than to show the extent of the Jewish race. The author of the First Book of the Maccabees—this book was written between 106 and 63 B. C.—informs us that the Roman senate sent letters to those nations among which Jews had settled (I Macc. xv, 21-23), warning them not to molest the Jews in any way, and ordering that Jewish conspirators who had fled to them, be extradited to the High Priest Simon. The letters were dispatched to the Kings of Syria, Pergamum, Cappadocia, and Parthia; and to the regions of

Lampsacus, Sparta, Delus, Myndus, Sicyon, Caria, Samus, Pamphilia, Lycia, Halicarnassus, Cos, Sidon, Aradon, Rhodus, Phaselia, Gortyna, Cnidus, Cyprus, Cyrene—twenty-three in all.

A similar list of names is found in a letter addressed to Emperor Cajus Caligula (37-41 A. D.). The Emperor is to be impressed with the great extent of the Hebrew nation. If he grants the favor asked for, he will be blessed by the inhabitants not of one city but of "ten thousand in every region of the habitable world," in Europe, Asia, and Africa. Expressly mentioned are Egypt, Phoenicia, Syria, Pamphylia, Cilicia, Bithynia, Pontus, Thessaly, Boeotia, Macedonia, Aetolia, Attica, Argos, Corinth, Peloponnesus, Euboea, Cyprus, Crete. "I say nothing," the writer continues, "of the countries beyond the Euphrates, for all of them . . . and Babylon, and all the neighboring satrapies, which have any importance whatever, have Jews settled in them." [4]

Most of the names given in both these lists refer to Greek-speaking localities, and have therefore been omitted by St. Luke.

Among the three lists, that of St. Luke, though compiled for a special purpose, is unquestionably the grandest. It brings out the extent of Judaism most clearly. In its stately progress over three million square miles it alights only on the more important regions. It points out a number large enough to be imposing but not so large as to cause confusion, and moves with deliberate ease over oceans and countries, never losing sight of its aim to demonstrate the greatness of the "Miracle of the Tongues."

[4] *Philo Judaeus,* tr. by C. D. Yonge, London, 1855, Vol. IV, p. 161.

III

WHAT, AFTER ALL, ARE THE CATACOMBS [1]

WE all have heard of the Catacombs. They are underground places where, so we are told, the first Christians assembled for the celebration of the sacred mysteries, and where they also buried their deceased brethren. This general and often very hazy idea of the Catacombs unfortunately is not rarely mixed with errors concerning the very nature of these sacred places. It is the aim of these few lines to rectify some of these misconceptions.

First, we must give up thinking of them as subterranean chapels or even larger rooms. *The first and dominating purpose of the Catacombs was to serve as burial places.* In ancient Christian literature they are known as "Cemeteries." The name "Catacombs" was coined for them nearly a thousand years after they had gone out of use. The Catacombs consist of long corridors or galleries hollowed out in the rock, with recesses on both sides for the bodies of the deceased. There are four or five such recesses one above the other. These cavities opened sidewise, and the bodies were deposited parallel to the direction of the corridor. After a body was placed in its "loculus" the opening was tightly closed by a slab of marble or was walled up with bricks. As a rule the galleries were about ten feet high. But in some places they have double that height and have ten or twelve rows of

[1] *Catholic Daily Tribune,* July 2, 1935.

tombs above one another. In such cases the workers had deepened the floor of the galleries and continued making recesses below those already existing. The corridors are very narrow, about four or three feet wide, so as to have just space enough for a body to be carried through to its resting place.

These tomb-lined galleries form a real network, crossing one another commonly at right angles. Below the first level thus created a second, third, and even a fourth and fifth level was excavated. Before me is a detailed map of the *Catacomb of Domitilla*. Students of the Marquette School of Engineering measured on it the length of the corridors on the first and second levels and found that, if stretched out in one line, they would amount to more than seven miles. The third and fourth levels of this catacomb are much less extensive, but would probably add another mile. The *Catacomb of Calixtus*, as far as it has been investigated and its dimensions measured, counts fourteen miles. Reliable authorities give it as their estimate that the Catacombs of Rome alone contain about four hundred miles of galleries, and that more than two million Christians have been buried in them.

The Catacombs do not form one continuous system but are *found in groups, each of which is named after some Saint or other prominent person,* such as the ones just mentioned, of Domitilla and Calixtus. There are around Rome forty or more such underground cities of the dead, some of which have not yet been explored. All the Catacombs are situated outside the old walls of ancient Rome, since burial inside the walls was not permitted by Roman Law. Modern Rome, however, expands far beyond the old walls, and so it is that Catacombs may be located below the buildings of the present city.

The Roman Law declared sacred and inviolate all places, large or small, where human bodies had been interred, and the Catacombs were no exception to this rule. They enjoyed this privilege even during times of fierce persecution. We know only of two cases of violation of this sepulchral sacredness in Rome, namely, in the years 257 and 303 A.D.

That these long narrow passages *could not have been intended as places for assemblies* of the faithful or as dwellings is evident. They were the ordinary burial grounds of the Roman Christians. Some scholars say that the Catacombs were started in Rome about 150 A.D., though others prefer the last decades of the first century. Since that time the bodies of those who departed in the Lord found their resting place in these ever and ever lengthening silent galleries, both in the years of actual persecution and when the Church enjoyed periods of peace. Shortly before the year 300, and after Constantine had given full liberty to the Church, small parts of the Catacombs received more elaborate treatment and were often beautifully ornamented. This was especially the case with the so-called "Cubicula," rooms or chapels, which were fitted out for divine services though they were never very large. Most of the pictures of the Catacombs which are current in our books represent such "Cubicula." While these "Cubicula" with their wall paintings and the articles found in them (and elsewhere in the Catacombs) are of the greatest importance for the history of the times, these representations are apt to mislead us as to the real character of the Catacombs. We rarely see pictures representing one of the narrow passages with the recesses opened, and still more rarely, if ever, photographs of so-called "intact galleries," showing the niches still sealed with marble or masonry, and perhaps marked with names or other inscriptions written or engraved on them.

Many are under the impression that during the whole period of persecution, which lasted roughly three hundred years, all the Christians in all the parts of the wide Roman world entombed their dead in Catacombs. This is another error. *Such underground burial places, as the Roman Catacombs were, existed only in certain spots.* Rome possesses the larger number known to us. Others have been discovered near Naples in Italy, Syracuse in Sicily, some cities in northern Africa, and isolated places in Gaul, and these are partly as interesting as those of Rome, though few of them have been explored. But generally speaking the Christians buried their deceased brethren the same way as we inter our own.

During the last century one could find the statement that the Catacombs were simply *quarries* adapted to burial purposes. *Nobody who knows the nature of these underground narrow galleries* will entertain such an idea. Quarrymen would certainly have widened the avenues considerably both to be able to cut out larger blocks and to carry them away with greater ease. As one writer says, one can make a quarry out of a Catacomb, but not a Catacomb out of a quarry. It is true, however, that entrances to Catacombs were often located in quarries or sand pits. The rock by the way in which the Roman Catacombs were hollowed out is of *a soft kind* (*tufa*), which can be cut with a knife, though, on the other hand, it has no little resistive power. The making of the Catacombs was, therefore, much simpler than mining operations. No propping of the sides or ceilings was necessary. In some other places, such as Naples, Christian Catacombs are formed in a much harder kind of rock, and the passages as well as the larger cavities (*cubicula*) could be made wider than at Rome.

After the Church had entered upon the era of complete peace under Constantine in 313, the Roman Christians continued burying in the Catacombs until the beginning of the fifth century, when this mode of burial was made unsafe by the inroads of the barbarians. The bodies of the Saints were gradually transferred to the city churches, the shadow of oblivion sank upon the Catacombs and by the year 800 they were completely forgotten. They were rediscovered by chance in 1578 and became the object of systematic study by Catholic archeologists.

Numerous pictures and inscriptions are found in the Catacombs, all of which testify that the faith of those who deposited their deceased friends and relatives in them had the same Faith which we ourselves profess. They believed in the immortality of the soul, the Redemption by Jesus Christ, the Blessed Sacrament, the veneration of the Saints and their intercession for those on earth. The words of piety and hope, which we read on the graves of the Catacombs would fit on our tombstones as well. Let us greet with reverence and love those millions of our brethren whose mortal remains expect the day of the Resurrection in the countless recesses of those mysterious galleries. "Their hearts and ours are one." When "the hour cometh wherein all that are in the graves shall hear the voice of the Son of God," we shall meet all these men and women, not as strangers but as children of the same family of Our Lord and Redeemer.

BOOKS ON THE CATACOMBS:

BARNES, ARTHUR, *The Early Church in the Light of the Monuments*. New York, 1920.

MARUCCHI, ORAZIO, *The Evidence of the Catacombs for the Doctrine and Organization of the Primitive Church*. New York, 1929.

IV

PTOLEMY THE GEOGRAPHER [1]

CLAUDIUS PTOLEMAEUS, the great Alexandrian of the second century after Christ, is probably known to many of us only as the man who gave a definite shape to the theory that the earth is a globe situated in the center of the heavens, and that it is the point around which the sun and moon and stars move in daily and yearly cycles. The Ptolemaic System of the universe held undisputed sway in the minds of the learned and unlearned for nearly fifteen centuries. However, although historical atlases and even high school textbooks frequently give some world map under Ptolemy's name, his importance as geographer is not frequently alluded to. Yet Ptolemy is the true Father of our science of geography. It is he that perfected the art of cartography and introduced or cleared up the mathematical principles which still govern it.

I

Ptolemy's geographical ideas are chiefly contained in four books: the *Almagest*, the *Tetrabiblos*, the *Geography*, the *Astronomical Tables*.

The word *Almagest*, the title under which this work is commonly known, is Arabic. Its Greek title, translated literally into Latin, is *Syntaxis Mathematica*. But it is far from being a handbook of mathematics. It is

[1] *Thought*, Vol. IX (1934-1935), pp. 449-457.

rather a handbook of scientific astronomy. Here the author also treats of those facts which the present usage assigns to what we call "Mathematical Geography." The Geocentric System is here discussed and in particular the roundness of the earth explained and substantiated by a large number of interesting arguments, some of which are still found in present-day geographic primers.

The *Tetrabiblos* (a work consisting of four books) is almost wholly devoted to the pseudo-science of astrology. It is, indeed, odd that so serious a mind as Ptolemy's should have been subject to that rank superstition. He treats of the influence of the stars upon human life and human character with the same solemn mien with which he views the geographical longitudes and latitudes of cities and mountains. Countless people who cared little for the other works of the great Alexandrian knew the *Tetrabiblos,* which, indeed, was the cause of very much of Ptolemy's renown. The third work, the *Geography,* will occupy us in this article.

The fourth is a collection of astronomico-geographical tables of the longitudes and latitudes of prominent places, chiefly cities. These *Tabulae Manuales* are only now being recognized as a separate publication, whereas formerly they were frequently considered as a part, a sort of appendix, of the *Geography.* They have come down to us either in fragments attached to the *Geography* or in separate, but often very confused, individual manuscript codices. They were, however, really compiled by its great author after the other works had been completed, and in not a few cases items which occur also in the *Geography* have been corrected by Ptolemy himself according to better information.

2

The third work, commonly known as *Geography* is really the heart of the whole astronomico-geographical system of Ptolemy. Though six of its eight "books" are descriptive of countries and oceans, the author's real purpose was to furnish a systematic instruction on how to draw correct maps. Since the earth is a globe, any representation of its surface must be that of the surface of a globe. The drawing of maps on a real globe would be the most natural, but it has the disadvantage that one cannot see the whole of the globe-map at once glance. Moreover, since the inhabited earth (the *oikumene*) as far as it was known to Ptolemy, covered only a small part of the globe, the greater part of it would remain unused.

Ptolemy thus faced the problem of representing the spherical surface of the earth upon a flat surface, which, of course, is not possible without a sacrifice in accuracy. To reduce this sacrifice to a minimum and at the same time not to make the drafting of his maps too difficult, he devised several projections differing according to the size of territory to be represented by a map. His work is illustrated by three world maps, which cover the whole of the inhabited earth as far as known to him, and a large number of country and province maps. For the world maps he drew the middle meridian and the middle parallel as straight lines, while all the other meridians and parallels became curved. For the numerous country and province maps he still further simplified his network by omitting all curvatures. The parallels remained straight lines running east and west, and the meridians were straight lines converging towards the north. In this network he entered the individual cities, islands, and other points according to their geographical longitude and latitude. In his scientific way of procedure these two elements were to determine the place of a locality on the map; and he gives geographical longitude and latitude of some eight thousand places with all the exactness possible in his days.

It should be noted, however, that the genuine Ptolemaic world maps which have come down to us in the Greek manuscripts, do not show the projection described by Ptolemy in the text. World maps so drawn, though they may go by his name, are not found in the oldest and best Greek codices. The original maps were, perhaps during the master's lifetime and under his eyes, redrawn by another geographer, Agathodaemon, upon a similar projection with the meridians as straight lines converging towards the north, only the parallels being curved.

We now possess an excellent edition of this fundamental work of Ptolemy by Prof. Joseph Fischer, S.J., of Stella Matutina College, Feldkirch, Austria. Its title is: CLAUDII PTOLEMAEI GEOGRAPHIAE CODEX URBINAS GRAECUS 82, PHOTOTYPICE DEPICTUS. EDIDIT JOSEPH FISCHER, S.J., CONSILIO ET OPERA CURATORUM BIBLIOTHECAE VATICANAE.[2]

This brilliant publication consists of four volumes. One, in large folio, contains facsimiles in original size of the twenty-seven maps of the *Codex Urbinas Graecus* 82, the twenty-seven maps of the *Vaticanus Latinus* 5698, and three maps of the *Urbinas Graecus* 83. The other three volumes are in large quarto size.

[2] Published for the Bibliotheca Apostolica Vaticana by Otto Harrasowitz, Leipzig, Germany, and by R. J. Brill, Leiden, Holland.

They furnish, first, a complete facsimile edition of the text of the *Urbinas Graecus* 82, which is the best existing Greek manuscript, with a paleographic and critical Introduction to this Greek text, by Pio Franchi de Cavalieri; second, a monograph entitled *Prodromus,* a volume of more than 600 large quarto pages on the life and works of Ptolemy, especially his *Geography,* its character, transmission by manuscripts, and influence in ancient and modern times; third, a volume with twenty-four Greek, two Arabic, and fifty-seven Latin maps, taken from a large variety and number of manuscripts. The *Prodromus* and the last named (third) volume of facsimile maps are Professor Fischer's personal contributions.

3

Father Joseph Fischer, S.J., has been styled the Sherlock Holmes of ancient maps. He has been discovering, working, and studying in the field of geography for more than thirty-eight years. His successes began in 1899 when he was rummaging among the literary treasures of the library of Wolfegg Castle, an ancient residence of the Prince of Waldburg-Wolfegg-Waldsee. He there came upon a copy of the oldest map with the name of America, issued in 1507 by Martin Waldseemüller, and another map of 1516 by the same famous cartographer. There also came to light a beautiful manuscript of Ptolemy's *Geography,* which proved to have served in the preparation of two early printed editions of the Alexandrian scholar's work (Ulm, 1482 and 1486).

In the desire of unearthing more copies of Waldseemüller's maps Father Fischer, with the financial support of the Austrian Institute of History, made three journeys to Italian, French, and English libraries. He found no Waldseemüller maps, but an unexpectedly large number of manuscript maps and texts, both in Greek and Latin, of the *Geography* of Ptolemy. He resolved in consequence to devote his studies entirely to investigations concerning that great Alexandrian geographer. Monsignore Achille Ratti, then Librarian of the Ambrosian Library in Milan, now Pope Pius XI, called his attention to a Greek manuscript of the same work, which that library possessed, a hint which turned out to be of unexpected importance. This manuscript was different from all those so far seen by Father Fischer. It helped to lead him to the recognition of a double class of Greek manuscripts, which he calls the A-Redaction and the B-Redaction. Both have a very definite character. Those of the A-Redaction have only twenty-six part maps, beside the world map; those of the B-Redaction have, beside the world map, sixty-four or even sixty-eight country and province maps. They are also distinguished by the number and character of the entries of localities, and by the place they assign to the maps in the text. The numerous Latin translations made from the Greek text are all based upon Greek codices of the A-Redaction.

Father Fischer's greatest discoveries were made in the Vatican Library. Among its very numerous Ptolemy manuscripts there was especially the *Codex Urbinas Graecus* 82, dating back to the year 1200 A.D., which turned out to be the best Greek copy of the A-Redaction; and the *Codex Urbinas Graecus* 83, a remarkable copy of the B-Redaction; and besides the *Codex Vaticanus Latinus* 5698, which holds a key position among the Latin translations.

After much consultation with scholars of all coun-

tries, the authorities of the Vatican Library conceived
the plan of the grand publication which is now completed, and which is preeminently based upon the life-
long labors of its editor, Father Fischer. This noble
edition will for a long time remain the standard work
for the study of Ptolemy's Geography, and will have
to be consulted also, when the great geographer's other
works are made the subject of research.[3]

4

We should add a few remarks concerning Ptolemy's
lasting influence on the science of geography.

Within the Greek-speaking world the *Geography*
served as source of information and as regular textbook. We still have a manuscript of a summary produced by some schoolmaster for his pupils, and this
summary was probably not the only one. In view of the
enormous disturbances in the Orient, especially the
destructive wars waged by Mohammedan Arabs and
Turks and the havoc wrought by them in all kinds of
literary productions, is it surprising that we can still
point to the works of at least five scholars of the
Hellenistic times who based similar geographical elucubrations on it, partly with their own emendations.
Even a geography written in Syriac betrays its dependence on Ptolemy in numerous points. We also
know that, at the time when Arabic scholars cultivated

---

[3] The results of Father Fischer's first historio-geographical studies
are laid down in the following publications: (i) *The Discoveries of
the Northmen in America,* by Jos. Fischer, S.J., London, 1903. (ii)
*Die älteste Karte mit dem Namen Amerika aus dem Jahre 1507
und die Carte Marina aus dem Jahre 1516 des M. Waldseemüller,
herausgegeben von Jos. Fischer, S.J. und Fr. R. von Wieser,* Innsbruck, 1903. (iii) *Map of the World by Jodocus Hondius of the year
1611.* Edited by Edw. L. Stevenson and Jos. Fischer, S.J., New York,
1907.

the science of ancient Greece, several translations into Arabic had been in existence. The large Latin work of Ammianus Marcellinus is most extensively based on Ptolemy.

But generally speaking the Roman Latin writers kept aloof from the Greek geography. Ptolemy was too scientific for them. They cared nothing for geographic longitude and latitude. All they wanted was the information how to get from one place to another. So they simply compiled lists of stations leading, for instance, from Rheims to Trier. Or they produced their itinerary maps, in which they entered the cities or towns and marked the distance between them by the number of miles, without regard to the position of places or countries on the globe. On the most famous of them the Mediterranean Sea has the shape of a somewhat broad river.[4]

The Middle Ages made no progress in the line of geography or map making. If they followed any lead it was that of the Romans, and they emancipated themselves from this also. One of the most brilliant productions of that period, the *Mappa Mundi* of Ebstorf, shows an idealized world. The upper part of the map is devoted to Asia, the lower left side to Europe, and the lower right side to Africa. All the cities appear with turreted walls. Jerusalem forms the center, and is a broad picture, like Rome, each of these cities being larger than the island of Sicily. Maps like these were

---

[4] *Weltkarte des Castorius, genannt die Peutingersche Tafel* (reproduced in colors), by Konrad Miller. Strecker und Schröder, Stuttgart, Germany, 1885. To this belongs the large work, *Itineraria Romana: Römische Reisewege, an der Hand der Tabula Peutingeriana dargestellt,* by Konrad Miller, 1915. Same publisher. On both, see "Roman Itineraries," by F. S. Betten, article in *Catholic Historical Review,* Vol. VII (1921-1922), pp. 296-302.

not intended to serve any practical purpose, much less were they based upon mathematical reality.

Both the idealistic medieval map and the ultra-practical Roman map were bound to remain without influence upon the development of geographical cartography. It was the arrival in the West of the Ptolemaic maps and their scientific explanations which started the geographical movement from which our present-day maps have originated. The change came with the Renaissance. About 1400, at the time of the great Councils, began the influx of Greek scholars into Italy, who brought with them, among other treasures of Greek literature, copies of the Alexandrian geographers' work. Italy took to Greek geography. As early as 1406, the first translation of the *Geography* into Latin was finished by Jacobus Angeli, and thereafter Latin translations, complete and partial, with and without maps multiplied rapidly. More than thirty of them, all dating from the fifteen century, are described by Father Fischer in his *Prodromus,* and he omits countless others. Ptolemy's *Geography* really became the vogue. By the middle of the century the art of printing was invented, and at once several complete expensive printed editions of the large work helped to satisfy the common desire for this particular study.

Then followed the period of the great geographical discoveries, when new islands, coasts, and countries were continually reported to the astonished geographer, none of which fitted into the mathematical network devised by Ptolemy. However, the eager students of the Alexandrian were equal to the task. At first they helped themselves by producing sectional maps for the new lands. But soon, very soon indeed, geographers courageously set to work at a grander problem, the production of a new world map with all the radical alterations and extensive additions demanded by the discoveries. In this way the Ptolemaic map itself more and more fell into oblivion. For two centuries the ancient details slowly gave way to the new entries and improvements and by 1800 every trace of the Ptolemaic inheritance had entirely disappeared from the maps of the modern world.

5

Yet though the name of the great Alexandrian no longer figures on the new maps, he remains the Father of modern geography and cartography. He had laid down for all times to come the principles on which any representation of the earth's surface must be based, namely, scientific observation and mathematical exactness. The mapmakers of the fifteenth and following centuries continued in his footprints when they charted the world according to their more extensive acquaintance with geographical facts. It was the study of Ptolemy's "Geography" which had schooled their minds in correct geographical thinking and in the appreciation of exact cartographical representation. A problem of no small magnitude lay before them, namely, the devising of a network of meridians and parallels suitable to cover the whole earth, not merely one fourth of it. But they had not been studying their Ptolemy in vain. The large wall maps of the world by Waldseemüller and others testify to their ability in handling map projects of the largest dimensions. Nor was their work a revolution against Ptolemy's teachings. On the contrary, it grew organically from the masterpieces they had admired in the works of the Alexandrian geographer and from the principles they had learned from him. They were his disciples, probably the greatest and boldest he ever had. They themselves have been outstripped by successors who were helped by an ever-increasing amount of geographical facts and by a vast improvement in the instruments, methods, and materials available for map construction. But the principles have remained those of the Alexandrian Claudius Ptolemaeus.[5]

[5] Although we are a very young country we have known how to possess ourselves of a goodly number of ancient and very ancient manuscripts. Also some Ptolemy codices are on this side of the ocean.

The Henry E. Huntington Library and Art Gallery, San Marino, California, owns a Latin Ptolemy manuscript called the *Wilton Codex*, of the fifteenth century.

Five codices are in the Newberry Library, Chicago, Illinois. Two of them, in Latin, date from the fifteenth century; one in Greek, from the fourteenth; one, consisting of maps only, probably of the early sixteenth century; and one, with a German commentary, possibly also of the early sixteenth century.

The famous Latin *Ebner Codex*, of the fifteenth century, is in the Public Library of New York. Closely connected with this precious possession is a publication by E. L. Stevenson, one of the foremost American geographers, a friend and collaborator of Father Fischer: *Claudius Ptolemaeus' Geography;* translated into English and edited by Edward Luther Stevenson; based upon Greek and Latin manuscripts and important late fifteenth and early sixteenth century printed editions; including reproductions of the maps from the Ebner manuscripts; with an introduction by Joseph Fischer. XVI and 167 pages in folio. (Published by the New York Public Library.)

V

CHRISTIANITY LEGALIZED—THE DECREE OF MILAN [1]

AFTER the battle of the Milvian Bridge, A.D. 312, in which the usurper Maxentius lost his life, Constantine the Great and Licinius remained the sole emperors of the Roman Empire, Constantine ruling the West, and Licinius the East. In the following year, 313, both emperors jointly issued the Decree of Milan, by which they gave full religious liberty to the Christians. More than any other document emanating from secular authority this Decree has "changed the face of the earth." Constantine was the prime mover. Licinius, though at that time not unfriendly to the Christians, probably gave his consent chiefly in deference to his mighty co-emperor. He always remained a pagan. Later on he began to disregard the Decree in the administration of his own provinces, and finally started again a persecution of the Christians. This and various other causes led to a war between the two rulers, which ended in a complete victory for Constantine.

The text of the Milan Decree is preserved by Lactantius, the Christian Cicero, in his work, *The Deaths of the Persecutors*. And there is a Greek translation of it in the *Ecclesiastical History* of Bishop Eusebius. This translation, however, seems to have been based

[1] *Catholic Historical Review,* Vol. VIII (1922-1923), pp. 191-197.

upon a Latin original, which in some small items disagreed from the Latin text of Lactantius. The professors of the University of Vienna, who edited Lactantius' writings in their *Corpus Scriptorum Ecclesiaticorum Latinorum* supplemented the Decree here and there by slight insertions from Eusebius. The English translation given below is made from the text so reconstructed, which may be found in the *Enchiridion Fontium Historiae Ecclesiasticae* by Conrad Kirch, S.J., Nos. 352, 353.

In A.D. 311 the arch-persecutor Galerius, driven to despair by the pains of a horrible disease of which eventually he died, had grudgingly permitted the Christians to practice their religion. But this Edict of Toleration (Latin text in Kirch, No. 349) did not restore confiscated property, and worse than this, it did not assure to the Christians the use of citizens' rights. The clause "provided they do nothing contrary to good order" allowed of very unfavorable interpretations. And the announcement that more detailed directions would be given to the magistrates was apt still more to tone down expectations. This Edict had been published also in the names of Constantine (who had never joined in the persecution) and Licinius. Both, too, must have sent out the detailed directions, spoken of in the document, though we have no means to ascertain whether these were identical in the realms of both. But, however this may be, the two emperors by the Decree of Milan expressly and unequivocally withdrew and cancelled all the restrictions of religious liberty which either might be deduced from Galerius' Edict or were contained in the special "instructions" and "communications" dispatched to the magistrates.

—The Milan Decree was addressed to the imperial governors.

Part I. I, Constantine Augustus, and I, Licinius Augustus, at a propitious juncture meeting in Milan, and taking under consideration the whole range of public interest and safety, have come to the conclusion, that among all matters conducive to the public weal those ought to be settled in the very first place, by which the reverence due to the Deity is safeguarded (to wit) that we give to the Christians as well as to all (others) free permission to follow the religion which each one chooses, in order that whatever Deity there is on the heavenly throne may be propitiated and show itself favorable to ourselves and to all that are under our power.

Hence, listening to the demands of both public welfare and sound reason, we have thought it our duty to enact that leave shall be refused to no one whatever who has given his heart either to the teachings of the Christians or to that (other) kind of religion which he himself feels to be the most suitable to him; so that the Supreme Divinity, worshipped by us with full freedom, may be able to show to us in all things its wonted favor and benevolence.

Thy Lordship will therefore take notice of our pleasure that all the restrictions which are contained in former instructions concerning the Christians (super Christianorum nomine) and which appear to be very ill advised (sinistra) and out of keeping with our clemency, are all and entirely cancelled; and that each and everyone desirous to observe the religion of the Christians may do so without any fear, and without any disadvantage to himself. We thought it our duty to ex-

press this to thy Lordship in the plainest terms, so that thou knowest we give to the aforesaid Christians free and unlimited permission to practice their religion. Thy Lordship understands, that for the tranquillity of our times the same freedom as to religion and observance is likewise expressly and liberally granted to others, so that everyone may enjoy the fullest permission to worship what he chooses. We take this step with the intention of preventing the appearance as if we meant to slight anything deserving of honor or religious veneration.

Part II. As to the Christians we deem it our duty to issue still another enactment, (namely) concerning the places (buildings) in which they formerly were accustomed to assemble, and about which a well-known rule was laid down in the communications sent heretofore to thy Fidelity. Those persons who appear to have bought these identical places either from our treasury or from anybody else shall restore the same to the Christians without money and without charging any price, setting aside all deception and delay. Likewise those who have received them as presents shall immediately surrender them to the same Christians. If the present owners, however, whether they acquired them by purchase or by gift, shall wish to receive anything (as compensation) from our bounty, let them apply to our representative, so that provision may be made for them also by our clemency. It will be thy duty to see to it that all this property be returned to the community of the Christians without any procrastination.

And since the Christians, as is well known, possessed not only those places where they used to meet, but also others which belonged not to individuals but to them as corporation, that is to the churches, we comprise all these in the aforesaid ordinance (of restitution). And thou wilt cause them to be returned without hesitancy and without litigation, to the same Christians, that is, to their corporation and communities; observing, however, the above mentioned caution (to wit) that those who faithful to our order restore them without charging any price may expect indemnity from our benevolence.

Conclusion. In all these affairs thou shalt be obliged to yield to the body of the Christians thy most efficacious assistance, to the end that our ordinance be carried out as speedily as possible, and that at the same time through our clemency care be taken of the maintenance of public order. In this way the divine favor towards us, which as expressed above we have experienced on the most momentous occasions, will forever prosper our future enterprises and the happiness of our people.

But in order that the tenor of this our gracious ordination may come to the knowledge of all, thou shalt have copies of it (i.e., of this proclamation) certified by thy signature, posted up everywhere, and shalt promulgate it broadcast; so that the firm determination of our clemency may not remain in obscurity.

By the first part of this Decree the emperors made Christianity another state religion, as those who professed it were declared to be no longer subject to any loss of civic rights or privileges, nor to any sort of political disability. Henceforth the followers of Jesus Christ could no longer be molested on account of their Creed. They now could plead in the courts, and could accept state offices without being obliged to perform the pagan ceremonies connected with them. In short, they now possessed in full reality all the privileges of

Roman citizens. Before the law they now stood on the same level as the rest of the population. On the other hand, the emperors were careful to emphasize strongly and repeatedly that they did not in any way think of curtailing the religious liberty and rights of the pagans, who still made up, perhaps, nine-tenths of the population. Seeing the sentiments of hatred and supreme contempt with which the pagans looked upon the Christians, the Edict must have had a stunning effect upon the adorers of the old Roman gods, while, no doubt, to the despised, persecuted, and hunted Christians it must at first have seemed "too good to be true."

It should be noted how clearly and consistently the unity of the Supreme Being is expressed in the Decree. This certainly was a blow against the current polytheistic ideas of paganism. It was not entirely an innovation, however, since the neo-Pythagoreans and the neo-Platonists had already attempted to consolidate the cult of the many gods and goddesses into something like a crude monotheistic system. But farther than the unity of the Godhead the authors of the Decree do not proceed. They do not declare the God of the Christians the One True God, and they prefer to use such indefinite terms as Deity. They expressly refuse to enter upon that question at all, leaving it to the individual to decide for himself "what Deity there is on the heavenly throne." Nor did either of the emperors profess himself a Christian. Licinius, of course, could not. And as to Constantine, it seems that although he recognized the favors he had received from the God of the Christians, and realized the unquestionable superiority of the religion of Jesus Christ, he did not yet see his duty to embrace that religion.

While thus Part One of the Decree secures to the Christian religious liberty and civic rights, Part Two does away with one of the worst consequences of the persecutions. Although the great period of church building was yet to come, many Christian temples had been erected during the time of peace which preceded the fierce persecution by Diocletian. Diocletian had ordered these churches to be destroyed or confiscated and put to other uses. Many had passed into private hands. All these buildings without any exception were now to be restored to the Christian communities, no matter how often they might have changed hands. With the churches themselves was to go all other property once held by the Christian congregations. The present owners were told to apply to the imperial treasury, if they desired indemnification. The amount they might expect was not specified. But this was hardly possible. Nor was it necessary because the treasury officers, in whose hands would practically lie the settlement of such cases, all being pagans, were certainly inclined to allow rather too much than too little.

It does not appear from the Decree, whether churches which had been destroyed were to be built up at public expense. But considering the later zeal of Constantine in raising Christian temples we may presume that he had made provision for the rebuilding of churches by other enactments of which we have no positive knowledge. We cannot doubt, either, that church property of any kind which was still under the control of the Fiscus now reverted to the Christians. This was at any rate a lesser burden for the imperial exchequer, it would seem, than the redemption of those possessions which had passed into private ownership. But outside of these two points the Decree is certainly

very definite, leaving absolutely no loophole. Nor does
the language of the Decree admit of the slightest
doubt as to the determination of the Caesars to see
their will executed.

The imperial order to restore the alienated church
property had for the Christians another consequence
of far-reaching importance, in that it recognized the
several ecclesiastical units as corporations with the
right of holding property.

But while insisting in strong terms upon the restitution of church property the Decree stated unmistakably that private property lost by the Christians in
consequence of persecutions did not come under this
head. Confiscation of possessions had been one of the
most dreadful penalties inflicted on the faithful Christians, and Constantine knew very well that the estates
and movables taken from rightful owners amounted
to immense value. If he did not order their restitution,
he must have had good reasons. Perhaps, it was the
opposition of Licinius that prevailed on him not to
raise this demand. Possibly, too, both emperors were
convinced that such a restitution would cause great disturbance in the civic body, and that the evil thus
brought upon the state at large would be much greater
than the benefit accruing to a number of individual
Christians. .

The Milan Decree was in the course of time followed up by other laws calculated to remove obstacles
which stood in the way of a wholesome development
of the Church. Constantine exempted the clergy from
the duty of accepting municipal offices, and from the
taxes imposed by Roman Law upon unmarried persons.
He enjoined the sanctification of the Sunday, and gave

expressly to the churches the right of acquiring property by testament. He provided for military chaplains; each legion was to have a certain number of clerics and a large tent to serve as church in the camp. He promulgated laws for the protection of women, children, and slaves, though in these points he did not venture to go so far as the moral law of the Church demands. In A.D. 321 he indeed ordered the restitution of confiscated private property of individual Christians.[2] But this order may have applied to some particular provinces only, or it may have been limited to losses suffered during the persecution of Licinius. An investigation on this point is beyond the scope of the present paper.

It has been asserted that this document, coming from the Emperors, was not an "Edict" in the strict sense of the word, but merely an order to the governors, a "Rescriptum," according to which the governors were to issue edicts or regulations to the effect of giving full liberty to the Christians. But let us consider the document itself.

There is certainly not the slightest trace of any such order to inferior officers. It is the Emperors themselves who "give to the aforesaid Christians free and unlimited permission to practice their religion." It is the Emperors themselves who order the restoration of Church property, concerning which the governors are not told first to declare that property forfeit, but to see to it that it be returned "without procrastination."

Concerning the imperial document, the governor is not told to make it the subject of a publication of his own, but to have copies of it made and posted up everywhere. (See last paragraph of the document.)

[2] Sozomenos, *Ecclesiastical History*, Book I, Chap. 8.

He will have to publish it such as it reaches his hands, *haec scripta,* (this proclamation) as written. The whole tenor, besides, shows that it was not considered as an instruction destined for one particular governor, especially the solemn introduction. Eusebius expressly calls it "Imperial Constitution."

Finally, there is visible in the whole document, in particular in the third paragraph of Part I, the fear it might be misinterpreted and its enforcement delayed. It is not probable, therefore, that the execution of it should have been entirely put into the hands and the good will of the governors, all of whom were pagans. They might first take their time for issuing their own proclamations, and then neglect to carry them out.

But even if we presume that the document was merely destined for the governors, its enormous importance remains the same, since all the governors' edicts received their whole force solely and entirely from this "Decree of Milan."

VI

The Death of a Medieval Sinner [1]

IN medieval history we occasionally meet with the report that men who had led a very sinful life and committed outrages of the worst kind against their neighbors and the Church, became converted upon their deathbed and received the sacraments. It is evident that this exterior conversion could not benefit their soul, unless it included a true contrition, by which the unfortunate man was sincerely sorry for his transgressions, and with his whole soul turned to God his Creator and Last End. We have reason to presume that this was commonly the case. Deep in the heart of medieval man was his strong Faith in the doctrines of the Christian religion. He knew that an eternity depended on his condition at the moment of death. And when that terrible moment was approaching, his Faith got the upper hand in his thoughts, and caused him to make his peace with God. It is interesting and instructive to read of the death of one such medieval sinner as told us by an eye witness. We refer to the Emperor Otto IV. After receiving countless benefits from Pope Innocent III, to whom indeed he owed the imperial crown; and after promising by the most solemn oaths that he would respect the rights of the Church; he became, almost immediately upon being crowned, the most determined enemy of Pope and Church, threw to the winds all his sworn pledges, and

[1] *Historical Bulletin,* Vol. VIII (1929-1930), pp. 8, 9.

brought misery and devastation upon countless communities and individuals. After a life of crime he was, in 1218 A.D., prostrated by sudden illness, and soon became convinced that death was fast approaching. Let the author of the *Origines Guelficae* tell us the rest.[2]

The illness which exhibited the worst symptoms of diarrhoea progressed with devastating rapidity, shattering in the shortest space of time his once healthy system. He had now spent eight years under excommunication, and though he had made a number of attempts to procure absolution from Rome, his efforts had been of no avail, as he remained stubborn in his refusal to fulfill the prescribed conditions. Only with death imminent could he come to see the matter in another light. On Tuesday, May 15th, 1218, the Cistercian abbot of Walkenried learned of the severe dysentery that had laid low the Guelf, and sent him red wine and apples to alleviate his sufferings. Otto sent word that he urgently wished to see the abbot the next day, his purpose being to give whatever security might be necessary for receiving absolution. As the Wednesday passed without the abbot appearing, the Emperor had the provost of the Cistercians of St. Buchard in Halberstadt called. To him he swore that he would submit to each and every command of the Pope, and received absolution, extreme unction, and holy communion from the provost. From then on to the day of his death, he communicated daily. On Tuesday the abbot of Walkenried arrived, and the sick man expressed to him his displeasure at the delay. He asked

[2] The report as here given is a translation from the work of Emil Michael, S.J., *Geschichte des deutschen Volkes vom dreizehnten Jahrhundert bis zum Ausgang des Mittelalters,* Freiburg im Br., 1915, Vol. VI, pp. 214-218.

him to go to the neighboring town of Goslar, and to return early on Friday. The Emperor was greatly delighted at his appearance on Friday morning, and caused all those present except the abbot, the other priests of whom there were nine, the Empress, and a few noblemen to withdraw from the room. Then he had a blanket spread out before the bed, rose from his sick-bed and remained standing upright, leaning upon the provost who had administered to him the sacraments of the dying. Then all sang with devotion that moving antiphon *Media vita,* so beloved in every affliction, especially in calamities of war: "In the midst of life we are surrounded by death. What other aid can we seek, than Thee, Oh Lord, who art justly angered by our sins? O most holy God, omnipotent and merciful Saviour, do not deliver us up to bitter death." At the invocation "O great God . . ." the sick man shed tears, raised his eyes and his hands to Heaven, and became dead to the world in silent prayer. Then he bade the priests put on their stoles. He himself laid down upon the blanket that had been spread on the floor, threw the end of the abbot's stole about his neck, and requested those present to pay close attention to what he was about to say: "Beneath this stole, I acknowledge to all of you that I have sinned grievously against the Chair of Peter, and that from the time that God had brought me to honor through the agency of the princes, who selected me unanimously for the kingship, and the Pope who after confirmation of that choice consecrated me Roman Emperor, I have through stubborn malice wronged the Pope himself together with the Roman Church and ill treated his envoys, and I also seriously injured other churches. Besides, Lord Abbot, at my absolution I have sworn upon the relics of Simon and Jude, which I had brought from Goslar, that I will bow in all things to the commands of the Pope, save the imperial dignity, to which I was legitimately elected and solemnly consecrated." (This reservation, the narrator adds, he expressed constantly and to everyone.) Thereupon he made a general confession, and added the following disclosure: "Since after my election and consecration to the Emperorship I did not know how I might prove my gratitude to the Lord God for that favor, I consecrated my body and soul to Him who had assumed the Cross for me, and on the departure from Rome called the Bishop of Cambrai apart and received from his hand the cross that I have worn unto this day about my neck, but have not revealed to anyone. I constantly waited for an opportune time, to undertake the pilgrimage in a manner befitting the imperial majesty, for the praise and glory of the Crucified One as well as for the redemption of the Holy Land. Nevertheless the devil has to this day succeeded in hindering the carrying out of this resolution." Thereupon the Empress unfastened the cross from his neck, and the abbot imposed it upon him a second time for the remission of his sins, with the injunction henceforth to bear it openly.

But the penitent was not yet satisfied. He had willow switches brought in, and now he requested that every priest take a switch thereof and scourge him, while he had stretched himself naked upon the floor. During this flogging the psalm *Miserere* was sung by those present. And he called out to his scourgers: "Come on, O scourge this sinner more vigorously!" At the conclusion of the psalm he urgently entreated that they scourge him still more, and all were moved to tears.

The prayers customary after the *Confiteor* were said, the *Misereatur* and the *Indulgentiam,* and though he thought he had not been scourged enough, he was lifted into his bed, and he was told that it was enough for him and for Almighty God; that it must not be carried to the point where blood would flow. After the Emperor again recovered some strength, he said to the Abbot: "Now go and eat, and then return immediately." After the latter's return, the Emperor again dismissed all with the exception of the Empress, a few of his secretaries and Count Henry of Waldenberg, and said, "Of what use is it to speak of my life? For indeed there is none of it left. It is better that we speak of something else, namely that we put everything in order. I pray that my testament be carried out unchanged, both as to the castles and the individual persons." He entrusted this to Count Henry with the task of going to Braunschweig and bringing from the great store of money that he, Otto, had there, 500 marks, which he wanted to give to the poor and to his servants. He then gave detailed directions about his burial. When those present shed tears, he comforted them saying: "Do not cry, because I shall not die to-day. To-morrow morning between 6 and 9 o'clock be ready for my passing on." And, the narrator adds, "so it happened."

About midnight between Friday and Saturday, the 19th of May, the venerable Bishop Siegfried of Hildesheim came to the sick-room. The dying man exhibited great joy on noticing him, repeated his earlier acknowledgment of his grievous sins against the Roman and other churches, gave the necessary guarantees, and after he had in accordance with his wishes received another scourging, was given absolution by the bishop also. The patient then conversed with the bishop much in detail regarding the welfare of his soul, gave him a written statement of the conditions under which he had received absolution, and had the imperial seal put upon this document.

In the morning of May 19, there ensued a considerable weakening of his condition, and the dying man said to those about him, "it seems I am losing my senses." Once more he asked of his confessor the last consolations of the Faith. They were given him, and shortly thereafter Otto IV was no more. He was buried according to his wishes in the church of St. Blase at Brunswick beside his first wife Beatrice and his parents.

*   *   *   *

This is indeed the death of a truly repentant sinner. On the point of meeting his Divine Judge, Otto began to realize the enormity of his crimes. He wished to do what he could to atone for them, and in this desire voluntarily inflicted on himself the severe acts of penance. With good reason did the two ecclesiastics who absolved him, says Father Michael, disregard the dying man's declaration concerning the imperial dignity. Otto must have been convinced that this had nothing to do with the reparations which he knew he was bound to make, and for which he had amply and minutely provided in his Testament. From the Testament, too, it is evident that he was far from expecting a full reinstatement into his imperial position.

"His testament, his death-bed confessions and acts of voluntary penance indicate that he was in earnest when he made the break with his entire past. Only a soul both strong and filled with genuine faith could thus turn around and disavow the mistaken policy of a full decade of years. In the last days of his earthly pilgrimage the dying prince directed that will power which he had so long displayed in the service of injustice towards higher and nobler aims, and if in his life he was never great, at least the victory he won in death over himself and the passions which he had permitted to dominate all his actions during so long a time, proved him to possess the greatness of a hero." [3]

[3] Michael, *op. cit.*, p. 220.

VII

A Belated Viking Adventure—The Kensington Stone [1]

THE Kensington Stone is one of the latest discoveries bearing on the history of America. To see it upon the right background we must briefly recall the daring expeditions of the Norse navigators to the northern lands of our continent. In 984, Eric the Red discovered Greenland, which grew into a prosperous little republic and maintained permanent trade and other relations with Iceland and Norway. About 1000, Leif, Eric the Red's son, asked for missionaries from Norway and introduced Christianity. The same Leif Ericson also discovered the coasts of American proper, and founded the colony of Vinland the Good somewhere in Nova Scotia or Massachusetts. It is commonly held that the last expedition on record to Vinland the Good was in 1121. *The Kensington Stone* will among other things add one more record to our knowledge of Scandinavian expeditions.

Kensington is a small village of some 300 inhabitants in Douglas County, near the western boundary of Minnesota. Here in 1898, a farmer discovered a stone thirty-one inches long, sixteen inches wide, and six inches thick, with an inscription in the Norwegian language, which covered one of its large sides and one of its narrow sides. It was written in runic script, and contained the date of A.D. 1362. It attracted the

[1] *The Historical Bulletin,* Vol. XII (1933-1934), pp. 66 ff.

widest attention chiefly among the Scandinavian settlers and naturally also in their European homeland.
Few inscriptions have been so carefully examined.
Everyone of its sixty words and each of its two hundred and twenty characters were subjected to a most
searching scrutiny. Facsimiles of the stone were exhibited in France and Norway and in numerous learned
societies in America. Geologists and chemists made
microscopic examinations of its surface and its sub-
stance, and philologists and historians eagerly studied
its text and message. By the year 1908 the stone had
simply been swamped under a deluge of addresses,
articles, and booklets. It was definitely set down as a
forgery.

The *Runes,* by the way, are a kind of script used by
the Teutonic nations, chiefly the Scandinavians, before
and long after the Migration of Nations. Their origin
is obscure, since the idea that they developed from the
Latin has been given up. Though the runes were also
used in the writing of books, the runic literature consists chiefly of inscriptions on wood, metal, and most
frequently on stone.

As stated the case of the Kensington Stone was lost.
But an ardent scholar of Runic literature, Mr. Hjalmar Holand, of Ephraim, Wisconsin, when visiting
the finding place, obtained the stone from the owner
in order to keep it as a curiosity in his home. While
reading and rereading the exactly chiseled lines of the
runes, he gradually began a new study. He reexamined
the literature, weighed again the arguments which
spoke pro and con, and came to the conclusion, that
though the stone might merely represent the work of
a counterfeiter, it so far had been rejected on false evidence. All the arguments put forth against its genuine-

ness really proved nothing, because all of them were based on false premises. The article in which the result of his investigations appeared provoked another flood of literature much larger than the first. Again scholars and learned societies in both continents studied, spoke, and wrote about the Kensington Stone, with the result, however, that all the difficulties gradually vanished, and that the inscription is now generally recognized to be a true historical record.

The text of the inscription is this:

We are 8 Swedes and 22 Norwegians on an exploration journey from Vinland over the West. We had camp by a lake wherein are two skerries [small rocky elevations], one day's journey north from this stone. We were out and fished one day. After we came home we found ten of our men red with blood and dead. Ave Maria. Save us from evil. We have 10 of our party by the sea to look after our ships, 14 days journey from this island. Year 1362.

When found the stone was entirely encircled by the roots of an aspen tree, which embraced it tightly and in their natural growth had even flattened themselves against its surfaces. The stone had therefore been lying in its position when the aspen tree was very small. In 1898, the tree must have been some seventy years old, which brings us back to about 1830. This was about twenty years before the State of Minnesota began to be settled by white men, and there were only some trappers and townsite speculators, who had other things in mind than chiseling a fake inscription upon a stone in a language unknown to them and in a writing some hundreds of years out of use. The first group of Scandinavian farmers settled in the surrounding country in 1868. In the centuries before these the whole country was inhabited by none but Indians, save the

French trappers who rambled through the forests in search of skins. The idea of fakery, therefore, must be entirely given up.

Even if we had not these facts concerning the region in which the stone was discovered and its inhabitants, the invocation of the Blessed Virgin Mary could never have been thought of by the Protestant Scandinavians of the nineteenth century, and this alone would bring the origin of the stone back to the time before the Reformation.

Moreover, the spot on which the stone rested when discovered is called an island in the inscription. It is not an island now. The stone was found on an elevation which rises some forty feet above the nearest environs. Close by extends a swamp with a narrow gully at the northwest which carries off excessive water. Were the level of the water in the swamp only fifteen feet higher, that elevation would be an island. It is not at all impossible that this was the case in the year 1362. If we presume, that the gully underwent an erosion of fifteen feet, which indeed could have happened very easily after the date given on the stone, we have a very simple and natural explanation of the term "island." Professor Winchell, formerly state geologist of Minnesota, does not hesitate to declare:

I am convinced from the geological conditions and the physical changes which the region has experienced, probably during the last five hundred years, that the stone contains a genuine record of a Scandinavian exploration into Minnesota and must be accepted as such for the date named.

On the other hand, it seemed quite unthinkable that a forger in the nineteenth century should have spoken of that spot as an island, and this one word makes the assertion that the stone and its inscription is a fraud untenable.

Another significant consideration is this. The stone has been exposed to the air, as far as we know for certain, for not fully forty years, and even during much of this time it was partly covered. Before its discovery in 1898, it lay in the ground beneath the aspen tree, sheltered against direct atmospheric influences. And yet it appears so thoroughly weatherbeaten that all observers declare it must have been at one time unprotected against wind and weather for a very considerable number of years. This condition of the stone of course excludes its having been produced as a fakery during the time when any white settlers existed in the country where it was found.

A difficulty has been found in the phrase, "a day's journey." To fit this phrase into the geographical conditions of the land Mr. Holand presumes that it means "a day's journey by sailing," an assumption which he makes quite plausible. However, even though perhaps these words remain obscure, that does not interfere with the clearness of the rest of the inscription. Nor does it undo the force of the arguments in favor of the stone.

Mr. Hjalmar Holand has set down the results of the investigations carried out by himself and his numerous friends and opponents in a book entitled, *The Kensington Stone: A Study in Pre-Columbian American History* (privately printed). From it the few points briefly dwelt upon so far have been taken. Other interesting matter must be omitted, such as the finding of Swedish battle axes in Minnesota, or the very detailed discussion of the runic and linguistic character of the inscription. Nor can we follow the author as he determines the place of the massacre, and gives us his conjectures as to the purpose for which this expedition was inaugurated and the fate of the survivors. But the question, whether the stone is of significance to history may be briefly touched upon in conclusion.

The importance of the Kensington Stone with its runic message is of course not equal to that of certain other stone inscriptions found in the course of the years. It does not compare, for instance, with the amount of knowledge made accessible by the Rosetta Stone. But we should not underrate it either. It is the oldest document of American history written on the new continent itself by white men. It is the only runic inscription found in America, and it belongs to a period almost devoid of runic literature. It adds a significant item to the fragmentary sources we possess concerning the doings of the Northmen in America, and it helps to show that the discoveries of Eric and his son about the year 1000 were not isolated incidents without any historical sequence, but were followed by an intercourse between America and Scandinavia for some four hundred years.

In a lengthy and thorough review of Mr. Holand's book in *Speculum,* Vol. VIII, pp. 400-408, Dr. S. Eynarsson of Johns Hopkins University enters upon a very detailed discussion of the runic inscription. "Whereas there is no doubt as to the correctness of the translation as a whole," he says, "many words, forms, and letters do not tally with the shape or use they have in other runic inscriptions of the same period." But these observations cease to be historic. They are linguistic. The historian's (and archeologist's) task is to find out and prove from facts that this stone with its message really comes down to us from that faraway time of A.D. 1362." This has been proven, and Dr. Eynarsson himself grants it at the end of his review. Thereby the historians have gained a most interesting bit of information for themselves. But they have also furnished an addition to the availing number of runic inscriptions. It is now for the runic scholars to step in. Let them investigate the character of this well attested piece of runic literature and draw from it conclusions for the practical and theoretic knowledge of that ancient writing. Possibly some divergencies may be set down as mistakes made by those sailors whom we need not suppose to have been experts in the handling of script and language. But whatever linguistic difficulties remain unsolved cannot interfere with the genuineness of the Kensington Stone and the reliability of its message.

VIII

THE "CODEX AUREUS"—A MASTERPIECE OF HAND COPYING [1]

IN some collections of manuscript books of the ancient monasteries there was a *Codex Aureus,* a Golden Book. Sometimes this name was given because the binding was entirely or partially ornamented with gold, or there was much gold in the writing itself, or the whole writing was carried out in gold, or all these causes came together. When hearing of a *Codex Aureus* we cannot tell which of these causes gave that name to the manuscript. In classic Latin the term *Codex* means a book, originally one written on wooden tablets, later on simply any kind of book. In the parlance of present-day archeologists it denotes a hand-written book dating from the time before the invention of printing. Some of the Codices are of unusual importance, and are named after the place where they were written, or where they were once preserved, or where they are now kept.

The *Codex Aureus,* which I wish to describe, is in the possession of the Bavarian State Library at Munich. It is, however, often referred to as the *Codex Aureus* of St. Emmeram, Ratisbon, where it has been preserved for more than eight hundred years. This masterpiece of ancient book-making fully deserves its name. It is written throughout in golden letters upon the white ground of the parchment. It is a Gospel

[1] *The Historical Bulletin,* Vol. VI (1927-1928), pp. 24-27.

Book, containing the four Gospels, in Latin of course. It has two hundred and fifty-two pages of the size of a large missal. Each page is divided into two columns, and there are forty lines to each column. The letters are large capitals, called "Uncials" by the paleographists. The letters are so exactly and uniformly executed that at first sight one has the impression of viewing a printed book. The *Codex* uses very few abbreviations, which otherwise are numerous in most codices, and those here employed are so simple that they can be understood without a special key.

Broad margins like frames surround the pages. They are executed in a great variety of colors. The margins of each two opposite pages show the same patterns. But no two pairs of margins are the same in the whole book. Each couple is different from every other couple. Each two pages also have a page heading tastefully worked into the upper margin, and consisting of the two words, SECUNDUM MARCUM (according to Mark), or SECUNDUM JOHANNEM, the word SECUNDUM always occupying the place on the left-hand side. A narrower band, resembling the frames, runs down the middle of the page to separate the two columns. Thus each page is a work of art in itself, a marvel of exactness and originality, radiant with the golden letters, and resplendent with the rich colors of the frames.

Each Gospel is preceded by several introductory pages. There is first one with the words, INCIPIT EVANGELIUM SECUNDUM MATTHAEUM, or SECUNDUM JOHANNEM. (Here begins the Gospel according to St. Matthew, or according to St. John.) Then follows a concise Preface setting forth the character of the sacred writer and the peculiarities of his Gospel. After this there is a *Breviarium* of the Gospel, that is, a short summary of its contents, somewhat like the chapter headings in present day Bibles, put together and forming a sort of Index. The next page is a picture of the Evangelist. St. John, for instance, is represented as a venerable old man with white hair and beard, looking up to an eagle which appears in the clouds. Each Gospel begins with a grand initial page. The initial page of the Gospel of St. John contains only the words IN PRINCIPIO ERAT VERBUM. The syllables IN PRIN occupy the whole upper half of the page. From a network of gracefully intersecting lines the letters I and N stand out clearly in their bold strokes. The vertical strokes of the N are five inches in height. The I is in the center, and is not repeated for the Syllable PRIN. The other letters of PRIN are placed within the space covered by the outlines of the big N, and interwoven with one another.[2] The next cross line gives the letters CIPIO, which are less prominent, but still more than an inch high. The two other words, ERAT VERBUM, are much smaller, one word above the other. The spaces left free by the letters are filled out with artistically interlaced mathematical designs. (Coils, so effectively used in the Book of Kells, are entirely avoided.)

If a glance at the brilliant pages justifies the designation of "Golden Book," this is still more the case with the front cover. (The rear cover evidently never had any ornamentation.) According to an estimate made by a modern goldsmith the ornaments lavished upon this wonderwork of art must have required six ounces of gold at the least. Eighty precious stones, dis-

[2] Compare the picture of the "Monograph Page" of the Book of Kells in Betten's *Ancient World* (Boston), p. 614.

tinguished by eighty different hues, are scattered over the surface. No words can express the brilliancy, accurateness and good taste here displayed.

As stated before, the characters used in this much admired manuscript are "uncial," that is, capitals all through. They remind one of the writing employed in the *Codex Amiatinus,* which dates from a much earlier century.[3] Specialists of paleography hold that the letters, as well as the sundry elements of the profusive ornamentation of the *Codex Aureus,* betray a very strong Roman influence together with features common to Byzantine, Frankish, Anglo-Saxon, and Irish manuscripts. As in all the oldest manuscripts the words are not separated from one another, nor is there any real system of punctuation. One peculiar feature, however, deserves a few words.

Bible scholars consider it an undoubted fact that in the first centuries two ways were in vogue of writing the sacred books. One was the same as the one commonly followed at the present day. The scribe filled out the entire lines across the writing surface, without paying any attention to the divisions of the text into sentences, or the subdivision of the sentences, and also without separating the words. This required great skill in the reader, especially if he was to read to an audience. (At that time the books were produced much more for such public readings than for private perusal.) For the benefit of the readers another method was followed. Each sentence was carefully divided into its natural parts, such as had to be distinguished in intelligent reading. Each of these sections, called "Colons," would then be given a whole line by itself. A manuscript written according to this method

[3] See illustration in Betten, *Ancient World* (Boston), p. 16.

looked almost like a long poem. For instance, Mark i,
9, 10, would appear thus:

> And it came to pass in those days
> Jesus came from Nazareth in Galilee
> and was baptized by John in the Jordan
> And forthwith coming up out of the water
> He saw the heavens opened
> and the Spirit as a dove descending
> and remaining on him

The *Codex Amiatinus* represents this method of
writing, which no doubt renders the task of the reader
much easier. The *Codex Aureus* does not go quite so
far as older Codices had gone. It fills the entire lines
of the columns. But it clearly distinguishes the several
"Colons," and marks the end of each by a dot. No
other punctuation marks are employed, except the in-
terrogation point which is put above the last syllable
of a colon.

Archeologists are at a loss to which of three ancient
abbeys, St. Denis, Reims, or Corbie, must be adjudged
the honor of being the place where this admirable book
was produced. The names of the scribes, however, are
known. Two brothers, priests, Beringar and Liuthard,
wrote this wonderful Gospel book for King Charles
the Bald. Later the *Codex Aureus* was presented to
Arnulph of Carinthia, King of the East Franks, who
eventually became emperor. Arnulph in turn made it
over as a truly royal gift to the abbey of St. Emmeram,
Ratisbon. Here the precious volume found a resting
place during eight centuries. In the literature of these
centuries it is frequently referred to. Visitors to the
famous Abbey, both lay and ecclesiastic, admired it and

extolled its incomparable beauty. In 1812, the Bavarian government declared the Abbey suppressed, took possession of its property, and transferred the *Codex Aureus* to the Bavarian State Library at Munich.

After the World War a Munich firm (Hugo Schmidt Verlag) reproduced it by scientific methods with faultless accuracy. The reproduction itself is a work of high art. It is the most beautiful Gospel book now in existence, surpassed only in some unimportant features by the original itself. Whereas formerly the priceless *codex* could be admired only by the relatively few visitors of the Munich State Library, it is now at the disposal of the world of savants and admirers of medieval works of art. The libraries, the rich bibliophiles, will acquire it; the scholar can consult it far away from the resting place of the original. Scholars cannot buy it. Scholars are poor. They must rely on the generosity of others.

The work is sold in three editions, either in six volumes bound in parchment at 360 goldmarks ($90.00) each, or in six clothbound volumes at 300 goldmarks ($75.00) each; or unbound in ten sections at 120 goldmarks ($30.00) each. In these editions is not included an extra volume of text at 220 goldmarks ($55.00). This seems much. Yet considering the labor of reproducing, the expensive processes which were necessary; the exactness with which every detail had to be attended to, the fact that skilled workmen embodied several years of labor in the work—the price is far from being too high. One journey to the original would cost as much as the parchment-bound edition and more, and would benefit only one man and his work, whereas one copy placed in an American library will render precious services to dozens of serious workers, and would fill with joy the hearts of countless admirers of ancient art. Let us hope that many American book collections will incorporate this wonderful book, both to enhance the completeness of their treasures, and to enable American scholars to utilize it in their scientific investigations.

The present writer had the pleasure of seeing and examining a copy of this golden book in the library of St. Vincent's Arch-Abbey at Beatty, Pennsylvania. He desires to express to the Benedictine Fathers of that great institution his sincere thanks for their Benedictine hospitality which it was his privilege to enjoy.

IX

Printing—The Divine Art—Who Invented It?[1]

IT is impossible to give an exact date for the invention of printing, the greatest of all inventions after that of writing. We may say, however, that it took place about the year 1450, though some sort of real printing was done, as we are going to see, one or two decades before that year.

In order to concentrate our attention entirely on the question of the inventor of printing proper, i.e., printing with movable type, we leave aside the discussion of what may be called preliminary arts, such as printing with dies, or the reproduction of pictures or short texts by block printing. We shall concern ourselves exclusively with that art of book production which spread by leaps and bounds over the continent during the half century following the year 1450. Nor do we enter into any sort of investigation concerning the possible dependence of European printing on the practice of the same or some similar art which had been in vogue for several hundred years in China. In a very recent book, *The Invention of Printing in China,* Dr. Thomas F. Carter, a specialist in this field, gives it as his opinion, that documentary evidence does not indicate any such dependence.

For several centuries a literary feud has been waged as to who is the real inventor of printing: John Gutenberg of Mainz (1400-1464), or Lourens Janszoon

[1] *Historical Bulletin,* Vol. VI (1927-1928), pp. 4-7.

Coster of Haarlem (1396-1484). This question now seems to be definitely settled by a book which appeared in 1921.[2] After a lifelong study the author was able to apply to this controversy the old scholastic principle, *Qui bene distinguit, bene docet,* "He who distinguishes well, teaches well." The book has been issued with the financial assistance of the Dutch Society of Knowledge of Haarlem, a fact which shows that Coster's compatriots fully approve of the publication. The information embodied in the following pages is chiefly culled from this work. Zedler's discussions will at the same time serve to clarify the several steps which were necessary to lead to the final perfection of the typographical art.

The first step, the use of movable metal type, was made by Coster. Dr. Zedler reproduces the two most important statements of Dutch authorities who claim for him the honor of being the inventor of printing. An unprinted book by Zurenus Junior of Haarlem, who lived in 1507-1591, recounts how Coster was robbed by a faithless assistant, who carried away the whole outfit and began printing at Mainz. Another testimony dating from 1561, tells the same story. Dr. Zedler thinks that there must be some kernel of truth in these traditions, though they appear nearly a century after Coster's death and are embellished with a wreath of fabulous details. He gives a very exhaustive study to the remnants of the earliest Dutch prints— too lengthy to reproduce or even summarize—and comes to the conclusion that they represent a stage of procedure which is more primitive than the methods followed by Gutenberg. These ancient Dutch prints are generally, and without contradiction, ascribed to

[2] Gottfried Zedler, *Von Coster zu Gutenberg,* Leipzig, 1921.

Coster. A number of them Dr. Zedler finds to be older than any of the productions of the Mainz typographers. There is no doubt that Coster employed movable type. Nor can it be questioned that the characters used by him were of metal. *Lourens Janszoon Coster must be considered the inventor of the art of producing and using individual metal characters for the making of books.*

Many of us may imagine that this really was the art of printing such as we have it now; if it was not, what was still lacking? What remained for Gutenberg to invent? Let us first state that the invention Gutenberg made must have been very essential. It must have been radical. We see this from its results. Coster printed only rather small books, almost exclusively schoolbooks, especially the Latin grammar by Donatus, the most popular textbook in medieval schools. Dr. Zedler thinks he can distinguish two more Dutch typographists, though their names are unknown. One of them printed only Donatuses. Practically, therefore, Coster had no imitators. The later flourishing condition of typography in the Netherlands took its origin from the introduction of the Mainz craft. The remnants of the "Costeriana" are nearly exclusively mere scraps, rescued from the covers of later books.[3]

It was different with Gutenberg and his disciples. Their art spread rapidly from Mainz to other places. When Coster died in 1484, there were printing establishments in about fifty other cities, among them at

---

[3] Coster printed on parchment. When the number of printed books increased, the bookbinders took the durable leaves of former works and pasted them on the wood and pasteboard covers of the new books. A large number of remnants of very early manuscripts and other books have thus come to us, which in many cases have rendered valuable service.

least thirteen in Coster's own country, the Netherlands. After his death Coster's metal type, consisting
of lead and tin, was melted down and changed into
wine tankards. Coster's method, though representing
in itself a step of vast consequences, had gone out of
date, and given way to the typographical devices of
Gutenberg.

The whole difference lay in the way of producing
the type. Coster cut each character first into wood, and
used the wooden type as form for the casting of the
metal type. With the wooden form he made moulds
in sand, which, when filled out by fluid metal, would
shape a metal character of exactly the form of the
wooden one. His type metal was lead. (The procedure
was not quite so simple as it may seem from these
few words, but this is not the place to enter more
deeply into the details of his craft.) Gutenberg who,
in or about 1436, had made the acquaintance of Coster's Donatuses, at the very first beginning employed
methods similar to those of the Netherlander. But very
soon he took the step which has made the art of printing what it now is. The sand mould had to be remade
each time after one metal type had been produced in
it. *Gutenberg substituted the metal mould.* Starting
with a wooden type, he first cast a brass type. This
he hammered into lead, and thus gained a much more
durable mould, a real "matrix." Experiments have
shown that five hundred perfect lead types can be cast
in a lead mould before it begins to deteriorate per-
ceptibly. This was an enormous advantage over Coster's methods. Gutenberg's associate, Schoeffer, who
later on separated from him, further perfected the art
by engraving the letter in steel and driving this into
copper. The copper mould was practically indestruct-

ible. He also invented a better type metal and the printers' ink, both of which are still in use today. But the principal progress was the metal mould, and this is due to Gutenberg.

Coster's sand mould admitted of little progress. It excluded the casting of very fine type. In fact, all the letters of the Coster prints are of nearly equal size, the small "a" being about one-eighth of an inch in height. Naturally, too, the letters had to be rather massive. In spite of other differences which allow the distinguishing of several kinds of type, all the Coster prints, though covering a period of nearly fifty years, appear as having been produced with what we now call heavy-faced type. The oldest Mainz prints, too, show much of this character. But after the disciples of Gutenberg had been at it much less than fifty years, they had produced an incredible variety of type, differing, not only in general character, but also in size. Each tried to outdo the other in elegance and accuracy. All this had become possible by the use of metal matrices.

The most important feature, however, of Gutenberg's invention, was the *hand mould,* a little instrument by means of which the casting of metal characters could be carried out conveniently and rapidly. Dr. Zedler says the construction of this contrivance is hard enough to understand when you hold it in your hand and can examine all its many parts, but it is next to impossible to grasp it from description. He gives more than thirty delineations, vertical sections, cross sections, component parts, etc., to illustrate his description. But I confess I am unable to follow him in his discussions. If the instrument is so difficult to understand, it must have been much more difficult to devise.

It seems to have taken Gutenberg several years to bring it to its final shape.

The hand mould was the real secret of the Mainz printers. It crystallized, as it were, into a concrete thing the principle that characters could be made by metal moulds. That general principle might be known the world over. It could help only those who possessed a means to carry it into execution in a way which secured quick results. Gutenberg's hand mould made it possible to commercialize the invention. With it printing could be made a well paying business. (It is exactly this feature that was lacking in the Chinese printing, which remained a very costly affair.) Be it said to the honor of the greatest printers of the fifteenth century, that they looked upon their craft as an ideal means to multiply good books. Many of them were educated men and genuine lovers of books. Hence the great perfection of so many *incunabula* (books printed before 1500), which makes them objects of admiration for all later typographers. But if there had been no money in it, those men could not have afforded to devote their time and thought and capital to the production of printed books, though indeed they considered printing more as a fine art than a mere handicraft.

Thus the investigations of Dr. Zedler have enabled us to give honor to whom honor is due—honor to Lourens Janszoon Coster, the dapper Dutchman, who really gave the first start to the new art that was to change the face of the intellectual world; honor to John Gutenberg, who actually sent forth the art upon its rapid march of triumph.

A few points of additional information may be added. The kinds of type used by the first printers north of the Alps were what we now style Gothic (type), or as this kind is often called Black Letter. But historians of the art distinguish a large number of classes of type, which is sometimes truly bewildering. The reason is very simple. The printers who settled in any given locality tried to match exactly the best kind of manuscript books of the city or monastery. In this, however, the various places differed. The shape of letters, and the sort of abbreviations of words, were not the same everywhere. The printers would ascertain these peculiarities and produce their letters accordingly. In Rome, for instance, they from the first printed in what we call Roman type, that is, the type now in common use.

There were in the beginning many itinerant printers who plied their trade especially in monasteries. These acted exactly the same way. They did not arrive with a complete printing outfit. They probably brought nothing but their hand mould. Their first care was to study the sort of writing found in the manuscript books of the institution and duplicate it on their type. Meanwhile the paper could be procured, and the press made by the carpenter of the monastery. The amount of lead and other metal necessary for types and matrices was not very great. The first craftsmen never printed all the pages of one sheet in one operation, but only one page at a time, dissolved the type after one page was finished, and used the same type to set up the next page. That much metal was probably already in the possession of the monastery. (The productions of these itinerant printers are not always very perfect.)

For four hundred years each printing house, large or small, produced its own type with the hand mould.

It is not a century since the mechanical production of type has begun. Whereas formerly the individual printer could make 400 types in an hour, the machine used in our type foundries throws out some 15,000 in the same time, and these are so perfect and accurate that they need no inspection, but may at once be shipped to the customers.

X

PRINTING—THE DIVINE ART—WHY IT SPREAD RAPIDLY [1]

TO practice his art Gutenberg entered into partnership with a citizen of Mainz, Fust (Faust), who in a very ignoble manner forced him out of the business and continued it with his son-in-law Schoeffer. Meanwhile, however, the art was kept a secret. But in 1462 the city of Mainz was besieged by the rightful Archbishop Adolph of Nassau, and on this occasion the quarters of the Fust-Schoeffer concern were so badly handled that printing had to be suspended. The men who had worked there and who were of course in possession of the secret, dispersed and established themselves in other cities. The knowledge and practice of the art now extended rapidly. About one decade from the time of the seizure of Mainz, printing shops were scattered over all of central Europe. (Archbishop Adolph, a lover of arts and sciences, gave his protection to the new craft, and found means to reward the outraged Gutenberg in a suitable manner for his service to mankind.) About a thousand typographical firms, mostly with German names, are known to have carried on a flourishing business before 1500. Rome alone by that year possessed a hundred and ninety presses, more than any other city in the world. The art spread from Cologne to the Netherlands and thence to the

[1] *Historical Bulletin,* Vol. IV (1925-1926), pp. 21-23.

British Isles. In 1472, a German issued in Italy the first printed edition of Dante's *Divina Comedia*.

The new invention could not have made such rapid strides had there not been a plentiful and low priced material at the disposal of the printers. During the Middle Ages people wrote on parchment,[2] that is, skins of animals, as sheep, goats, pigs, etc., which were so treated as to offer a smooth surface for writing. Parchment, though a very durable material, was naturally dear and rare. But the manufacture of paper from rags, preferably linen rags, had been for several centuries previous to Gutenberg's invention, steadily increasing in the lands of Europe. It had been introduced from the Moorish portions of Spain and Sicily, and these in turn had received the art of making paper from some Asiatic nation, undoubtedly China.

In Gutenberg's time there existed paper mills in the neighborhood of Mainz. The printers began at once to employ paper almost exclusively, the number of books printed on parchment being insignificant. Unquestionably the extensive production of books by the new process could not have been possible had it not been for the cheap material, and the activity of the presses in turn gave a powerful impetus to the paper industry. But it would be going much too far were we to assert that the existence of paper mechanically called the presses into being. If that were the case, the press would have originated among the Arabs in their Asiatic or European homes. The papermaker's art was a necessary condition for the rapid increase of the printer's art. But it alone could never have been the motive

[2] The term *vellum* signifies in a strict sense a peculiar kind of parchment of great fineness and whiteness, made of the skins of very young calves. In practice the two words are often used interchangeably.

for men to think and brood and plan for another and quicker way of producing books. There had to be above all a lively demand for books, a general craving for reading and study.

Offhand we are ready to ascribe this "book hunger," as some writers aptly called it, to the rising tide of Humanism, the literary feature of the extensive Renaissance movement which just at this time began sending its waves all over Europe. But when printing was in full swing, this movement had not yet reached the Rhine Valley, the starting point of the new art. The first products of the press were not intended for Humanists. The population which eagerly grasped for the first printed books was still unaffected by the Renaissance. This population had acquired its intellectual propensities in the old schools of the Middle Ages. That exalted love for Latin and Greek literature which already swayed other countries of Europe, showed the first traces of its influence in the cities on the Rhine as late as 1460, some ten years after the invention had been made. The first classic book was printed in Germany in 1465, and it was the *De Officiis* of Cicero, which medieval teachers utilized for moral instruction. *The Orations* of the great Tullius would have been much more in keeping with the aspirations of the Humanists.

What sort of (hand-written) books were actually in demand when typography appeared in the field, we glean from the catalogs of a bookseller who plied his trade in the small Alsatian town of Hagenau. Besides books in Latin for the clergy, he offered in German the greater epics, books of minor poems, rhymed translations of parts of the Bible, legends of the Saints, prayer and meditation books, sagas, collections of popular songs. This catalog shows that the desire for reading was by no means confined to the so-called higher circles, which were conversant with Latin, the language of the educated; that the "book hunger" which brought forth the art of printing had not been produced by Humanism but was of a different and earlier origin, and that this craving for books extended to all classes of the population. It goes without saying, however, that once the new process of bookmaking had taken root and demonstrated its eminently practical value, the Humanists in their desire for good editions of the classics did not fail to enlist its services. They gave great encouragement to the printing fraternity, while on the other hand the output of the fast spreading presses enormously fostered the study of the ancient writers.

The first productions of the art were exactly along the lines represented by the catalog of the Hagenau bookseller. It is evident, however, that the smaller popular books do not attract the attention which writers dealing with this subject bestow upon the large brilliant Bibles and similar prominent prints.[3] Among nineteen German Bibles the Koberger edition is the most famous. Canisius College, Buffalo, N. Y., is in possession of a lavishly illustrated two-volume copy of the Koberger Bible which was printed in 1486.

The members of the clergy, partly because of their superior education, partly because they at once discerned in typography a most powerful means for the promotion of the spiritual welfare of the people, were, as the printers gratefully owned, the most liberal buyers of printed books and, as it were, the professional

[3] See Guggenberger, *Hist. of the Christian Era* (St. Louis, 1901), II, p. 135.

protectors of the craftsmen. The Benedictine Abbey of Subiaco near Rome put up the first printing press outside of Germany. As early as 1467 and 1469, two cardinals invited German printers directly to Rome. A large number of monasteries following the example of Subiaco soon possessed their own presses. Bishops hailed typography as a "divine art." "Most commendable," wrote Pope Innocent VIII in 1487, "is the art of printing, inasmuch as good and useful books are thereby easily multiplied."

During the centuries preceding the invention of printing, a brisk trade, national and international, in handwritten books had grown up. In how businesslike a manner it was carried on we see from the catalog of the Hagenau dealer. There now arose at once the trade in printed books which followed the same channels but soon assumed much greater proportion. The Koberger firm sold its books in Poland, Hungary, the Netherlands and Italy. Lyons was its headquarters for France. On one occasion a consignment of three hundred copies of a single book was despatched to that city. "In the principal cities," writes a contemporary, "Koberger has as many as sixteen stores. He manages his affairs so well that he is cognizant of the condition of each branch and can supply the wants of one shop from the superfluous stock of another."

How eagerly often the books were bought, we learn from the letter of a scholar at Basel to a friend. "At this moment," he writes, "Wolfgang Lachner is having a whole wagon load of classics of the Aldine editions brought over from Venice. Do you wish for any of them? If so, tell me immediately, and send the money. For no sooner has such a freight arrived than thirty buyers start up for each volume, merely asking the price and tearing each other's eyes out to get hold of it." Generally every printer also acted as agent for every other printer. The accounts were settled, as is still the custom in Germany, at yearly conventions. These took place first at Frankfurt on the Main, and later on at Leipzig, which is still one of the greatest book marts of the world.[4]

[4] See *Catholic Historical Review,* Vol. VIII (1922-1923), pp. 512 ff.

XI

THE TUDOR QUEENS: A COMPARISON [1]

THE comparison between the two Tudor queens of England is a theme frequently discussed by both Catholic and non-Catholic authors, and one which almost obtrudes itself to anyone who gives some study to the two reigns. A point most strongly insisted upon is the number of executions which took place under them.

"Mary burnt 288 in five years; Elizabeth killed less than 200 in forty-five."

The conclusion is that Mary was cruel, while Elizabeth was humane. These numbers, however, can bear a closer investigation. Nor are they the only criterion on which to base the charge of cruelty. We shall take up the question of the numbers first, and after that examine another viewpoint commonly neglected in the discussion. [2]

[1] *Catholic Historical Review,* Vol. XVII (July 1931), pp. 187-193.
[2] The positive information for our first part is chiefly gleaned from Rev. John Lingard's great work, *History of England,* which though written about a hundred years ago, "still stands firm and immovable." (Rev. E. Ryan in *Church Historians,* edited by P. Guilday, p. 286.) For the second part we rely on Arnold Oskar Meyer's *England and the Catholic Church under Elizabeth,* translated by M. McKey (St. Louis, Mo., 1925). This work, written by a German Protestant, enjoys the reputation of thoroughness and fairness. (It is hardly possible to take exception to any of the facts adduced by this careful investigator. Views may occasionally differ when it comes to the evaluation and interpretation of the facts; a circumstance which does not affect the passages to be utilized here.)

I

The Number of Executions. Among the 288 victims who suffered under Mary the Catholic there were some sixty who had been found guilty of rebellion, chiefly in connection with the several attempts made to put Lady Jane Grey on the throne.[3] The remaining number were punished for heresy according to old English laws. But if rebels are included among the victims in the case of Mary, the same must be done in the case of Elizabeth. Now the fact is that under Elizabeth none were formally executed for religion, all condemnations being pronounced on the charge of rebellion. To deny that Elizabeth was the "Supreme Head under God of the Anglican Church" was construed as high treason. It is evident that this was a religious cause, since all those who refused to save their lives by abjuring the primacy of the Pope really died for their religious conviction. The number of those formally sentenced to death upon this plea is commonly given at about 180. But outside of these 180 executions there were numerous others, carried out in consequence of the suppression of risings. After the revolt in the northern counties, known as the

---

[3] I find it extremely difficult, at least with the sources of information at my disposal, to determine how many after all were executed as heretics. Lingard (Vol. V, pp. 485-6) states that after expunging "the names of all who were condemned as felons or traitors, or who died peaceably in their beds, or who survived the publication of their martyrdom, or who would for their heterodoxy have been sent to the stake by the reformed prelates had these been in possession of the power . . . it will be found that in the space of four years almost two hundred persons perished in the flames for religious opinion." Rev. Herbert Thurston, S.J., on the other hand, asserts that within four years 277 persons were burned to death for heresy. (*Catholic Encyclopedia,* IX, 767.) Other writers, such as Innes in his *History of England under the Tudors* and Gairdner in his several works, do not give any total at all. Both these non-Catholic historians speak with admirable fairness of the Catholic queen. It would probably be difficult to find a more just and truthful account of her personality and government than is that presented by Innes.

second Pilgrimage of Grace, "those among the insurgents who possessed lands or chattels were reserved for trial in the courts of law, that their forfeitures might furnish the queen with an indemnification for the expenses of the campaign. . . . But the meaner classes were abandoned to the execution by martial law." Before setting out upon his expedition of blood, the Earl of Sussex, Elizabeth's commissioner, wrote to Cecil concerning the number of his intended victims:

> the number whereof is yet uncertain, for that I knowe not the number of the townes; but I gesse that it will not be under 6 or 7 hundred at the least that shal be exequuted of the comon sorte, besides the prisoners taken in the felde.

That the earl meant what he said is evident from the following words of Lingard:

> Sussex . . . whether it was through the natural severity of his disposition, or his anxiety to convince the queen of his loyalty which had been doubted rightly or wrongly, exercised his authority without mercy. In the county of Durham alone more than three hundred individuals suffered death, nor was there between Newcastle and Wetherby, a district of sixty miles in length and forty in breadth, a town or village in which some of the inhabitants did not expire on the gibbet as a warning to their fellows.

In view of the forecast of Sussex and of the statement of our reliable historian we certainly are right in concluding that the number of "6 or 7 hundred at the least" was reached. These hangings, moreover, were prompted no less by religious hatred than by political reasons, because when at length pardon was offered to the survivors, they had to take not only the oath of allegiance but also that of supremacy; that is, they had to renounce their faith. We may therefore justly put these many hundreds of executions on the same level with the two hundred put to death under Mary for the sake of religion.

To these six or seven hundred must be added those slain during "the horrors committed in Ireland by the lieutenants of Elizabeth." I have not been able to obtain any definite or approximate figures of their numbers. Lingard, however, states that at the end of the English operations Ireland was no better than an extensive wilderness, a term which evidently does not merely denote destruction of property but above all destruction of human life.[4] This condition of Ireland was indeed partly due to famine, and to disease caused by famine. But the famine had been brought on by English aggression and treachery. A certain author who otherwise wishes to show how unfairly Catholics treat the "Protestant historical attitude," and who makes much of the "less than 200 killed" under Elizabeth in forty-five years, grants that the "horrors committed in Ireland by the lieutenants of Elizabeth" are possibly the worst brutalities of that cruel age. If we presume that the number of the victims of purposely inflicted punishments in Ireland amounted not to hundreds but thousands, we are perhaps not far from being right.

Here is the place to point out how Queen Mary acted on a similar occasion.

In the first two years of her reign there were two risings for the purpose of making Jane Grey Queen of England. The second in particular was by far more formidable than any of those later on directed against Queen Elizabeth.[5] The chief seat of the revolt was the county of Kent. When the danger was over, some five

---

[4] Lingard, *History of England,* Vol. V, pp. 431-434.
[5] Lingard, *op. cit.,* Vol. VI, p. 630.

hundred men "of the common sorte" were in the hands
of the government. About fifty of these paid for their
crime on the gallows, and these are, as far as I can see,
included in the 288 executed under Mary. She had the
rest, some four hundred, brought to her presence, pronounced their pardon, and without imposing any oath
or other condition told them to go home in peace. Nor
did she dispatch any commissioner to that county with
powers such as Elizabeth had given to the Earl of
Sussex.

To be entirely fair, it is still necessary to call attention to an important circumstance: Americans are
justly proud of being assured by their Constitution that
nobody shall be sentenced to any penalty *without due
process of law*. The summary proceedings of court-
martial are to be the rare exception and reserved for
times of extraordinary danger. The frequent use of
this form of trial would certainly not be looked upon
as indicating a good government. Under Queen Mary
it was resorted to in those fifty cases mentioned just
before. Under Queen Elizabeth it was overwhelmingly
the rule. In comparing the two queens this fact ought
not to remain without careful consideration.

It is not the fault of the present writer if the reader
is left under the impression that as far as the number
of the executions is concerned, Queen Mary has nothing to fear from a comparison with Queen Elizabeth.
But people have figured out that there were under
Mary on the average fifty-five executions every year.
Had she ruled forty-five years like Elizabeth, an enormous number of men would probably have fallen
through the hand of the executioner. This calculation
is based on the supposition that her executions would
have continued at the same rate as long as she would

be on the throne. This, one should say, is utterly improbable. The causes of the executions were bound to decrease in number and with them the executions themselves. Protestant writers tell us that at the time of Mary, heresy and sedition were almost convertible terms, and if the punishments took place in unprecedented number, it was because heresy existed on an unprecedented scale in England. It is not at all likely that these extraordinary conditions should have lasted long. Nor is it impossible that other counsels would have prevailed at the royal court independently of change or permanence of conditions.

2

Torture. Both queens lived at a time when torture was still considered an indispensable adjunct of every criminal court. Even if we had no express knowledge of the methods of the English courts, we should suppose that it was practiced under Mary as well as Elizabeth. Now in deciding which of the two governments, or which of the two queens personally, should be accused of special cruelty, we think that the extent to which the rack was employed, and the manner in which pain was inflicted, possess a great determining weight. Though in the courts of Mary the torture probably was not put out of use, I have never seen it alluded to in any way. It is very different with Elizabeth. Arnold Oskar Meyer's *England and the Catholic Church under Elizabeth* contains remarkable pronouncements on the rôle torture played in the courts of that queen. In a long passage on this horrible subject the author refers to Richard Topcliffe, the professional torturer, who had obtained the "privilege" to take prisoners to the private torture chamber in his own dwelling, which was fitted out with instruments of his own invention. Nobody knew as exactly as he how much pain the human nervous system is capable of enduring. Dr. Meyer has the following to say about him:

> No blot is more foul on the history of Elizabeth's latter years than the name of Richard Topcliffe. Every inhuman quality which the most heated imagination can picture is embodied in this example of unspeakable degradation. Greed and perverse delight in inflicting suffering rather than religious fanaticism were the motives of Topcliffe's conduct. "Topcliffian customs" was a synonym for brutality; *topcliffizare* became a slang term for hunting a man to ruin and death. . . . Only a man like Topcliffe was capable of torturing afresh one who had already been broken on the rack. . . . *Had he not been sure of the queen's approval,* the wretch could not have plied his trade.[6]

This statement, made by a writer who enjoys the reputation of invariable fairness, throws a very sinister light on the methods of the Elizabethan government as well as the personal character of the queen herself. It is natural to ask, did Queen Mary also have a Topcliffe? Did she employ a man about whom some responsible writer would be willing to duplicate the verdict given by Meyer on Topcliffe? And if there was one, was he allowed as Topcliffe did to boast of the personal approval of the queen? It is not necessary to dilate on the conclusion which follows from the fact that all these questions must be answered in the negative.

Mention may be made here of a proceeding which, though legal under all governments, was nevertheless

[6] Meyer, *op. cit.,* p. 183. (Italics inserted.)

so frequently resorted to under Elizabeth as to form
a true peculiarity of her reign, namely, the *domiciliary
visits* of suspected Catholics. With his soldiers and a
horde of volunteer helpers from the rabble of the
county, the sheriff would, commonly by night, burst
into the house of some prominent Catholic. Every bed
and box and cupboard and wardrobe were searched
and the contents thrown about; the wainscoting and
floors were torn up; holes were made in the walls to
discover hiding-places of priests or some other signs of
their presence; and the house was left in a state of
complete devastation. If there were domiciliary visits
under Mary, and I have never seen them mentioned,
they certainly were not so numerous as we find them
to have been under Queen Elizabeth.

But Dr. Meyer assists us in comparing the two
queens as to the practice of torture by another statement:

Fairness is rightly held to be a strongly marked characteristic
of the English people. How deeply this quality can be impaired
by religious fanaticism is shown by the judicial murders sys-
tematically inflicted on those suspected of conspiracy. And yet
the administration of justice presents still worse features than
false witnesses and unjust judges. Torture (*peine forte et dure*)
was applied in England from the time of Edward I only when
the accused refused to plead. Under the Tudor monarchy torture became a royal prerogative in cases in which the safety
of the state was held to be in danger. *The climax of this
development was reached during the reign of Elizabeth.* Not
only were the great majority of those who were tortured during
this period Catholic priests, considered *ipso facto* dangerous
to the state, but the persecution of Catholics was at its height
*just when torture had developed into a fine art, and the treat-
ment* of prisoners was barbarous in the extreme.[7]

[7] Meyer, *op. cit.*, p. 179.

No further comment is needed on words like these. They indicate in whose favor our judgment should incline when comparing the two queens and their methods. In fact the italicized lines settle the question peremptorily, even if we did not have the passage on Topcliffe.

Our comparison of the two queens, therefore, results decidedly in favor of Mary the Catholic. She was indeed severe in dealing with both secular and religious criminals, but the 288 executions of her reign, if there were that many, cannot compare with the hundreds and thousands of the victims of Elizabeth's wholesale killings in England and downtrodden Ireland. If the question is raised which of the two female Tudor rulers deserves the epithet of the "Bloody," the facts we have seen give an unequivocal answer.

XII

THE PONTIFICATE OF POPE CLEMENT VIII
(1592-1605)[1]

"HE who enters the conclave as Pope, will come out as cardinal." This Italian saying came true in the conclave from which Clement VIII proceeded as the successor of Peter. In all the secret and open transactions among the cardinals which may make a conclave look like an ordinary political election affair, it is the Holy Ghost Who appoints the next Head of the Church. Cardinal Santori, a prelate in every way worthy of the papal tiara, believed he was already as good as elected. In the early morning after the first night spent in the rooms of the conclave, Santori's party was ready to proclaim him pope by acclamation. But an opposition made up of sixteen cardinals refused to participate and forced a regular balloting which showed clearly that Santori had no chances ever to secure the required majority. The great dream of his life was irreparably shattered. But most edifying is his entry in his autobiography:

The night which followed was more painful to me than any misfortune that I had ever endured, and the great grief and

---

[1] *The History of the Popes from the Close of the Middle Ages.* Drawn from the secret archives of the Vatican and other original sources. From the German of Ludwig, Freiherr von Pastor. Edited by Ralph Francis Kerr of the London Oratory. Volumes XXIII and XXIV: Clement VIII (1592-1605). (St. Louis: B. Herder Book Co., 1933. Pp. xxxviii, 542; xx, 592.) *Cf. Catholic Historical Review,* Vol. XX (1934-1935), pp. 420-426.

93

anguish of soul that I felt produced, incredible though it seems, a sweat of blood. But when in my sorrow I humbly turned to the Lord God, pondering how deceitful and wretched is all earthly happiness, and how true joy is only to be found in the contemplation of God, I felt myself freed from all disturbance and all human passion. I was further confirmed in this blessed exaltation of my spirit when, on the following morning, during holy Mass, I thanked God for His mercy to me, a poor sinner, and for all the favors that He had bestowed upon me. I also prayed for my enemies, who marvelled greatly when I sought to comfort my inconsolable friends.

Cardinal Santori proved himself a faithful servant of the new Pope and placed his eminent talents unselfishly at the service of the Church under the direction of Clement VIII.

The new pontiff, though of the nobility, did not bring to the papal chair the renown of a great and ancient family—he himself had begun his life's task as a clerk in a Roman bank—but he was an experienced prince of the Church with a wide knowledge of the conditions and needs of the Catholic world and well acquainted with the practices of every kind of diplomacy, a man who sought unselfishly the true welfare of the flock of Christ, an indefatigable worker who did not spare himself whenever the interests of the Church called for special efforts. And Clement VIII's piety was that of a saint. Every day was begun with a lengthy morning devotion including his Mass, and was finished by a confession made to the Oratorian Cesare Baronius. At all times the pope took part in public religious functions. On special occasions, for instance when the danger of a Turkish invasion threatened, or before some important decision, special devotions, such as the exposition of the Blessed Sacrament, were ordered, and nobody participated more earnestly in them than the Pope himself.

The greatest task before the new Pope was no doubt the settling of the affairs of France. Henry of Bourbon, claimant to the crown, had several times abjured Calvinism and several times returned to it. He was opposed by a league of Catholic grandees, while at the same time prominent Catholic noblemen were members of his own party. Philip II, King of Spain, sided with the league, whose victory would, so he calculated, not only be the defeat of heresy in France but also an increase of Spain's influence in European politics. Several of the previous Popes, too, had assisted the league with money and soldiers. What was Clement VIII going to do? For some time he followed the policy of supporting the league. But when Henry Bourbon's star began to rise, when the power of the league dwindled more and more, and when Henry, seeing that his own Catholic friends demanded a serious change of his attitude, made the best promises of a Catholic administration and of his own conversion, the Pope began to relax and entered into private negotiations with him. The French bishops did not await the result of these transactions. On July 25, 1593, they received his abjuration of Calvinism and absolved Henry from excommunication, reserving the confirmation of their act by the Holy See.

After his abjuration, although Henry showed in his political actions that he was resolved to treat Catholic affairs in a Catholic manner, Clement VIII still refused to receive his envoys officially. One of the conditions finally demanded by the Pope—the official acceptance and promulgation of the Tridentine decrees—was bound to meet the resistance of the Gallican bishops and clergy of France. In fact the refusal on the part of the Pope to treat with Henry strengthened the anti-Roman tendency of many French ecclesiastics who did not hesitate to suggest a special patriarch for France. It was this consideration, too, which strongly prompted Clement VIII to incline toward a reconciliation with the Bourbon prince. The obstacles were still many and great. Spain tried everything, from the direst threats to the lowest intrigues, to obstruct the Pope's endeavors. But with commendable singleness of purpose, having in view nothing but the welfare of France and of the Church at large, after many prayers and solemn and private supplications, Clement VIII took the step which gave to France ecclesiastical peace on a solid foundation. On September 17, 1595, in a solemn assembly in St. Peter's, the elaborate ceremony took place of Henry's absolution, and for the first time the pontiff styled him "The Most Christian King of France and Navarre."

France badly needed a religious reform. The material devastations caused by the Huguenot wars were terrible, but not the worst of the evils. Seven of the fourteen archbishoprics and almost forty of the one hundred bishoprics were vacant; and many of the actual bishops had been intruded into their dioceses illegally and were leading the life of secular noblemen. In wide territories the morality of the clergy, secular and regular, was deplorable. In the older religious Orders the abominable custom of abbots *in commendam* (lay abbots) had worked enormous evil. A change soon began to appear. A brilliant galaxy of new bishops, an ever increasing army of zealous and saintly priests and religious, appear in the field, through whom was literally renewed the face of Catholic

France. The improvement came not without the active coöperation of the Most Christian King, though in many important points he failed to live up to his promises and so caused much annoyance to the Pope.

The jealousy of Spain and of its sovereign, Philip II, was one of the obstacles to the absolution of Henry IV of France. Spain was in alliance with the French league and at war with Henry of Bourbon. Clement VIII did all he could to demonstrate that if he received Henry back into the Church, it was not on account of any aversion to Spain. Nevertheless, Philip II felt it as a blow against himself. Actually it had the result of weakening considerably the power and influence of the Spaniards in Rome. Philip II so far, in many questions, had almost dictated to Pope and cardinals what attitude to take. To the best interest of the Church at large this policy was now at an end.

The Pope was, however, forced to wage a constant war against the Spanish monarch's Cesaro-papism which indeed in many points closely resembled Gallicanism, and he was by no means satisfied with the results. Especially were the Spanish Governors of Naples and Milan guilty of much violent interference with canon law and rights of the sovereign pontiff. The Pope had serious complaints also against the Spanish Inquisition. His constant endeavors, however, to bring about peace between France and Spain were finally crowned with success. He prized this fact very highly because it promised to bring nearer to completion his lifelong dream of a common enterprise of Christianity against the common foe, the Turk, whose attitude was becoming more and more alarming.

Like his great predecessors, in particular Saint Pius V and Gregory XIII, Clement VIII worked indefatigably for a general reform of the Church. While the great ecclesiastical interests in France and Spain seemed to absorb all his attention, the eye of the supreme shepherd did not lose sight of any of the smaller portions of his worldwide flock. His nuncios, to whom fell the practical part of his endeavor, were all picked men, inspired with the zeal of their master. Their work was supplemented by special envoys dispatched to cities and provinces and kingdoms. The Pope eagerly studied their reports and kept in touch with them by a brisk correspondence. No bishop or abbot fulfilled his duty conscientiously, no secular ruler supported the work of the reform, but received a papal letter of praise and encouragement, a distinction shared by cities and little towns alike. Letters urging the enforcement of the Tridentine decrees and threatening canonical penalties in case of neglect went out unceasingly to those who were remiss in this duty. Though the Pope did not succeed in all cases—his elaborate attempt, for example, to regain Scandinavia was a complete failure —he had the joy of seeing the return to the faith of many lost districts and the vigorous revival of religious life in countless others. This was in particular the case in Germany, where many of the institutions founded by Gregory XIII were now beginning to bear ample fruit. The Dukes of Bavaria and the Archdukes of Austria excelled by their zeal in the promotion of Catholic reform.

A highwater mark in this grand flood of Catholic revival was the celebration of the Jubilee of the year 1600. Extensive preparations had been made in repairing roads and bridges and in providing provisions and lodging accommodations. Apparently, the 1,200,000 pilgrims were becomingly taken care of, and it was chiefly Roman charity that accomplished this enormous task. The hospice of the Trinità de' Pellegrini alone gave food and shelter to half-a-million pilgrims. Among the priests none was more zealous and indefatigable than the supreme highpriest himself. Protestants who had come to see how the pope was raking in money, were dumbfounded when they saw how everybody in Rome, Clement VIII above all, was spending heavy sums for the benefit of the pilgrims.

Shortly before the solemn opening of the Jubilee the Eternal City was stirred by the news that the remains of the virgin-martyr Cecilia had been discovered in the church named after that saint. The body, covered with a costly gold-embroidered dress, lay in the casket of cyprus wood, in which it had been placed by Pope Paschal I in the year 821. The onlookers, including the Pope, were so struck with awe that none ventured to touch the veil which was thrown over the whole figure. For several weeks all Rome went to admire the majesty of the virgin and martyr, so suddenly brought near to them from a distance of centuries.

It was hardly possible for any Pope to carry out more literally the word of St. Paul: "I am the debtor of all." While his searching eyes beheld the needs of the nations of the world, his attention was also given to the city of Rome. A thorough canonical visitation was ordered of all the churches, beginning from St. Peter's down to the smallest house of prayer. All the institutions of piety and charity and all the houses of the Religious were examined. In many cases the Bishop of Rome appeared personally and not rarely unexpectedly in some church or convent or college, bestowing praise on what he found to be good and not mincing words when things were wrong.

In his general care for the reformation of all classes
of faithful the religious claimed a great share of his
endeavors and those of his legates. His legate, Della
Torre, succeeded in uniting the Benedictine abbeys of
Switzerland into a particular Congregation and to revive the Benedictine Congregation of Suabia. With
incredible difficulty but very efficiently Cardinal de
Vaudemont restored the Benedictine abbeys of French
Lorraine to their original fervor and formed of them
and others two flourishing Congregations. These successes are instructive to show that the Church has the
power of reform within herself and is able to regain
her vigor instead of succumbing to external or internal
obstacles. In like manner the other religious bodies, if
necessary, were taken care of, and both the older establishments and the younger organizations found in Pope
Clement VIII an ardent promoter and protector.

As already indicated, Clement VIII like his predecessors conducted a very considerable part of his pastoral
office through the activity of his nuncios, whose number he increased, and by his numerous special envoys,
who were travelling all over Europe to carry out his
plans of reform. His extreme care in appointing cardinals resulted in a splendid assemblage of men conspicuous for piety, learning, and general ability. The
corporate influence, however, of this body naturally
decreased in the same degree as the amount of business
which was now settled by the newly established cardi-
nalitial Congregations grew in extent and importance.

During Clement's pontificate the Jesuits played a
large part, and not entirely according to their liking.
Indeed, countless papal letters went out to princes and
peoples and ecclesiastics in praise of their indefatigable
labors. But the Pope had his doubts about their organ-

ization and teaching. Members of the Society, backed powerfully by King Philip II of Spain, objected to life-long incumbency of the Father General and to several other points. Above all the divergence between the new Society of Jesus and the venerable Order of St. Dominic concerning the doctrine on grace called for a decision, which was eagerly expected by Protestants and Catholics. Pastor's treatment of the end of these intrigues and of the attitude finally taken by Clement VIII in the controversy on grace makes interesting and thrilling reading. The Jesuits had also become involved in the affairs of England, where Elizabeth was displaying the cunning devices of her last years. The first Stuart king had endeavored to gain the support of the Catholics for his succession by liberal promises which he never meant to keep. The persecuted Catholics themselves were split into two hostile camps, and Elizabeth even tried to enlist the Pope's assistance against one part of her Catholic subjects.

Ever mindful of his position as champion of Christian civilization, Clement VIII followed in the footsteps of his great predecessors by promoting with everything in his power the war against the growing influence of the Turk. He met with little success on account of the jealousy between Spain and France, the selfishly commercial views of Venice, the almost general apathy of the Christian states, and last but not least the incredible stolidity of the Emperor Rudolph II. Once the Pope with the assistance of several Italian princes equipped a small army which he sent to Hungary. For a short time this helped to stir up the parties immediately threatened, the Hungarians, Translyvanians and others, to a more active resistance and gained some small advantages. But the army had to be disbanded on account of the lack of coöperation.

Nothing is more surprising than that this man who led so prayerful a life and exercised such astounding works of penance should have been subject to the weakness of nepotism. It can perhaps be forgiven if he raised two of his nephews to the cardinalate, because both were worthy and able men; but it is less pardonable that he enriched them with large sums of money beside the revenues they drew, and that his secular relatives were similarly favored with offices and wealth. However, none of them led a scandalous life, nor did their uncle proceed so far as to establish, after the example of several of his predecessors, a new principality for them. The two cardinals, besides, spent their treasures largely on the promotion of arts and literature. Like most of the papal families of this period, that of the Aldobrandini was of short duration, the last of its male representatives dying in 1637.

In spite of this weakness Clement VIII is a great figure among the successors of St. Peter. His personal piety places him almost among the saints. As a diplomat he was extremely wary and careful, preferring to reach a goal by small steps rather than by sudden violent actions. With unalterable single-mindedness he strove for the welfare of the Church under all circumstances, and was at the same time guided by a strict sense of justice toward all concerned. His reform activity was a lifelong activity. The perusal of this biography produces the impression of one who stands upon the watchtower of the universe, noticing with keen eye the needs of the Old World and the New, conscious of his duty toward all men and all nations.

His great pontificate was doomed to a long oblivion,

due to the timid policy of his relations in not permitting access to the *acta* of his government. These documents were finally returned to the papal archives, which Leo XIII threw open to the scholars of the world, thus making possible the production of works like Dr. Ludwig von Pastor's *History of the Popes*. The German original of this gigantic work, covering the period of 1300 to 1800, is finished. It is greatly to be deplored that the English translation proceeds very slowly, having reached, by the present volumes, no farther than the year 1621.

XIII

CARDINAL BELLARMINE AND THE GALILEO AFFAIR [1]

IT is not generally known that the great Robert Cardinal Bellarmine, just raised to the honors of the Altar and declared a Doctor of the Church, was rather closely connected with the measures taken by the Church concerning the heliocentric system as advocated by Galileo Galilei in the beginning of the seventeenth century. On one occasion he had to act officially in this matter. But far more interesting is his own personal attitude. In a way the Cardinal was surprisingly modern. He was and remained perfectly fair both to the defenders and the opponents of the new theory. But to understand his position it is necessary first briefly to recall the progress of the controversy and the circumstances under which the Church finally decided to take official notice of it.

After making a number of discoveries and inventions in the field of physics Galileo, famous also in the realm of mathematics, tried his hand at astronomy. By 1610 he had become an enthusiastic admirer of the heliocentric theory, devised ingeniously by Copernicus some seventy or more years before. During these seventy years the Church had never taken a stand concerning it, while Martin Luther and the other Reformers condemned it as open heresy as soon as it appeared. A point rarely stressed sufficiently is the fact that there was no proof for it. As mathematical device it could

[1] *Historical Bulletin*, Vol. XI (1934-1935), pp. 5-7.

serve for the simplification of astronomical calculations. But neither Copernicus nor Galileo nor any other
astronomer had been able to show by a cogent reason
that it was more than a fine and even useful idea.
There had been much and heated discussion about it,
but only within the charmed circles of astronomers and
other scientists and in their professional Latin publications.

Galileo began to discuss it before a wider public. As
he commonly wrote his publications in Italian, he also
explained and defended the Copernican theory as it
were in the open. It was natural that the people and a
large number of the educated classes were shocked at
the seeming contradiction between it and the language
of the Bible. Holy Scripture speaks of the sun as rising
and setting, and as moving across the sky, while the
new theory maintained that the sun stands still, and
that it is the earth that moves. Preachers inveighed
against the new theory, and in strong language warned
the people not to adopt such unbiblical ideas. It was
unfortunate that Galileo, the layman, entered the theological arena and in several letters endeavored to harmonize the language of the Bible with the Copernican
theory. These letters spread rather widely in manuscript copies and were eagerly read by friend and foe.

As the controversy increased in animosity and even
acrimoniousness, the Church authorities thought it
their duty to take a hand in the matter. For the Church
the question turned around those expressions found
everywhere in Holy Scripture which refer to the relation of sun and earth, and which had always been
understood in a literal sense. Could it be permitted to
understand them in a figurative sense, namely, as denoting only the apparent motion of the sun? It was the

time when the religious innovators had thrown open
the Bible to the interpretation of each individual as the
last instance. So since there was no real proof for the
necessity of such a change, the Church decided, in
1616, to uphold the literal interpretation of these
expressions. Galileo personally was ordered not to
hold the new system any more as a fact, though he
might continue his studies about it and might even look
for genuine proofs for it.[2] (He continued drawing a
salary as honorary professor of the University of Pisa,
which amounted to a considerable sum, and which ulti-
mately came from ecclesiastical funds.)

Seventeen years later, in 1633, Galileo was again
summoned to Rome. He had flagrantly violated the injunction given him in 1616. This time he was obliged
formally to retract his teaching as a heresy, and was
sentenced to life-long imprisonment, his prison being
his own beautiful villa Arcetri near Florence. (He was
in no way prevented from following up his other
studies and investigations in the line of physics.)

We can now turn our attention to the Cardinal
Saint. Our task is facilitated by the appearance of a
large work on Cardinal Bellarmine in which several

[2] The verdict of the Theologians of the Holy Office declared the
teaching that the sun is the center of the universe and void of local
motion as heretical, and the proposition that the earth moves, as at
least erroneous in the faith. Cardinal Bellarmine was to admonish
Galileo "to abandon the said opinion," as stated later in this article.
This might seem to be much severer than simply to avoid asserting
it as a fact. But there is an official explanation of this "abandoning
the said opinion." At the same time the great work of Copernicus,
De Revolutionibus Orbium Caelestium, was put on the Index *donec
corrigatur*. The corrections were pointed out. They consisted in alter-
ing the passages in which Copernicus asserted his theory as absolutely true into an hypothetical form. These alterations could be
made with pen and ink and have actually been entered with pen and
ink in a copy to be found in the Vatican Library. The book so corrected was in no way forbidden, and could be read and studied and
even taught and discussed by Galileo as well as by everyone else.

pages are devoted to the reproduction of the most telling of Bellarmine's utterances concerning Galileo, to which are added illuminating passages culled from a work of an Italian historian, Bricarelli, who had made Cardinal Bellarmine's attitude towards Galileo the object of special investigations. Upon these well selected extracts we base our own study.

Long before the matter was brought officially to the attention of the Roman authorities, Bellarmine had opportunities to show sincere interest in Galileo's physical studies and was on the best terms with the enterprising scientist. Especially his astronomical discoveries had attracted the Cardinal's attention. The same was true of Bellarmine's brethren in religion, the Jesuits of the Roman College. When Galileo began to broach the Copernican theory, he found in the Cardinal a benevolent listener. Bellarmine indeed was convinced, and this showed his large-mindedness, that a different interpretation of the respective phrases of the Bible was not at all out of the question and might even become necessary. But as a true scholar he did not fail to call attention to the fact that there was so far absolutely no proof for the new system. The possibility of harmonizing the new theory with the biblical expressions, by referring the latter to the apparent movements instead of to the real, he fully admitted. But such a possibility, he rightly declared, was not by any means an argument for the truth of the Copernican theory. It merely did away with one serious objection against it.

Galileo had roused the opposition of both exegetes and adherents of the teachings of Aristotle. With precipitate zeal these went to extremes in their denunciations of the heliocentric system and loudly demanded its condemnation by the Inquisition. On the other hand, Galileo himself and his enthusiastic followers knew no bounds in proclaiming the reasonableness, grandness, and perfection of their ideas.

The saintly Cardinal strongly counselled moderation on both sides. Most remarkable is an utterance which he made to a friend when the strife was going on. "This is not a matter to hurry over or to fly into a fury about. Nor should these opinions be censured at all." His view of the affair was that the matter should be studied more dispassionately, more thoroughly, and in a truer scientific spirit, with the sole end in view to find out the truth. Nor should it be discussed before the public at large, which could only be scandalized by even hypothetical statements of this kind. "Had the moderation urged by the learned and saintly Cardinal been really practiced," says Bricarelli, "there would have been no condemnation of Galileo." It was the mutual incriminations of both parties which brought the conflict to a head. Galileo's attempt to harmonize his theories with the expressions of the Bible by his widely circulated letter added fuel to the flames.

After the condemnation of the system was passed by the Holy Office in 1616, St. Robert was chosen for the painful task of acquainting the great scientist with it. No reason why just he should have been selected to deliver this message appears in the documents, nor did he hold any office which would have imposed this duty on him. He was evidently chosen because both he and his brethren had shown to Galileo so much benevolence in the past. On this occasion the Cardinal also gave him a written testimonial of his good faith and religious sincerity.

With this ended the relation of St. Robert to the

Galileo question. The great Cardinal died in 1621, long before the second act of the drama, which took place in 1633. At this second trial, however, Galileo exhibited that testimonial of orthodoxy which the Saint had left in his hands.

In a letter to Foscarini, one of the fighting champions of Galileo, Bellarmine makes clear his standpoint towards the heliocentric system. The letter is dated April 12, 1615, about a year before the first process. It is really the standpoint which not only every Catholic but every true scholar had to take at that stage of development. There was no undoubted proof for the new hypothesis, and as long as that was the case the words of the Bible had to be understood as they were understood by the Fathers of the Church. Concerning the arguments, which were actually advanced by Galileo, the Cardinal says: "I have the most serious doubts (*ho grandissimo dubbio*)"; and in case of doubt we are obliged to retain the current interpretation of Holy Scripture. "I shall not believe that there is such a demonstration, until it has been laid before me."

But for the case that a valid demonstration be forthcoming, the Cardinal is equally determined. The few sentences in which he gives his attitude show him to be possessed of a thoroughly scientific mind. If a valid argument is presented, that which is now a mere hypothesis will be an undoubted fact, which cannot be given up. It will then be necessary to adjust to this fact the interpretation of many Biblical expressions. This he thinks is possible, without changing the real sense of the Bible. He evidently has in view the tenacity with which all mankind at his time stuck to the geocentric system, when he states that in case of a factual proof of Copernicus' theory "we must go carefully into the explanation of those biblical passages" which seem to contradict the new system. Should we not succeed in explaining them satisfactorily, we must not therefore give up the system. We should then "rather confess to a lack of full understanding, than admit a demonstrated fact to be untrue." The great principle that supernatural revelation cannot conflict with the teachings of genuine science has rarely been more forcibly expressed. Science, of course, must present real facts, facts based on arguments, which hold water. Revelation cannot permit its interpretation to be changed to accommodate some theory which still hangs in the air. It may be useful to broach a theory or hypothesis, perhaps even as "working hypothesis," but the honor given to real facts must not be granted to it.

St. Robert Bellarmine appears as a man with an open mind. Galileo's discoveries at once attracted his attention and won his sympathy. But he was both too Catholic and too scientific to overlook the weakness of the great scientist's astronomical contentions, though he did not underrate what real value they possessed. Had his warnings been heeded by both sides, there would have been no "Galileo affair." The Church would not have been obliged to take measures against the pseudoscience of an otherwise eminent scientist. Science, true science, would have had a more natural and wholesome development.[3]

[3] For more details see the article "Galilei" in *Catholic Encyclopedia* or the briefer notice in Betten's *Historical Terms and Facts* under "Galileo." There is a long chapter, "The First Troubles of Galileo" in *The Life and Work of Blessed Robert Francis Cardinal Bellarmine, S.J.,* by James Brodrick, S.J., London, 1928.

XIV

HARTMANN GRISAR, S. J., HISTORIAN (1845-1932)[1]

WHEN the news of Father Hartmann Grisar's death appeared in our papers, the members of the historical brotherhood knew that their profession had suffered a severe loss. It was a sad consolation that the great historian had reached the age of eighty-seven years, and had been active until death took the pen from his ever busy hand. Father Grisar, born at Coblenz on the Rhine, was ordained priest and joined the Society of Jesus in Rome in the year 1868, after finishing his theological studies at Innsbruck. As if with a presentiment of his future occupation, he utilized the two years of his novitiate to familiarize himself with the churches, places of historical interest, and the archeological treasures of the Eternal City. Appointed rather early and unexpectedly to the professorship of Church history at Innsbruck, he found it at first a difficult task to keep up to the standard set by such men as Hurter, Nilles, and other prominent members of the faculty. But he soon felt "the writer's itch." After testing himself on smaller subjects he became in 1877 one of the founders of the *Zeitschrift für katholische Theologie.* His first great contribution, the result of original studies, was a treatise on St. Gregory the Great's social activity among the various classes of people who lived on the estates of the Holy See, a publication which still fully retains its value.

[1] *Catholic Historical Review,* Vol. XVIII (1932-1933), pp. 229-232.

He deciphered, from the author's almost illegible handwriting, the important addresses of Father James Laynez, S. J., given at the Council of Trent, which until then had been considered unusable, and published them under the title, *Jacobi Lainez Disputationes Tridentinae.* Occasional lengthy visits to Rome enabled him to write a number of valuable historical contributions for the Roman monthly, *Civiltà Cattolica.* (He handled Italian with the same ease as his German mother tongue.)

As his special talents appeared more and more, his superiors relieved him of the duties of his Innsbruck professorship and transferred him to Rome, where he was able to devote all his time to historical and archeological studies. He spent several years in visiting the libraries, archives, churches, and museums of the Eternal City and central Italy. In spite of the great hardships caused by heat, malaria, and the ill-suited food of the Roman Campagna he ever looked back upon these years as the most pleasant time of his life. As a first fruit of these labors appeared the *Analecta Romana,* a collection of exhaustive studies on a great variety of subjects, a publication which won for him the admiration of the learned world of Europe. His ultimate aim, however, was the composition of a scientific *History of Rome and the Popes in the Middle Ages,* of which to his great regret he was not able to publish more than one copiously illustrated volume (in the English translation three volumes). His health, greatly weakened by his studies and the Roman climate, forced him to return to Innsbruck, where, far from the fields of his particular research, he found it impossible to pursue these studies any further. Several attempts in later years to return to Rome and take up the work again, regularly resulted in failure. But to the end of his life the importance of this enterprise and the intention to continue it were uppermost in his mind. Indeed the fact that non-Catholics in ever increasing numbers were entering that period of history made a truly scientific and extensive work by Catholics imperative. One of his last joys was the assurance of his superiors that the *History of Rome and the Popes* would be carried on and concluded.

Father Grisar now returned to a subject to which he had already successfully devoted himself in his early years, namely, the Reformation. After a preparation of ten years appeared his *Luther* (three volumes in the original German, six in the English translation) which not merely brings out the true facts of the reformer's opposition to the Church but lays the greater stress on the various conditions, previous studies and experiences, both religious and secular, the influence of other persons, of success and the opposite—upon the progress and retardation of Luther's activity. The work is rather a psychology than a biography of Luther. Its most remarkable feature, perhaps, is the absolute impartiality in the treatment of his subject. In his chapter on "Luther Fables" for instance, he shows that while many of the stories accepted by Protestants about Luther are unhistorical, some also, current among Catholics, are without foundation in fact. He did not fail, either, to recognize good traits in Luther's character. Together with this impartiality are united moderation and dignity of language which never stoops to the use of opprobrious words in the refutation of adversaries. The enormous amount of new material which Grisar brought to bear on the evaluation of Luther aroused considerable enthusiasm

among Catholics. Non-Catholic critics—they had given
unanimous praise to his *History of Rome and the
Popes*—were greatly divided in their attitude. Their
reviews ran all the way from unstinted praise to determined condemnation, the latter often being expressed in the most insulting terms. Of late, Protestant
authors prefer not to mention Grisar and his work at
all, which, however, does not mean that they take no
notice of it. His researches are too far-reaching, too
thorough, to be ignored. Page after page in works by
non-Catholics show that they have consulted Grisar
and that his quiet but irrefutable deductions have had
a lasting effect upon them. In his highly scientific manner, Grisar took the offensive in the Luther controversy and forced the adversaries into the defensive.

Sixteen years after the appearance of this epoch-
making work the author, now more than fourscore
years old, summarized the results of all his studies on
the Reformer in a one volume book, written with
youthful freshness in a more popular vein, though
with the same degree of scientific accuracy: *Martin
Luther, His Life and His Work*. This work, too, we
possess in English, though in an abbreviated form.

In 1883, Pope Leo XIII had thrown open the Vatican Archives to the students of history at large, Catholics and non-Catholics alike. Thereby and by his special
utterances and general attitude he indicated that the
Church is best served by the exposition of the truth,
even when it appears contrary to her interests and the
wishes of her children. One of the noblest fruits of this
new policy was the great work of Ludwig von Pastor,
*History of the Popes from the close of the Middle
Ages*. This new tendency was followed by the practice,
inaugurated by prominent writers, of divesting the

lives of the saints of those tales and stories which
historical criticism refuses to recognize as authentic.
Many Catholics, educated Catholics too, refused to
approve of this policy. A controversy ensued, which
sometimes became rather acrimonious. Father Grisar
also took sides in it. In a convention of Catholic scholars at Munich, in 1900, he decisively and energetically
pleaded for genuine historicity in describing the lives
of the saints, even at the sacrifice of edification and
rather ancient traditions. His address met with much
opposition, but the correctness of his stand was eventually recognized by all competent persons, including the
bishops, and it helped greatly to clear the atmosphere
for both the historical writer and the reading public.

The period of dissension, however, was by no means
over, when in 1901, Father Grisar appeared in the field
with the *History of Rome and the Popes*. In compiling it, he had applied his principles, the true principles
of history writing. He endeavored to tell the truth,
the whole truth, and nothing but the truth, and discarded a number of cherished Roman legends, which
had been accepted for a long time as a matter of
course. There was then much dissatisfaction, sorrow,
and indignation among devout people. "In Rome,"
said a book-dealer to me at that time, "they are making novenas for Father Grisar's conversion." Prayer
is always good, but its effect, though infallible, does
not always take on the form that was expected. Father
Grisar remained unconverted. A change seems to have
taken place, however, in the Catholic body, which is
now certainly not only willing but positively eager to
have the real truth from the pen of historians. People
realize, too, that the strictly historical procedure works
both ways, and indeed it has worked by far more in

favor of the Church than against her. Father Grisar is among the foremost Catholic scholars who champion a fearless application of genuinely historical methods in the exploration of the Christian past.

Father Grisar ever remained a true son of the cheerful Rhineland, a most agreeable companion, ready to help all those who approached him in any sort of difficulty or perplexity, and always anxious to avoid anything that might aggrieve or disconcert those with whom he had to deal. Inflexible in all points where truth came into question, he was obliging and yielding wherever charity suggested, and above all he never failed to treat his adversaries with the politeness of a true gentleman. While his works are highly apologetic by way of fact, they are not so in their form. His objective was simply to represent things as they appear when seen through the medium of honest and unbiased historical research, whether favorable or unfavorable to those who advocate or condemn them. It is this characteristic which among other causes gives their lasting value to the publications which bear the name of Hartmann Grisar, S. J.

XV

Saint Peter Canisius (1521-1597)
Doctor of the Church

1. THE PROTESTANT REFORMATION IN GERMANY

AT the beginning of the sixteenth century Germany, like all Europe, was entirely Catholic. Its churches and monastic establishments were numerous, charity flourished, the divine services were conscientiously attended. But abuses also existed. One might have discerned an overestimation of external observances, a considerable lowering of morals among the people, a remissness on the part of the pastors of souls in performing their sacred duties, and great laxity in many convents and monasteries. The various payments made by ecclesiastics to the Roman Court, though by no means unjust or excessive, were an object of complaint and helped to nourish a perceptible current of anti-papal feeling. Similar evils existed in all countries, but they were more noticeable in Germany. As yet, however, few if any so much as dreamed of a rebellion against Rome or a separation from the Church.

Then, in 1517, arose Martin Luther, the Augustinian Friar of Wittenberg, to pose as a reformer of the Church. He grew bolder day by day. He attacked not so much the immorality among the laity and clergy or the neglect of religious duties, or the carelessness of the shepherds of the flock, as certain doctrines and in-

stitutions of the Church themselves. He denied the
divine origin and power of the papacy and the priesthood, the Sacrifice of the Mass, most of the sacraments, the necessity and usefulness of good works.
Faith in Christ alone, he maintained, is sufficient for
salvation. He declared the Bible to be the sole source
of the doctrines he chose to retain. The temporal
rulers were to take the place of the bishops and might
seize all the rich property of the Church. Many attempts were made to win him back by kindness, but in
vain. Finally, in the beginning of the year 1521, the
public excommunication was pronounced against him
and his followers.

The death of Emperor Maximilian I, 1519, contributed towards the growth of these disorders. For
two years there was no Emperor, a time well utilized
by the innovators to spread their pernicious errors.
Then Maximilian's grandson, Charles V, already in
possession of Spain and all its dependencies, became
emperor. He entered Germany a few months after the
excommunication of Luther and summoned the princes
of the empire to a solemn Diet at Worms. To please
the potent friends of the reformer he allowed Luther
to appear before the august assembly. The apostate
friar, backed by his protectors, refused to recant his
errors, and the Emperor not only forbade the new
religion, but also placed Luther as a heretic under the
ban of the empire, May 8, 1521. This act made Luther
an outlaw and obligated his immediate territorial
prince to proceed against him. But that prince, the
powerful elector of Saxony, just appointed head of the
imperial regency which was to represent the emperor
during the long absence which his affairs in other portions of his vast dominions required, favored Luther's

cause in his own land and did nothing to stop its progress in other parts of Germany.

Thus things went rapidly from bad to worse. Eight years later, in 1529, Emperor Charles V found the adherents of the Lutheran heresy well entrenched in Germany. He was hard pressed by the Turks and the French, and in order to obtain military help he suspended the Edict of Worms for the Protestant principalities, forbidding, however, the future extension of the Lutheran heresy. This injunction was heeded as little as the Edict of Worms, and a quarter of a century later nearly half of Germany had become Protestant.

By the so-called Religious Peace of Augsburg, 1555, the Emperor made further concessions, allowing every prince to determine the religion of his subjects, and stipulating only that, should a bishop or other prelate turn Protestant, the temporal possession connected with his office was to be retained by the Church. Even this restriction was grossly violated in the following years. Germany was drifting farther and farther from the Church, the source of its former greatness.

But there stood already in the field the power which God's Mercy had provided to stem the tide of defection, to defend and strengthen what was still Catholic, and to reconquer much of what had been lost. In 1540, Pope Paul III gave his approbation to a new religious Order, the *Society of Jesus,* founded by St. Ignatius Loyola. Its purpose was to work for the Greater Glory of God in whatever place and occupation the Holy Father might see fit to employ its members. The Jesuits devoted themselves to preaching, teaching, and hearing confessions, and to various works of charity. They at once extended their labors to France, Spain, and Portugal, and in 1541 St. Francis Xavier set out for the foreign Missions in India and Japan.

Distracted Germany soon became a special object of the Society's active care. "All work of Catholic reform," says Johannes Janssen, the great historian of this troublesome period, "which has had any permanence, owes its origin to the exertions of the first three Jesuits who labored in Germany, (Blessed Peter Faber, Claudius LeJay, and Nicholas Bobadilla." [1] They were natives of Savoy, France, and Spain respectively. But this did not prevent them from pursuing their apostolate in Germany. The boundaries of nations and states did not yet divide Christendom in the same degree as now. Besides, Latin was still the common language of the educated classes of all countries. The much threatened Church of Germany had found able defenders before them, it is true. But the Jesuits followed a new program. They believed that the soul of all reform is the reform of the soul. They began by instructing the ignorant, high and low. They laid great stress upon the thorough education of children and youths in religion as well as in secular branches. By the "Spiritual Exercises" of their Father, St. Ignatius, they guided many to a higher and more perfect life of virtue. Their able and indefatigable defence of Catholic doctrine and discipline made them objects of fear and hatred to the Protestants. The secret of their success, however, lay in the incessant care which they bestowed upon the religious welfare of the Catholics themselves.

Blessed Peter Faber was the first to enter the empire and he remained there longer than the others. It was his privilege to win for the great work of genuine reform the man destined to enlarge beyond expectation

[1] *History of the German People*, Vol. III, p. 215.

the beginnings made by the first comers. This new paladin of Holy Church was Saint Peter Canisius, the Second Apostle of Germany.

2. CHILDHOOD OF SAINT PETER CANISIUS

Saint Peter Canisius was born on the 8th day of May, 1521, the Feast of the Apparition of St. Michael the Archangel. It was a memorable day and year. On the very same day Luther's doctrine was solemnly rejected by Emperor Charles V in the Diet at Worms. And in the same year St. Ignatius Loyola received in the defence of Pampeluna that wound which eventually caused him to change his life as officer of a worldly army into that of a soldier of Christ. Nymwegen, Canisius' home town, at the present time belonging to the Kingdom of Holland, was then a "Free and Imperial City" of the Empire.* Jacob Canees, or Canis, the father of the future apostle, belonged to a wealthy and prominent family. He repeatedly held the office of Burgomaster, or Mayor, of his native city, and was employed in important political missions by the Duke of Gelderland and by the Emperor himself. He was sincerely attached to the Church. A pious mother watched over the first years of Saint Peter's childhood, and often with tearful eyes recommended him to the protection of the Almighty. When she suddenly died, after giving birth to a daughter, the two little ones found in their father's second wife a genuine mother, who bestowed on them the same love and affection

* The question is sometimes asked whether St. Peter was a German or a Netherlander. He was both, just as a man can be a Californian and an American, or a Lancastrian and an Englishman. At that time all the Netherlands were part of the one Holy Roman Empire of the German Nation. See Historical Atlases,

as on her own numerous children. Peter himself, however, became the object of the special care of his new mother's sister, who lived almost the life of a nun in the world. He ever gratefully remembered the wholesome influence which this excellent aunt had exercised upon the religious training of his youthful mind.

The good seed fell upon fertile soil. The child was unusually given to prayer. He soon came to love to assist at the beautiful services in the churches, showed great delight when presented with holy pictures, and learned to serve in the sanctuary. At home he would, as little boys often do, imitate the ceremonies of the Mass, sing like the priests, and even give little sermons to the amusement and edification of the family and their friends. He early began to approach the sacraments. "Woe to me," he writes as an old man in his memoirs, "had I not under Thy kind guidance, O my Lord, availed myself frequently of the blessings of the Sacraments." It was by this means that he overcame the little faults from which his character was by no means free. Occasionally the bright, lively boy was rather irritable, even pert, resented admonitions, and showed more inclination for play and dissipation than his educators found it possible to approve. His stay of several years at a small boarding school, where nearly all the other boys were of poorer families and few as talented as he, made him proud and overbearing. But he evidently did not neglect his practices of piety. It was at this time that he was seized with an ardent desire to know his vocation. To find out what course God wished him to take in his life became the object of his fervent prayers at the reception of the sacraments and in his private visits to the churches. This sacred craving he called later on the "Teacher and Guardian Angel" of his youth.

3. THE DECISION FOR LIFE

God evidently watched over the pious lad. His father, who himself held the degree of Doctor of Law, intended to send Peter to a higher institution of learning. He no doubt knew of the conditions in university towns, and although the university of Cologne at that particular period had lost much of its former renown, the city was not by far so much infected with Lutheranism as was the case with other university towns. So Peter went to Cologne. On January 18, 1536, his name was entered in the register of the students of the Faculty of Arts.

The city of Cologne with its innumerable churches, its countless relics of Saints, its Catholic life, and its many excellent men attracted him at once and became for him like another home town. He was entrusted to a Canon of the Church of St. Gereon, a worthy ecclesiastic, who made it his practice to board promising students in his house. In order to take the better care of them he even salaried another priest to act as their tutor and look after their spiritual welfare. This priest, John van Esche, whom bodily infirmity alone had kept from joining the Carthusian Order, came across the path of Peter Canisius like an Angel from Heaven. The young student saw in him the living example of the highest virtue. From him he learned to control his passions, to check his impetuosity, to curb his desire for pleasure, to be kind and obliging to others. He adopted the practice of reading every day a chapter from the New Testament or some other pious book.

To this kind and firm spiritual father he repaired every night to give an account of the day and to receive words of praise or admonition or reproach. Van Esche did not spoil him. Once when Peter failed to return promptly from a vacation, the faithful shepherd suddenly appeared in Nymwegen and brought the lost sheep back with him to Cologne.

Among the young men who enjoyed the privilege of living in the same house there was one from Lübeck who had imbibed much of the errors of Lutheranism. But Father Van Esche, aided by Peter Canisius, succeeded in winning him back to the Church. The youth became Peter's familiar friend. Later on he entered the Order of the Carthusians, and is known to this day as the learned Laurence Surius, the author of many devotional books, as well as excellent works on dogmatical and historical subjects.

In 1540, Peter Canisius graduated from the Faculty of Arts. The question of his vocation, which he had recommended to God with undiminished fervor during all the four years, now became actual. To please his father he began the study of law. When, however, his father suggested marriage, he firmly declared it was not his intention to enter into that state at all. He also declined to accept an ecclesiastical benefice which it would have been easy for his father to procure for him. He did not as yet know his mind, except that he was resolved to study theology. After long discussions James Canis finally acquiesced in his son's desire, and Peter returned to Cologne to join the divinity students.

Years before this time, a lady who was highly respected by the people for her genuine virtue, had declared to him that he would some day render great service to the Church by the composition of books.

Another saintly woman had spoken to him of a new Order, through which God would send humble but efficient laborers into His vineyard; Peter she said would become their companion. In Cologne Peter made the acquaintance of a young Spanish priest. Alvaro Alphonso had come to Germany in company with Blessed Peter Faber, of whose virtue he gave the most glowing accounts. He praised him in particular for the ability with which he could handle a peculiar system of meditations and instructions, called "The Spiritual Exercises," which had been devised by Ignatius Loyola, a saintly Spanish priest. Ignatius, together with Faber and other zealous men, had established a new Order, whose members added to the usual three religious vows of poverty, chastity and obedience, a fourth one by which they obliged themselves to work for the salvation of souls in whatever field the Vicar of Christ would assign to them. A few years before, in 1540, Pope Paul III had given it his solemn sanction. Canisius' heart was burning. He now looked upon the prophetic words once spoken to him in another light. He resolved to put himself at least for a short time under the guidance of the saintly Faber. In the early spring of 1543 he set out for Mainz (Mayence) where Faber was then residing.

There he soon found that he was in the company of a thoroughly spiritual man, and Faber's hearty friendliness and winning ways contributed to inspire Canisius with unbounded confidence. He requested the favor of going through the entire Spiritual Exercises of thirty days under his direction. "Words cannot express," he wrote at the end of this holy seclusion to a friend, "how much light I received during these blessed days, and how condescending God was towards

me. These thirty days have made me a different man."
During this retreat the question of his vocation, the
object of so much prayer, was definitely settled.
"While scrutinizing my interior more carefully, I
learned how to pray to God in the Spirit and in Truth.
I understood that the mode of life as outlined by the
Constitutions of the Society of Jesus is exactly what I
need to live happily and to serve my God faithfully.
And hearing, like St. Matthew in his toll booth, not
obscurely the call of the Lord I am not at liberty to
resist his invitation." Without hesitating a moment he
wrote with his own hand: "In the year of the Lord
1543, on the Feast of the Apparition of St. Michael,
May 8, my birthday, entering into my twenty-third
year, after giving this important matter due consideration, I vow before God Almighty, the Blessed Virgin
Mary, St. Michael the Archangel, and all the Saints, to
place myself entirely under the obedience of the Society
of Jesus." Blessed Peter Faber received him into the
Order, and after a further stay of a few days, Peter
Canisius returned to Cologne as a novice of the Society of Jesus.

4. FIRST YEARS OF RELIGIOUS LIFE

The Society of Jesus possessed no house at Cologne,
in fact none in all Germany. So the young novice tried
to make up for the lack of the regular training in a
novitiate by works of charity towards the sick and
the poor, so much so that Faber, whom he kept accurately informed, saw fit to restrict his zeal, lest his
studies might be neglected. During this time he received the news that his father was seriously ill. He
at once hastened to Nymwegen. When he entered the

sick room, his father recognized him, but was unable to return his greeting. It would seem that the desire once more to see his first-born child had been the only force that kept him alive, because he died the very moment that he saw Peter and heard his voice. Peter ever kept him in loving memory and held him up as an example of Christian virtue to his young relatives.

No one as yet knew of the great step he had taken. He now disclosed it to his stepmother, but the good lady could not understand it. She thought him to be the victim of an impostor whose sole purpose was to get the money of the rich heir, and she even used violent language against Peter Faber. But a letter from Faber, full of meekness and charity, disarmed her completely. She not only put no more obstacles in Peter's way, but later on gladly allowed one of her own sons, Theodoric, to join the Society. Theodoric Canisius also became an able worker in the vineyard of the Lord. A touching love and affection always united the two distinguished brothers. When Peter returned to Cologne, three young Nymwegians followed him, two to enter the Carthusian Order, one, the Society of Jesus.

Part of his inheritance Peter Canisius distributed among the charitable institutions of his home town. The greater portion went to establish the first humble foundation of the Society of Jesus in Germany, the residence at Cologne, which soon harbored a little community of eight Novices with Blessed Peter Faber as superior. But the "enemy of the human race" suddenly roused a storm against them. They were to be expelled from the city. Professorships and other brilliant preferments were offered to Canisius to separate him from his brethren. The fact that as students they

were under the civil jurisdiction of the university pro-
tected them against the worst extremes of the persecution. But they were obliged to break up their common
life and dwell in private houses. In the course of time,
however, a better type of men came into power in the
city, and the vexations ceased entirely.

Though only a deacon, Canisius now began to
preach, first in a village near Cologne, then in the
famous church of "St. Mary in the Capitol," and the
élite of the city crowded to his sermons. But he always
showed a predilection for young students, who in large
numbers would visit him in his room, and whom above
all he sought to encourage to the frequent reception of
the sacraments. In 1546, he was ordained priest, a fact
which still more inflamed his apostolic ardor. It was
not long, however, until a peremptory letter from St.
Ignatius put an end to this activity. The farsighted
founder of the new Order desired him to devote all
his available time and energy to study. It was no small
sacrifice for the zealous and successful laborer, but he
obeyed without hesitation.

How high an opinion was entertained of the ability
of the young religious—he was just twenty-five years
old—appears from the fact that on one occasion his
superiors sent him into Belgium to conduct the negotiations for the establishment of a college of the Society at Louvain. He was to undertake missions of still
greater importance.

The several years which Peter Canisius spent at
Cologne were coincident with a grave crisis through
which the true religion in that city was passing. For
twenty years Hermann von Wied, Archbishop of
Cologne, had resisted the inroads of Lutheranism into
his diocese. In 1536, he celebrated a Provincial Synod

which enacted the most salutary decrees. But all this was rather the work of able advisers than his own. Goodnatured, weak, yet obstinate withal, in many ways, his deficiencies as a scholar were still more notorious. According to an angry utterance of Emperor Charles V he had not said Mass more than three times in his life, and did not even know the "Confiteor" by heart. During the stay of Canisius at Cologne shrewd Lutheran emissaries won him over to their heresy, while his faithful Catholic counsellors found the doors locked against them. Blessed Peter Faber made an unsuccessful attempt to open the eyes of the unfortunate prelate. Hermann's intention to resign his episcopal office, while retaining his position as a sovereign of the territory, subject to the Archbishop-Elector of Cologne, became more and more apparent. Such a development would have proved a grave misfortune not only for Cologne, but for the whole empire, because the Archbishop of Cologne was one of the seven "Electors," three of whom were already Protestant. Under the leadership of the indomitable Canon John Gropper, a Westphalian, the clergy and the university of Cologne offered stout resistance, and Peter Canisius was destined to play an important part in the struggle.

When, in 1544, Emperor Charles V came to Cologne, young Canisius was deputed to wait upon the monarch and implore his active interference. As the promises given to him were not carried out immediately, he followed the Emperor to Brussels, where he also met the Apostolic Nuncio. Things now began to move. The pope excommunicated and deposed the archbishop, and the Emperor declared his temporal possessions forfeited. During another embassy Canisius obtained financial aid from the Prince-Bishop of Liège,

and again went, this time in the name of the administrator whom the Pope had appointed for Cologne, to
treat with the Emperor at Ulm in Southern Germany.
Charles V's victory over the Smalkald League, an alliance of rebel Protestant princes, on whom Hermann
von Wied had relied, secured Cologne for the Church,
and its electorship for the Catholic cause.—Besides
Canisius' evident ability the double fact, that his
father, James Canisius, had rendered noteworthy services to the Emperor and was personally known to him,
and that Peter himself spoke the Flemish dialect which
was Charles V's mother-tongue, no doubt had had
much to do with his choice as spokesman and envoy,
and with the success that attended his efforts. He had
thus performed his first great services to the Church
and to Germany.

On his journey to Ulm, Peter Canisius met Cardinal
Otto Truchsess, Bishop of Augsburg, whose acquaintance he had made on a former occasion. The cardinal
now carried into execution the plan which he had long
cherished of sending Canisius as his theologian to the
Council of Trent, which had been opened in 1545 and
had meanwhile been temporarily transferred to
Bologna in Italy. Canisius there delivered several addresses in the consulting meetings of the theologians.
From Bologna, however, he was summoned to Rome
by Ignatius, and for the first time saw the founder and
General Superior of the Society, which he had embraced with such high-souled ardor. To try his virtue
the Saint did not allow him to join the community, but
kept him for several weeks among the candidates of
the Order. Canisius had next to go through that pro-
bation which the Institute of the Society prescribes for
those who have finished their studies. Then, while

many in Germany were urging his speedy return to
his fatherland, and while naturally he himself thought
of nothing else, St. Ignatius decided to send him not
to Germany but to Messina in Sicily, to become teacher
of a college class. Without the slightest murmur
Canisius went to his new destination and threw himself into the work as if he had never thought of anything else. He also preached in Latin and Italian, and
began to form far-reaching plans for the conversion
of Greece and other Eastern countries. But whether
St. Ignatius really intended him for Italy, or whether
he meant this disposition only as another kind of pro-
bation, after a year Canisius received orders to come
to Rome and to prepare for his return to Germany.

5. DEFINITE MISSION TO GERMANY

St. Ignatius had received an urgent request from
William IV, Duke of Bavaria, to send him a few
capable professors for the University of Ingolstadt,
which was suffering grievously from religious confusion
of the times. The Duke moreover had signified his
intention of establishing for the Society of Jesus a complete college, which would have been the first institution of the kind to be founded in Germany. Disregard-
ing all other petitions St. Ignatius resolved to send
three men to Ingolstadt. His selections were Salmeron,
one of the first seven Fathers of the Society of Jesus,
Le Jay who had formerly been in Germany, and Peter
Canisius.

Canisius alone happened to be in Rome. He received
Pope Paul III's apostolic blessing for the great mission
which he and his two brethren were to undertake.
From the audience with the Holy Father he repaired

to the Basilica of St. Peter to implore in fervent prayer the powerful assistance of the Most High. "It pleased Thee, O Eternal Highpriest," he writes in his memoir, "that I should feel impelled to ask Thy Holy Apostles, whose relics are venerated in the Vatican Basilica, for the confirmation and efficacy of the papal blessing. I experienced a great consolation and became conscious of the presence of Thy grace, which so kindly was granted to me through these powerful protectors. They on their part also bestowed upon me their blessing and sanctioned my mission to Germany. Thou knowest, O Lord, how often and earnestly on that day Thou has recommended Germany to me, that, as the good Father Faber did, I might surrender myself entirely to its welfare and live and die for that country."

While at Rome, Canisius was to take his final vows as a member of the Society of Jesus. Great interior favors were bestowed on him during his preparations for this important step. "While I was praying before the altar of the Holy Apostles Peter and Paul, a new grace was granted to me. Thou gavest me a special Angel to instruct and aid me by his guidance in the sublime life of a professed member of the Society of Jesus. There before me lay my soul in its whole ugliness, disfigured by countless faults and passions. The Angel, turning to the throne of Thy Majesty, pointed to my utter unworthiness, estimating it in quantity and number, to make me realize how little I deserved to be admitted to the act of profession. He emphasized the difficulty he would have in guiding such a soul on so sublime a way of perfection. Then, O Lord, thou didst show to me Thy Sacred Heart, didst bid me drink from that fountain, didst invite me to draw from

Thy sources the waters of salvation. I felt an ardent desire that torrents of Faith, Hope, and Charity should inundate my soul. I thirsted for Poverty, Chastity, and Obedience. I yearned to be entirely washed, clothed, and adorned by Thee. Then I had the courage to touch Thy most sweet Heart with my lips, and to quench my thirst from it. To cover the needs of my soul Thou didst promise me a garment consisting of three parts: Peace, Love and Perseverance."

Canisius had never had the opportunity of finishing up his academic studies by promotion to the degree of Doctor of Theology. In the same condition were the other two Jesuits, Salmeron and Le Jay, with whom he set out for Ingolstadt. St. Ignatius thought that this title would increase their authority as professors. Arrangements were therefore made with the University of Bologna for their promotion. "I was in great anxiety," Canisius writes, "on account of the rigorous examination. But Thou, O Lord, didst deign to give light and clearness to my confused mind. Thou even didst inspire me with the desire, that my ignorance which in my pride I had wished to remain hidden should be detected." He looked upon the promotion with the greatest religious respect and reputed it a high honor to be declared a professional "Teacher" (Doctor) of the sacred sciences. After the examination was over, we find him again in prayer, and consolations similar to those he had received before taking his last vows filled his heart. "All my patron Saints, it seemed to me, gave me their blessing, and became sponsors for my success and my reward as teacher. To Thee, O Father of all Wisdom, I give thanks for raising Thy humble servant to the dignity of the doctorate and putting me on the same level with my two excellent brethren." To be a Teacher of the Faith he ever deemed a great privilege and sincerely thanked God for having called him "into our Society and among the teachers, and given me the grace not to remain a dumb 'Canis' (dog) but to raise my voice in the chair of Orthodox Faith."

He ever remained devoutly conscious of the divine mission given him for the welfare of Germany. Having in mind the religious plight of his fatherland, he wrote a few years later to the Duke of Bavaria: "There is no land on earth which we Jesuits ought to have so near our heart as Germany." And in a memorial composed for Cardinal Hosius, Papal Legate at the Council of Trent, he says, "Among the German heretics there are very many, who err without stubbornness, without obdurateness. They err according to the manner of the Germans, who are by nature for the most part honest, and docile to what they hear in school and church." Rome, he was convinced would obtain the greatest results by kindness. In accordance with this principle he obtained dispensations, and leniency in applying certain ecclesiastical penalties, "lest the smoldering flax be extinguished." He tried to fill his brethren in religion with love for the unhappy country, and on suitable occasions, for instance when they came to confession to him, exhorted them to pray for Germany.

6. FIRST YEARS OF THE GREAT APOSTOLATE

The three Jesuits found Ingolstadt in a pitiable condition indeed. There were few students of theology, and some of these lacked even the necessary preliminary knowledge for this branch. Among the professors of the other faculties some inclined towards the innovations of the day, and others were openly Protestant. The town swarmed with Protestant books, even many textbooks used in the schools were un-Catholic. Church-going and the frequentation of the sacraments had fallen into disrepute, and the commandments of the Church were ridiculed. The three Fathers were, however, received with great demonstrations of honor.

They began their activity in their own characteristic manner. Besides the theological lectures they gave private instruction to the weaker students, and begged money and other alms for the poor ones. Canisius was soon busy with sermons and catechetical instructions for children and adults. The Fathers also procured temporal and spiritual aid for the poor, sick, and prisoners. The students, at first in very small numbers, to the surprise of the citizens, approached the sacraments more frequently. The non-Catholic and semi-Catnolic books disappeared.

In 1550, the university elected Canisius Rector, an honor which he was unable to decline. The teaching staff even desired to make him Vice-Chancellor for life, and after much resistance he accepted the duties of this responsible office for some months. It gave him a chance to impart to the Bishop of Eichstädt, who was Chancellor of the university, a clearer idea of the sad conditions which prevailed at Ingolstadt. This office also enabled him to introduce a little more discipline among the students. When admonitions, kind or severe, did not lead to the desired results, he proceeded resolutely to incarceration and dismissal. A new spirit became noticeable in the university.

His renown rapidly spread beyond the confines of Bavaria. Bishop Julius Pflug of Naumburg had been driven out of his diocese, but was able to return in consequence of the victory of Charles V over the Smalkald League. He most ardently desired to procure Jesuits for his nearly Protestantized flock. He wrote to this effect to Canisius, and although his request could not be fulfilled, it was a blessing of importance to the new apostle to have made the acquaintance of the worthy prelate by letter, as both of these men were destined to labor together for the sake of the Church on many an occasion. The Bishop of Eichstädt wished to send him to Trent, not in the capacity of a theologian but as his representative. The Cathedral Chapter of Strassburg tried to win him for the pulpit of the Cathedral. But all these endeavors were cut short by a new turn of affairs. Duke William IV had died soon after the arrival of the Jesuits in his land. His successor, Albrecht V, influenced by new counsellors, made no move toward the erection of the promised college. On the other hand, Ferdinand I of Austria, "King of the Romans," i.e., chosen to become Emperor when his brother, Emperor Charles V, would die, was on the point of establishing a college at Vienna, where Father Le Jay was already the superior of a small community. So Canisius received orders to join his brethren at Vienna. Albrecht V later on fulfilled the promise given by his father and founded the college at Ingolstadt. The year spent in Bavaria had been a real school for Peter Canisius. He was now fairly well initiated into conditions in Germany, and had accumulated a great deal of experience which served him well in his later years.

The outlook was dark in Vienna and a large part of Austria, much more so than in Ingolstadt and Bavaria. Opposition to the authority of the Church, contempt for the dogmas of the Faith, and neglect of ecclesiastical laws and usages were rampant. But the King of the Romans and many of his advisers were staunchly Catholic, and constituted well nigh the only support of the true religion. Canisius was given the task of supervising the younger students of the college and explaining the catechism to them. He also began to preach with so much success, that within a short while the largest church in Vienna after the Cathedral was assigned to him. The principal standard by which he gauged his success was the increase in the number of communions. He also took upon himself the regular care of the prisoners, and after a series of addresses to them, saw the greater part at the Holy Table. Under his direction his younger brethren gave weekly catechetical instructions in the prisons. The sacrifices which the Jesuits made when a pestilence swept the city, gained them increased popularity. For the poor inmates of the public hospital Canisius had printed in several languages a little prayerbook, which besides prayers contained short exhortations and instructions.

About Christmas we find him on a lengthy visit to an abandoned parish, which for many years had not seen a priest. He preached every day, gathered the children for instruction, and spent the rest of his time in the confessional. At the king's request he was freed from domestic duties for the time of Lent, and journeyed from parish to parish—countless parishes were without a priest—for similar work, undeterred by cold and snow, by the insults and intrigues of the evil-minded, and by the hardships of travelling upon rude country roads. When he returned the king requested his services as court preacher. Every Sunday Canisius

addressed the court in the royal chapel, and preached
to the people in St. Stephen's Cathedral.

His next apostolate was devoted to the institutions
of learning. The king made him visitor of the university and, upon his advice, promulgated new regulations, which did away with great abuses and diminished
the influence of the religious disturbers. Then the
king laid upon him the task of reforming two older
but very important institutions of higher learning, an
undertaking which caused him so much labor, anxiety
and worry, that he fell ill and for some time had to
interrupt his occupation.

The king's intention was to make Canisius Bishop
of Vienna. But the genuine son of St. Ignatius strove
with might and main to evade this dignity, and implored the assistance of his Superior General to the
same effect. Three times the king renewed his efforts,
and the pope was not disinclined. But finally Ferdinand
I wrote to his ambassador in Rome to let the matter
rest, "because I do not wish to cause to so saintly a
man, whom I love and esteem and whom I rather ought
to please, any more anxiety."

During this early activity in Vienna Canisius had
won the full and implicit confidence of King Ferdinand I, which was a great asset in his later work for
Germany. This confidence enabled him to strengthen
the good will of the prince, to encourage him to works
of piety and charity, to open his eyes to many dangers
and abuses, and to safeguard him against taking or
sanctioning objectionable measures. Through Canisius
the king learned that his eldest son, Maximilian, the
later Emperor Maximilian II, had as court chaplain
an out and out Protestant divine. The man was immediately removed and Ferdinand I gave serious and

energetic advice to his son. But Maximilian never became a really fervent Catholic. Ferdinand I, too, despite Canisius' restraining influence made several deplorable mistakes in his relation with the Church, though they never flowed from religious indifference or personal connivance at error. He did not waver in his confidence in Canisius and his reliance upon the zealous Jesuit's advice. On the contrary, he acted upon it at several of the most critical moments in the history of the Church of Germany.

Ferdinand's daughter was married to the King of Poland. Upon this fact Canisius built his hopes of gaining entrance to that kingdom for the Society of Jesus. In Poland, too, the Church was in a critical condition on account of the vacillation of the king. A large and powerful party among the nobility strongly favored Protestantism, chiefly because they craved for the rich property of the bishoprics and monasteries. Later on Canisius was sent to Poland by the Pope, and it is partly to his credit that at the diet of Petrikow the aspirations of the Protestants were not realized. He observed, however, that despite the machinations of the great, the people had retained much more religious spirit than those in the Catholic sections of Germany. He used to thank God for the consolation he had thus received. He thought, moreover, that through Poland the Society would be able to find its way to Russia and the Tartars, in the opinion of the time the wildest of all nations. To win this people for Christianity seemed to him a most worthy object of Jesuit ambition.

But while he thus burned with an unquenchable desire for the defence and extension of the Kingdom of Christ, Divine Providence had already devised another means by which Canisius was to multiply himself a thousand fold in his apostolic endeavors: the Catechism.

7. THE CATECHISM

We have noticed that one of the occupations which Canisius tried to take up as soon as possible was the instruction of children and the common people. It was the spirit of his Order. At Ingolstadt and elsewhere the particular spots are still pointed out in the street, where Canisius used to stand and explain the Word of God. Right from the beginning of his activity at Ingolstadt regular catechetical instruction became part of the course of education in the university. A good textbook, however, was lacking. The several catechisms with which Canisius was acquainted were not suitable for his purpose. He often mentioned this want in his letters to Rome, but without result.

The suggestion that he himself should write a catechism proceeded from King Ferdinand I. While pondering over the needs of his lands this prince had come to the conclusion that three books were needed, one for the instruction of the people, a summary of theology for the students of the sacred sciences, and a handbook for the clergy. Of course the overburdened Jesuits were to write them. Father Le Jay, then superior at Vienna, had accepted the arduous task, but he died shortly after Canisius' arrival from Ingolstadt, and the matter devolved upon Canisius. He confined himself, however, to the first, the textbook for popular instruction. The need for the other two was soon to be supplied by the official "Roman Catechism," or "Catechism of the Council of Trent," a work destined for the clergy.

Canisius first wrote the *Summa Doctrinae Christianae per Quaestiones Tradita, in Usum Pueritiae Christianae.* "Summary of the Christian Doctrine in Questions (and Answers) for the use of Christian youth." The language is fluent, without affectation, and very clear and perspicuous. "The book," says a Protestant critic, "is a wonder of brevity, precision, and teachability." The terms, statements, and admonitions used in it are almost exclusively drawn from the Bible and the great doctors of the Church, and are most dexterously woven together. Although there is a perfect unity of style, one feels all through the little book, that it is not Canisius who speaks but the Church and her authorities. This method supposes in the author an astounding familiarity with the productions of patristic literature. This catechism has one hundred and forty-six questions.

The *Summa Doctrinae Christianae* was written in Latin. Canisius had in view in the first place the students of the Jesuit schools, in which, as in fact in all the up-to-date institutions of the time, instruction was given in the international idiom. The *Summa* remained the basis of his catechetical works. He soon arranged a small edition of one hundred and twenty-two questions, which he called *Institutiones Christianae Pietatis sive Parvus Catechismus Catholicorum,* "Instructions in Christian Piety, or Little Catholic Catechism," and he attached to it a short collection of meditations and prayers. Both these Latin books were at once translated into German. But Canisius also composed two catechisms directly in German, one of one hundred and fourteen, the other of forty-seven questions and answers.

Ferdinand I, who meanwhile, after the abdication

of his brother Charles V, had become Emperor, prescribed the catechism for all the schools of his hereditary Austrian states. It spread rapidly through the rest of Germany. Its definite, brief, and yet detailed information was recognized as an incalculable boon to the true religion. Its method of appealing to passages of the Bible disarmed the Protestants, who had so far imagined themselves as possessing a monopoly in the matter of utilizing and interpreting Holy Scripture. The author aimed at a full and positive explanation of the Catholic Faith, but he also explicitly attacked the errors of the day, not indeed by hurling opprobrious epithets at the erring persons—he did not even mention the names of Luther or Calvin, or the word Protestantism—but by pointing to the contrary doctrine as it was embodied in the Bible and expounded by the great teachers of the Christian past.

Outside of Germany, too, the catechism entered upon a veritable march of triumph. After a short time Canisius could be truly said to be teaching Christian doctrine not only in Latin and German, but also in French, English, Scotch, Bohemian, Polish, Spanish, Italian, Ethiopean, Indian, and Japanese. One of the several editions published in France was begun in 1686 by order of the Archbishop of Paris and was reprinted four hundred times. In most parts of Germany it remained the official catechism until the end of the eighteenth century, when Josephism forced a shallower sort of instruction upon unsuspecting populations. In many districts, however, it maintained the field until far into the nineteenth century, and there are still living such as learned their Christian doctrine from their "Canisi."

The catechism was the cause of many conversions.

After Canisius' death it brought back to the fold Duke Wolfgang of Neuburg with his whole dukedom. It was one of the most powerful means employed by God to preserve and revive the Faith in Germany. Although it is now replaced by other catechisms thought to be more suitable to our own times and needs, it will ever remain a monument to its author's name, and a widely visible landmark in the development of the art of catechising.

The *Summa Doctrinae Christianae* was finished in Vienna. But much of Canisius' later work for the catechism was wedged in between the great labors of his apostolate, and was performed in the various places to which his numerous journeys happened to take him. In this way many of his other more occasional publications originated. Thus, when he stayed for a brief space at the court of Cardinal Otto Truchsess, Bishop of Augsburg, in Dillingen, there appeared there, with some additional exhortations, the *Litany of Loretto,* which up to that time had been unknown in Germany. No older print of this beautiful prayer has been discovered anywhere, and investigations have made it highly probable that this Dillingen print was prepared by Canisius. His pen was ever ready. As soon as his keen eye perceived the desirability of some particular publication, he was on the spot with a well planned and carefully worked out production to meet the demand. Saint Peter Canisius had in the best sense of the word "the writer's itch." He was not actuated by a blind passion to rush into print, but by the earnest desire to counteract the immense harm done by the countless heretical and otherwise unsound books and pamphlets which flooded the country.

8. IN BOHEMIA—CANISIUS IS MADE PROVINCIAL

On the occasion of a visit of King Ferdinand I to his kingdom of Bohemia the few prominent Catholic officials of Prague implored him to give them a college of the Society of Jesus. The religious condition of Bohemia was distressing in the extreme. Hussites of all shades, Lutherans, Calvinists, Anabaptists, and other heretics controlled the land, while not even the capital itself could boast of an eminent Catholic preacher. Canisius was invited to Prague, and after consultation with the leading men in Church and State he consented in the name of St. Ignatius to open the college. He wrote to Rome: "Those who are to come here must be armed with holy patience and an ardent zeal. I do not mean zeal to dispute with the heretics, but zeal to edify this country by their example." These words express one of the chief principles which guided Canisius in his apostolate.—The Saint himself once while saying Mass was greeted by a huge stone flung at him through the window, and once a man ran up to the altar to revile him.

The twelve Jesuits who arrived found themselves in great poverty. The buildings had not been finished, because the promised funds were not forthcoming, and even the means for their daily sustenance were scant. But they opened the classes, and their efficient instruction soon won the admiration and good will even of non-Catholics. The college of Prague, later on enlarged to almost gigantic dimensions, became the mother institution of a great number of others in Bohemia, Silesia, and Moravia. "From the time that the Fathers of the Society of Jesus came to Prague," writes a Bohemian bishop, "the Catholic religion began to revive and to increase gradually, so that every successive day presented a brighter aspect than the preceding." Between the years 1661-1678 the Jesuits in the above named countries brought back 29,500 erring souls to the true Faith.

During his stay at Prague Father Canisius paid a flying visit to Ingolstadt. There he received the official news, that St. Ignatius had erected the foundations at Vienna, Prague, and Ingolstadt into the Province of Upper Germany, and had appointed Canisius, who was himself the soul of all the undertakings, its first Provincial Superior. (The members of the Society in Belgium and Cologne were to form the Province of Lower Germany.) Two weeks later the news arrived, that the Saint had finished his earthly career. The appointment of Canisius as Provincial was St. Ignatius' last gift to Germany.

The new Provincial found a heavy burden to shoulder. The three colleges were in a precarious condition financially. It was, moreover, always to be feared that an outburst of Protestant fury, especially at Prague or Vienna, or the intrigues of liberalizing Catholics might put an end to their activity. As Provincial it was his duty to inspect the several institutions from time to time, to see to the observance of the Rules, to supply the necessary teachers, and to promote in every way possible the welfare of the houses and their individual members. He encouraged above all the spirit of prayer and of self-denial, on which, as he knew so well, everything else depended. Six years later Bohemia, and Hungary were separated from the Upper German Province and established as the Province of Austria. Canisius' influence, however, always extended much farther than his official jurisdiction. Twelve colleges—the college of those days consisted of the high-school classes and two or three years of what is called college in this country—owe their origin entirely or largely to his endeavors. These institutions he considered the most powerful agencies for a permanent reform of clergy and laity, and in them by far the majority of Jesuits in the country fulfilled their vocation by laboring for the practice and improvement of Christian education. Father Canisius was provincial from 1555 to 1569. But even after he had been relieved of this office, he remained the actual soul of the Order in Germany by the power of his personality, his sane and unerring judgment, and his indomitable spirit of enterprise.

9. THE RELIGIOUS "COLLOQUY" AT WORMS, 1557

Ferdinand I wished to have Father Canisius with him at the great Diet of Ratisbon in 1557, where important questions concerning religion were bound to come up. Incidentally it was understood, that while there, Canisius would give the sermons in the Cathedral. He preached on all Sundays and feastdays from the beginning of Advent to the middle of March, and during Advent he added three more sermons on weekdays. In the Diet the Protestant princes demanded, that to end the religious troubles of Germany a so-called "Colloquy" should be held. A number of theologians from both sides should come together, debate the controverted points, and come to some understanding. Such Colloquies had taken place several times, in Germany, Switzerland and France, but always without the desired effect. Each party had claimed the victory, a new strife of pamphlets and leaflets and handbills had followed the oral duel, and on the whole the Protestants by their quibblings and noisy boasting had gained more than the Catholics.

Canisius was strongly opposed to the measure, and submitted to King Ferdinand, who at that time was still acting as Regent and Representative of Charles V at the Diet, a memorial to this effect. The ecclesiastical princes also declared that there was no prospect of reunion except through the General Council of Trent, though this Council was now not actually in session. But Ferdinand was in greatest distress. An immense army of Turks was approaching the boundaries of Austria, and there was no force to ward off the attack. The Protestants made the grant of military assistance dependent upon his consent to the Colloquy, and the king yielded, stating, however, explicitly that the Colloquy should in no way form a prejudice to the Council. Each party officially appointed speakers. Canisius and another Jesuit were among the twelve representatives of the Catholics. The Protestants chose the famous Melanchthon as leader of their deputation. The Colloquy was to be held in the city of Worms on the Rhine.

As some months intervened before the opening of the Colloquy, Father Canisius in the meantime went to Rome, to take part in the election of a new Superior General of the Order. But the strife between Pope Paul IV and King Philip II of Spain prevented the arrival of the Spanish deputation, and the election had to be postponed indefinitely. While the Fathers were waiting for a better turn of affairs, Canisius employed his time in patristic studies in the Eternal City. There existed an edition of the works of St.

Cyprian, issued by Erasmus of Rotterdam, that erudite but shallow humanist of Luther's time, who despite an acrimonious feud with the heresiarch, and despite the saving mercy that he died a Catholic, had greatly contributed to the spread of error in Germany. Erasmus' Cyprian proved to be highly unsatisfactory, and Canisius had long ago resolved to issue a better edition. In Rome he noted down about a thousand emendations of the text, entrusting the rest of the work to his brethren. But he gave up the plan eventually, when he heard that other men were working at the same task. In fact several good editions soon appeared in Rome, Paris and Antwerp.

Germany, Catholic as well as Protestant, and in a way all Europe, eagerly looked forward to the coming Colloquy, which in the eyes of the non-Catholics stood far above the General Council in importance. A rather brilliant assembly of participants and anxious visitors gathered in the ancient city on the Rhine. For weeks the Jesuits were kept so busy that they had hardly time to say Mass and take their meals. Canisius, though not the official head, was by way of fact the intellectual leader of the Catholic deputation. The misgivings of the Catholics, however, began to disappear when they noticed the fierce contentions which arose among the strict Lutherans, the Zwinglians, Calvinists, and other factions of the Protestants. The Colloquy had been ordered by the imperial Diet to take place between the two religions which at that time were recognized in the Empire, namely, the Catholics and the "adherents of the Augsburg Confession," that is, the strict Lutherans. In the first official sessions a common ground was sought to proceed from, and common principles to decide the validity of arguments. The Protestants declared the Bible as interpreted by the individual the sole rule of Faith, while the Catholics demanded besides some other authority, the constant Tradition of the Church, to decide doubtful interpretations.

In the sixth session Canisius spoke at length on this subject. To show what mere private interpretation would lead to, he adduced the contradictory ways in which the Lord's words, "This is my Body," were understood by the Lutherans, the Calvinists, the Osiandrists, etc. A great and angry commotion arose among the Protestants. Then the president of the Catholic delegation put the pointed question, whether or not the Zwinglians, Calvinists, etc., were adherents of the Augsburg Confession. New and greater confusion followed, and the sixth session broke up in a turmoil. Subsequently five strict Lutherans were excluded from the Protestant delegation by the seven other members. They left Worms in a body.

Under these circumstances the Catholics could not continue the discussions, because they had no order to debate with any but adherents of the Augsburg Confession. Had they done so the Lutherans would have had a just cause to complain. An attempt made by the Catholics to revive the Colloquy through a new royal decree was frustrated by the peremptory refusal of the Lutherans to return. The sixth session was the last of the Colloquy, which was ended before it had really begun. The gathering, opened with so grandiose expectations of the Protestants, had only served to show to the whole world the hopeless disunion which split their ranks, and the glorious unity of the Catholic Church.

Although non-Catholic writers in a flood of vilifying and slanderous pamphlets tried to blame the

Catholics, especially Canisius, for the disruption of the Colloquy, intelligent persons could not help gauging the situation correctly. Even Melanchthon confessed, "now Canisius and the others of the papistic party are celebrating their triumphs over us." "From this moment," says the Protestant historian Maurenbrecher, "dates the ebb, the retrograde movement, the decline, of the Protestant current in Germany." No religious colloquy with the Catholics was ever again demanded in any Diet.

As soon as the deliberations connected with the Colloquy began to flag, Father Canisius utilized his spare hours in giving instruction to the children in the schools. A trip to Zabern in Alsace the residence of the Bishop of Strassburg, brought the indefatigable apostle to a number of Alsatian towns, where he also instructed the children and preached to the adults. He found many people there who faithfully adhered to the Church and religious practices. His interview with the bishop led to the establishment of the college of the Society at Freiburg in Breisgau.

10. CANISIUS AND THE COUNCIL OF TRENT

The Council of Trent had assembled in 1545. Two years later it was temporarily transferred to Bologna, where Canisius participated in some of the meetings of the bishops' theologians. After it had been reopened at Trent, in 1551, its sessions were suddenly interrupted by the treacherous inroad of Maurice of Saxony into the Tyrol. It remained prorogued until, in 1561, it was reopened again for its final and most brilliantly successful sessions by Pope Pius IV.

Canisius' whole soul was with the Council. He

preached about it; he exhorted the people to pray for
its success; by his order the students of the college of
Vienna, and probably of all the colleges under his
jurisdiction held special devotions every Monday to
implore for it the divine blessing. To his utter surprise he was himself called to Trent as one of the
Pope's theologians. Pius IV's order was transmitted
to him by Cardinal Hosius, the great defender of the
Catholic cause in Poland, and now one of the Presi-
dents of the Council. The Cardinal, whose esteem for
Blessed Peter bordered on veneration, was critically
ill, when Canisius arrived at Trent, but at the very
sight of the apostle he recovered immediately.

Besides being a member of the Commission for the
Prohibition of Books, Canisius took active part in the
consultations of the theologians, which were held twice
a day. The Blessed Sacrament was just then the subject of the debates, and in particular the question,
whether communion under both species should be allowed to laymen, was being spiritedly discussed. The
Spaniards and Italians spoke strongly against this concession. There was a great interest, when Canisius
rose. What was the German doctor going to say?
Canisius thought that the chalice should never be
granted generally, but it might, perhaps, be allowed to
those living in non-Catholic surroundings, as the refusal would expose them to unnecessary annoyances—
provided always, that the genuine doctrine of the presence of Our Lord under each species be inculcated.
This view gave great satisfaction to the imperial ambassador, who wrote to his master: "The Spaniards
and Italians spoke learnedly, but they know nothing of
our difficulties. Canisius alone hit the nail on the head."
As a matter of fact, however, the Council made no

regulation, but expressly committed the settlement of the question to the Pope.

This decision did not please Emperor Ferdinand I. This ruler, though personally above reproach, suffered keenly at the sight of the increasing boldness of the heretics. Many of his advisers represented the general concession of the chalice as the one great remedy against further defections, and an infallible means of regaining those already fallen away. There were also not a few echoes of the idea, once very general, that the Council is above the Pope and has power even to reform the Pope and pass laws over his head. When Canisius went back across the Alps, he and other theologians were consulted by the Emperor concerning the steps to be taken in this matter. Canisius reiterated the principles he had put forth at Trent and took occasion to remind the emperor forcibly, that there can be no salvation without close adherence to the successor of St. Peter.

But Ferdinand's mind had become confused. The religious difficulties in his hereditary estates were indeed extremely acute. Once it even seemed that he would be unable to retain the Jesuits in Vienna against the opposition that arose from various quarters. Like King Charles IX of France he had transmitted to the Council a long list of proposals and felt vexed that not each and everyone of them was taken up in the assembly. It was suggested to him to go to Trent and rattle the sabre. This step would have made the Sacred Synod appear an imperial council and would have undermined its prestige throughout the entire world. He took up his residence at Innsbruck, to be as near as possible to Trent. To Innsbruck he summoned a commission of theologians, among whom was our apostle, to aid him with their advice. Canisius prevailed on the Emperor to give up the idea of going to Trent, although even Cardinals were urging him on.

But the danger was by no means over. The Emperor demanded that a common memorial be submitted to him by the theological commission. And such was the spirit of that body, that the document jointly composed by them, of course not with the concurrence of Canisius, served only to irritate the Emperor the more. Had he acted on this memorial, the very existence of the Council would have been put in jeopardy. It might have broken up, and national synods, followed by schisms, would have been the almost infallible result, not to speak of the immense advantage that would have been afforded to the heretics by so pitiable a failure of the worldwide efforts made by the Catholic Church. Germany would have been practically lost. What should Canisius do? At first he thought of submitting a separate memorial, but finally he decided to ask for an audience. He showed the Emperor in detail how unsound were the suggestions made in the memorial of the commission. He implored Ferdinand to remember his position as protector of the Church and Papacy. Why should he not go hand in hand with Pope Pius IV, who was so seriously endeavoring to promote the renovation of Christendom? Why should he not consent to a personal interview with Cardinal Morone, the First President of the Council, who had come up to Innsbruck to show his willingness to arrive at an understanding? The Emperor was overcome. The same day he paid a visit to Cardinal Morone, and the imperial demands and proposals had been so modified, that the Cardinal failed to discern in them any serious difficulty. Saint Peter Canisius' prudence and courage had averted a grave crisis for the Tridentine Synod and the whole Church.

After the Council Pope Pius IV selected Canisius, who happened to be in Rome at the time, to take to the German bishops and Catholic princes the official decrees of the Sacred Synod and urge their execution. At the same time he was to call attention to the great importance of an Imperial Diet, which the emperor had called to meet at Augsburg in the spring of 1566. All the bishops and princes should attend it in person and be ready for the defence of the interests of the Church. Canisius was to go on his mission with all the powers and dignity of a papal delegate, but without any exterior display of pomp. Ostensibly he travelled as Visitor Extraordinary of the Jesuit houses in Germany.

In this disguise he journeyed to the bishops and archbishops of Würzburg, Mainz, Treves, Münster, and Osnabrück, and to the Duke of Jülich. Though this prince, who resided at Düsseldorf, had not fallen away from the Church, the clergy at his court could hardly be called Catholic. The zealous papal envoy tried every means to recall the duke to his duty, but seemingly in vain. With sadness in his heart he left Düsseldorf. But within three weeks he received the welcome news that the duke had banished the Protestantizing preachers, and insisted on the observance of Catholic ceremonies in his court church. Henceforth he was guided by the advice of better counselors.

Canisius carried with him a special papal brief for the City and University of Cologne, where he was received with great honor. The Pope allowed the university to draw the revenues of certain ecclesiastical benefices for the purpose of increasing its staff of professors. He then called attention to certain abuses, and the effect of this fatherly admonition was immediately noticeable.

Among the proposals which the apostolic envoy sent to Rome none was more important than that coadjutors with the right of succession should be given to all bishops. This would forestall the troubles and risks which regularly attended the elections after the death of the incumbents of episcopal sees, and which had already led to the loss of eight bishoprics. The Holy See eventually adopted this recommendation as a principle to be followed whenever circumstances would permit.

Incidentally the trip gave a welcome opportunity to several bishops of concluding their transactions concerning the establishment of Jesuit colleges in their dioceses.

While Canisius was on the lower Rhine, he could not well ignore the urgent invitations of his relatives and the magistrate of Nymwegen to honor his native city by a visit. Local historians assure us that this visit resulted in a wonderful strengthening of the Catholic part of the population in their Faith. Canisius' own numerous relatives remained Catholic under the most trying circumstances. It has recently been discovered that many of the families of the Catholic nobility of Holland today are in some way descendants of Gisbert Canisius, brother of the saintly Jesuit.

When in Cologne the apostolic wanderer learned that Pope Pius IV had been called to his reward, a fact which ended his own powers and duties as delegate. The new Pope, St. Pius V, at once sent him word to repair to Augsburg and await the opening of the Imperial Diet.

11. AT THE DIET OF AUGSBURG, 1566

Emperor Maximilian II had summoned the Diet chiefly to obtain aid against an army of 200,000 Turks which threatened the eastern boundaries. But everybody knew that the irrepressible question would come up again, and that the Protestants would make new demands to favor the diffusion of their errors. Upon the urgent suggestion of Canisius, Pope Pius V sent a special Nuncio to Augsburg, Cardinal Commendone, a prelate who thoroughly knew German conditions. Beside Canisius two other Jesuits and two secular priests were to act as his advisers.

The Protestant princes at once declared they would refuse to grant any subsidies to the Emperor, unless two important clauses of the Religious Peace of the year 1555 were abolished. By one of these clauses the adherents of the Augsburg Confession, i. e. the Lutherans, alone were to be tolerated in the empire; it was now demanded that the same toleration should extend to other Protestants also. By the other clause it was ordained that if a Catholic bishop or abbot should turn Protestant he was to lose his office with its temporal possessions, though without prejudice to his private property; this so-called Ecclesiastical Reservation they now desired dropped entirely.

At first it looked as if the dissensions between the strict Lutherans and the Calvinists, etc., would break up the Protestant front, as it had done in the Colloquy at Worms. But the Emperor waved this question, and left it entirely to the heretics to determine which parties were genuine followers of the Augsburg confession. This concession led them to drop their opposition to the Ecclesiastical Reservation. With the new imperial explanation of the first clause, the Religious Peace of 1555 was to be reenacted. But just at this juncture came, like a thunderbolt from the blue, the notification from Pius V to his legate, to oppose with a solemn protest any and every resolution which might be counter to the decisions of the Council of Trent. Was not this the case with the Religious Peace, which recognized another religion besides the Catholic? had not that document been solemnly condemned by Pope Paul IV? On the other hand, a protest under the present circumstances would form a most powerful weapon in the hands of the opponents. They would point to it as a proof that the Pope desired no peace, that he was meddling with the internal affairs of Germany. The emperor, known to be a lukewarm Catholic, might align himself against the papacy simply to obtain the necessary help against the Turks. Or a civil war might ensue.

Cardinal Commendone was in the greatest consternation. His advisers, above all Father Canisius, were kept busy day and night. Canisius was obliged to have himself replaced by another Father as preacher in the Cathedral. The three Jesuits and one of the secular priests, an Englishman, were convinced that the protest could not be made without grave injury to the Catholic cause. Only one of the five, an Italian, held the opposite opinion. The four convinced Commendone, that in 1555 the Catholics, being absolutely unable to enforce their just claims, had simply stated existing conditions and declared that they would refrain from an impossible enforcement of their rights. At any rate the re-affirmation of the Religious Peace would not be against the Council of Trent. They demanded, however, that the Catholic princes who were present at the

Diet, should in some official way declare their submission to all the decisions and enactments of the Council.

A messenger was dispatched to Rome with a letter from the Legate. Canisius and his two brethren sent a separate communication to their Superior General, St. Francis Borgia. St. Francis at once conferred with Cardinal Granvella, the Spanish ambassador, who fully realized the correctness of the attitude taken by the three Jesuits, but lacked the courage to intercede with the pope. In this quandary the Jesuit General himself undertook the office of peacemaker between the German Catholics and Pius V. At first the saintly Pope was utterly surprised, but, as he always did, he listened patiently to St. Francis' words. In the end he remarked he would pray for light. Francis Borgia also prayed. Two great Saints prayed. The protest was omitted. The Catholic princes at Augsburg gave before the Legate the desired solemn declaration of faithful submission. For the first time since the beginning of the religious troubles did the Catholics weather an Imperial Diet without suffering any disadvantage. On the contrary, "from this moment on," writes the Protestant Ranke, "a new life began in the Catholic Church of Germany."

12. CANISIUS' BOOKS ON ST. JOHN THE BAPTIST AND THE BLESSED VIRGIN MARY

In 1559, the Lutheran Matthias Flacius began the publication of a gigantic Latin work on Church History, in which he intended to prove that, while Catholicism was a degeneration, the Lutheran religion represented original Christianity. It appeared in eight huge volumes, and is commonly referred to as the *Magdeburg Centuries* from its division of universal Church History into periods of a century each. Flacius and his many collaborators had gathered material from countless libraries and archives (sometimes cutting the passages they desired bodily out of the original). This show of learning gave to the work a vastly overrated authority. The authors asserted numerous unproven facts and distorted others that were genuine so as to suit their preconceived purpose. The *Magdeburg Centuries* had a very large sale and did an immense amount of harm.

A number of smaller works had already been written against them, and at Rome plans were made by Cardinal Baronius to issue a complete refutation which later began to be realized by the appearance of the first instalments of the monumental *Ecclesiastical Annals*. But for the present Pope St. Pius V wanted a book equally deep but less extensive, and he gave to Father Canisius orders to write it. Canisius was to select several individual passages or features and expose the misrepresentations and false conclusions embodied in them, thus to show in a few instances the character of the method followed by the compilers. The humble religious had his misgivings concerning his competency in the field of history, but he went with a will at the assigned task. He selected three personages, whose character had been completely disfigured by the "Centuriators," namely, St. John the Baptist, the Blessed Virgin, and the Prince of the Apostles, St. Peter. His first step was to ask for the blessing of St. Pius V and of St. Francis Borgia, Superior General of the Society of Jesus.

He began his studies for the work in 1567 at

Dillingen, where the university library offered the best
material and facilities, and where he could enjoy the
advice of learned friends. Whatever he undertook
throughout the whole course of his life was done thoroughly, but for this work he made almost super-
human efforts. Some passages he recast as often as ten
times. His brethren became seriously apprehensive for
the health of the aging man. But in 1571 the first
instalment, a good-sized quarto volume on St. John
the Baptist, appeared and was greeted with words of
sincere praise by men of prominence all over Europe.
Canisius' wish for a plenary indulgence as his private
reward was joyfully granted by St. Pius V.

Meanwhile the indefatigable author had been relieved of his duties as Provincial. His successor, Father
Hoffaeus, was not so deeply impressed by the usefulness of work such as this. He and others were inclined
to think that a man with the experience of Canisius
could accomplish more good by devoting himself to
preaching and teaching and to the writing of more
strictly popular books. Canisius was to his great sorrow
transferred to Innsbruck as preacher for the court of
Archduke Ferdinand, a son of Emperor Ferdinand I
and then ruler of the Tyrol. This office it was presumed would not interfere much with his writing. Thus
he was deprived of the company of the eminent men
in the university of Dillingen. And although a wagon-
load of books, weighing fifteen hundred pounds, followed him to his new home, this could not console
him for the loss of the university library. His health,
also, suffered under the influence of the Föhn, a warm
wind which blows periodically on the northern slope
of the Alps. But faithful to his principle he made no
attempt to have the order rescinded.

In his sermons before the court he was far from imitating the example of those whom he was wont to call sugar preachers, who spoke ever of the Mercy but never of the Justice of God. He believed in pouring not only soothing oil but also sharp wine into the wounds of the sinful soul. Still he never demanded the impossible. Concerning the customs of the Carnival he said, "no king or Emperor, nor even Sts. Peter and Paul, could ever succeed in abolishing them. The preacher's task will therefore be to show the people how to enjoy themselves in decency, and without committing excesses." Upon his advice a regular crusade was inaugurated against bad books. But the wise reformer insisted that it was not enough to take the heretical writings from the people; good books must be put in their place. So the government made large purchases in Augsburg. The poor received Catholic books gratis. Those who could afford it were expected to refund half of the price.

To assist the zealous author in the composition of his volume on the Blessed Virgin, Archduke Ferdinand hired a copyist, and supplied the author, moreover, with money to buy books for his studies. "It is incredible," writes Canisius' step-brother Theodoric, then a priest of the Society of Jesus, "how much good Father Peter is bothering himself and others for this work. Everybody is surprised that he does not break down." Canisius knew that Cardinal Sirleto at Rome enjoyed the reputation of being most familiar with the Vatican library and other depositories of printed and manuscript books. To him he made bold to apply, and was happy to receive from him a number of contributions which it would have been impossible to find elsewhere.

While the author was staying a short time at Landshut, the residence of young Duke William, the later William V of Bavaria, it happened on a certain occasion that the laybrother to whom he used to dictate, asked permission to absent himself for an hour. Canisius, buried in his thoughts, remained seated at his desk. Then he heard the door open, but it was the young duke that entered. Without looking up Canisius, presuming it was the laybrother, began dictating. The prince at once grasped the situation, sat down and wrote on, until the brother returned. There followed, of course, much consternation and begging of pardon, all to the great glee of the duke, who modestly declared, that he was only too happy to have contributed a little to so worthy a work in honor of the Queen of Heaven.

The new volume appeared in 1577. It is a complete Mariology, treating of all questions that are connected with the dignity, position, and veneration of the Virgin of Virgins. It met with even greater favor than the volume on St. John the Baptist. The Catholic critics praised in particular not only the immense erudition, solidity, and reliability of the work, but also the enthusiasm of the author for his great subject, and the piety and unction manifested in every line. In spite of its size it was reprinted a few years later and several times in the course of the following centuries, the last edition being that of Paris which appeared in the nineteenth century. (If I am rightly informed another edition is now in preparation.)

Canisius had already gathered much material for the volume on the third object of Madgeburg misrepresentation, St. Peter, and the success he experienced with the first two volumes inspired him with the desire to finish the third one also. But Father Hoffaeus, the Provincial, thought differently. Men were too urgently needed for more direct work in the Vineyard of the Lord. The health of the celebrated author, too, seemed to be seriously on the decline. It was no small trial for good Father Canisius to learn of the Provincial's view. But, as he had always done, he entered heartily into his superior's plan. He himself remarked, that Gregory XIII, who had succeeded St. Pius V, would easily release him from the duty imposed upon him by the latter. Thenceforward he devoted himself, as of old, to the more or less ordinary duties of the members of the Society as preacher, catechist, and confessor. Several remarkable conversions of prominent Protestants soon were the fruit of his untiring zeal.

13. SAINT PETER CANISIUS AND THE SCHOOLS

One of the most striking features of St. Peter's activity is his incessant work for the rejuvenating of Catholic schools in Germany and the neighboring countries. This work really extends over all the years of his life. The schools of Germany, which in the beginning of the century had been in a very flourishing condition were now in a pitiful state. Countless institutions of learning had disappeared with the monasteries and other ecclesiastical establishments by which they had been formerly maintained. The Lutheran agitation had spread to the Catholic regions and had affected the teachers of those schools that were still in existence. The students were fewer, partly because the parents feared for the Faith of their children in view of the incorrect religious attitude of many teachers. The number of teachers, too, rapidly declined. The desire for knowledge was decreasing. The private tutors procured by noblemen for their children were often of doubtful orthodoxy. These tutors not infrequently accompanied their charges to the Catholic universities, and, because of the general dearth of professors, obtained positions as teachers. By the middle of the sixteenth century there was hardly a school in the Catholic lands of Germany in which not some member or members of the teaching staff were imbued with heresy.

St. Peter Canisius is rarely mentioned in handbooks of the history of education. And yet it was he that revived education in Catholic lands to the envy of the Protestants. He insisted above all on the use of the great means of education furnished by the Church. We have already seen how he acted at Ingolstadt and Vienna. He strove to induce the students to a more frequent reception of the sacraments. He encouraged general piety, frequent prayer, the practices of devotion. He wanted Catholics, but truly educated Catholics. Instruction in all branches was to be thorough. He went to endless trouble to procure suitable textbooks.

His carefully compiled catechism is only one feature of this endeavor. Wherever he had any influence he worked for the appointment of good, reliable teachers and for their decent remuneration. St. Peter was a firm believer in well stocked libraries. "Rather a college without a church" he used to say, "than a college without a library; we cannot be good soldiers unless we have good weapons." No Saint probably ever worked more unremittingly and went to greater personal trouble for the establishment and augmentation of libraries than St. Peter.

The plans of study which he drew up for Jesuit and other schools are believed by historians to have been the starting point of the Jesuit system as outlined in the *Ratio Studiorum*. The universities of Ingolstadt and Vienna, and of other cities, in particular the Saint's own Alma Mater, the University of Cologne, greatly profited by his suggestions, and by his influence with ecclesiastical and secular rulers. He laid greater stress, however, on "Colleges," which as remarked before comprised the high school classes with several years of college studies. Directly or indirectly he founded twelve such institutions. Though these "Colleges" were not expressly established to educate candidates for the priesthood, as a matter of fact they supplied an astonishingly large number of priests both secular and regular. About half a dozen "Seminaries" provided exclusively for young boys who purposed to become priests. Special institutions in connection with the colleges gave board and lodging to poor but promising boys from distant places. The Society of Jesus accepted no college unless it was endowed, because for very good reasons they did not want to charge tuition. This, however, greatly augmented the difficulties encountered in making new foundations. It is incredible how much begging, explaining, imploring; how much worry and anxiety each foundation cost the Saint; and how many cruel disappointments he experienced from lack of response even on the part of his friends. He sowed in tears, that the Church might reap an abundant harvest in joy and exultation.

St. Peter Canisius was himself a master in the art of teaching. Hence his renown as professor in universities, and as teacher in colleges. Above all he liked children. From the pulpits of the cathedrals, and from the council chambers of bishops and Emperors he always found his way to the children—in the schools, in the streets, wherever he could meet them. And the children loved him and eagerly awaited his coming.

The schools, high and low, were to him of paramount importance. It was indeed through them chiefly that, with his brethren in religion and his numerous friends and active collaborators, he saved what could be saved for the Catholic Faith in Germany.

14. SAINT PETER CANISIUS' BUSY LIFE

If ever a man made full use of every moment of his life, it was St. Peter Canisius. We have seen how on certain occasions he most powerfully, in union with other able and farsighted men, furthered the interests of the Church. We have also mentioned several of the productions of his pen. The works on the Blessed Virgin and St. John the Baptist required the hard and painstaking labor of years. The first of his catechisms, the little book with the one hundred and forty-six questions and answers, was definitely given to the press after the best part of three years had been devoted to its composition. We cannot enter upon the rest of his numerous literary productions. We must confine ourselves to the statement that the reprint of their titles alone covers some fifty quarto pages in the large bibliography of his Order.

A very considerable part of his apostolate was carried out by his letters, which have been edited in eight heavy octavo volumes. These letters represent an enormous amount of work and study. The overwhelming number of them treats of the most momentous affairs, especially those addressed to Popes, Emperors, cardinals and bishops. They are extensive memorials on the conditions of dioceses and countries and impart practical advice as to the remedies that ought to be employed. When reading these lengthy documents one is inclined to think that they alone would suffice for a man's lifetime. Here might be added that we have also several thousand manuscript sermons of the Saint, mostly written out in full, or at least very carefully sketched.

But along with all this and with the occupations indicated before went the cares and worries caused by the beginning colleges, the direction of the increasing number of laborers in the Lord's vineyard, and the government of the young Jesuit province, in which things and offices and methods had first to be planned and created before they could be in anything like smooth operation.

And yet this was not all. To make the reader realize, to some degree at least, the untiring zeal and give a better idea of his personal character and many-sided activities, we take occasion here to recount briefly some other noteworthy undertakings of his busy life. While in Rome in 1568 he had several audiences with Pope St. Pius V. The appointment of a Commission on German affairs consisting of several cardinals was greatly due to his suggestions. This Commission accomplished much in the interest of the Church in Germany, especially under the next Pope, Gregory XIII. So long as his sojourn in the Eternal City lasted, Canisius did not cease to exert influence upon the proceedings of this Commission. On one occasion the cardinals had decided to deal severely with certain German bishops. The papal briefs were ready to be despatched. Our apostle heard of it, and by his explanations and representations brought it about, that the plan was abandoned, and gentler measures were tried with eminent success.

Pius V intended to raise Canisius to the cardinalate. But the humble religious, so writes the imperial ambassador, "got wind of it, and is now beseeching the cardinals to change the Pope's mind." A personal audience with the holy Father had the desired result, and Canisius was allowed to return to Germany without the cardinal's purple.

The Protestant elector of Saxony and the landgrave of Hesse tried to influence the Prince-Abbot of Fulda to expel the Jesuits and hand over their college to Protestant teachers. Under the pressure of rebellious subjects the abbot seems to have wavered. When Canisius received the news, he at once wrote to the Bishop of Augsburg, and through him prevailed on the duke of Bavaria and the Emperor to put a stop to those machinations.

The Hapsburg rulers of the Tyrol had been for a long time engaged in a dispute with the Bishops of Trent concerning certain territorial privileges. Archduke Ferdinand, though a very pious man, was so convinced of his right that he would listen to no proposal even of a compromise. Upon the request of the Papal Nuncio Father Canisius made a new attempt and succeeded. Ferdinand was now ready to yield, and thus a feud, which had assumed the proportions of a standing scandal, was brought to a satisfactory conclusion.

In 1556, King Ferdinand followed his brother Charles V as Emperor. But Pope Paul IV, who strictly adhered to the medieval idea of the Holy Roman Empire, could not make up his mind to recognize as Emperor a man in whose election heretics had cooperated, and who claimed the imperial title after his predecessor, Charles V, had abdicated without the Pope's consent. Blind zealots helped to widen the breach between Pope and Emperor. In Rome, Ferdinand was considered no less than a semi-heretic. "And still just now," wrote Canisius to Rome, "nobody tries more seriously to stand with a clear conscience before God and good men than this prince does." As Provincial of the Jesuits in Germany he had many Masses, prayers, and works of penance offered up to end the dissension. The Superior General of the Society also informed him that in Rome everything possible was tried for the same purpose. At last Divine Providence interfered. Paul IV, personally a most blameless character, died and under his successor, Pius IV, all the difficulties disappeared.

Since 1559, Father Canisius had been preacher at the Cathedral of Augsburg. This position was by no means a sinecure. It called for a sermon on all Sundays and Feastdays, the latter then much more numerous than now, and for three additional sermons every week during Advent and Lent. The zealous Canisius added two catechetical addresses every week all the year round. When he accepted the office hardly eight thousand of the eighty thousand inhabitants of the city could still be called Catholics. At first St. Peter had often no more than thirty or fifty persons present at his sermons. Their number increased rapidly. At the next Easter, there were nine hundred communions more than the year before. Slanders by the Protestants, and small nagging on the part of the very men who had enthusiastically greeted his coming were not lacking. But when seven years later he surrendered the post to one of his brethren, half the population of Augsburg was Catholic.

The boys who sang in the choir of the Cathedral of Augsburg and attended the Cathedral school were forced to find lodgings in the city among surroundings in which they were exposed to many dangers. When Canisius observed this, he suggested to the bishop the plan of founding a common home for them. He himself collected part of the funds by begging among the rich citizens and the Catholic princes who happened to be at Augsburg for Imperial Diets. A suitable building was acquired, and Canisius composed the rules of discipline for the new institution. As preacher in the Cathedral he ever kept these poor students in sight and continued begging for them and appealing to his hearers on their behalf. "It is now cold," he once said in November, "and they need warmer clothes. Please give your contribution as you did last year. They pray and sing for us every day, and they are forbidden to beg."

In 1566, Cardinal Otto Truchsess, Bishop of Augsburg, asked Father Canisius to spend some time at the residence of Count Helfenstein, who was considering to return to the Faith of his fathers. The count had forcibly introduced Protestantism into his district, only to find that morality was visibly declining among his people. Of himself he confessed: "Since that step I can no longer pray as I could before." Canisius stayed with him for a week and cleared up his difficulties. The apostle improved the occasion by instructing in the Catholic religion two women who were under sentence of death on the charge of witchcraft and had been abandoned by the Protestant preachers. The little County of Helfenstein has ever since remained an oasis of fervent Faith in the midst of Protestant neighbors.

In the same year we find Canisius at Würzburg to lend his assistance to the negotiations for the establishment of a Jesuit college in that city. He had to promise to give the Lenten sermons the following year. During that Lent he preached three times every week and gave besides two catechetical instructions in another church. At the same time he prepared the regulations which were to be discussed at the Diocesan Synod during Easter week.

The Roman publisher, Paul Manutius, was in possession of a privilege which prohibited under pain of excommunication the reprint of any work issued by him. Some of his publications were, of course with impunity, reprinted in Germany by Protestants, and often with grave errors and even falsifications, while the cost of transportation made his genuine works prohibitively expensive in Germany. Canisius seized the occasion of the visit of a prominent Roman prelate to show how much this interfered with the interests of religion in Germany. After a short while Manutius saw his privileges curtailed in favor of German printers.

Pius V ordered the Jesuits of Upper Germany to prepare a German translation of the Roman Catechism. It was written by Father Hoffaeus but Canisius himself took great pains in revising it. About the same time a Spanish Jesuit, Jerome de Torres, consulted him concerning a Latin work, *The Creed of St. Augustine.* The German Provincial saw immediately the usefulness of such a publication in the struggle with the Protestants who constantly appealed to the great Doctor of the Church, and requested the author to have it printed in Dillingen. But he himself, upon his own responsibility, toned down several strong expressions, which the fiery Spaniard employed in treating of the heretics of the day. "Father de Torres," he said, "would not write that way if he knew Germany." (In the same spirit he prohibited in the houses under his jurisdiction the reading of the works of certain Catholic apologists who failed to keep within the bounds of charity when speaking of the religious innovators.) He also gave encouragement and assistance to the Augustinian Friar Panvini for works on the history and the antiquities of the Church, in particular Panvini's work on the catacombs.

In Rome, Father Canisius saw the Latin reports of the missionaries from India, Japan, and other foreign countries. He sent some of them to Duke Albrecht of Bavaria, on whom they made a deep impression. "The Word of God," Canisius said in an accompanying letter, "is not identified with any nation. If ungrateful Christians in Germany reject it, it goes to races of which our fathers had no idea." Later on he planned a regular publication under the title of *Indian Letters*. It was the beginning of a whole literature on missionary activity, a literature to which is due much of our knowledge of the history and work of Catholic missions in all countries, America included.

In a similar way Canisius extended a helping hand to the friend of his youth, the Carthusian Lawrence Surius. He searched the libraries to find material for *Surius' Collection of the Councils,* and his critical *Lives of Saints.* (The last-named work made Surius the forerunner of the great enterprise of the Bollandists.)

When Pope Pius V proclaimed a Jubilee to obtain God's aid against the Turks, secular and ecclesiastical authorities applied to Canisius for a detailed plan of announcing in an appropriate manner to the people this great means of winning Divine Assistance for the enterprise.

While occupied, at Innsbruck, with the writing of his work on the Blessed Virgin, he composed an instruction for the clergy of the diocese of Brixen, concerning the administration of the sacraments. It had been discovered that many abuses had crept into these sacred functions. The Vicar General sent this instruction to all the pastors.

A Zwinglian preacher, John Brunner, had been converted in consequence of his studies in the works of the early Doctors of the Church. As he was married, however, he could not think of entering the ranks of the Catholic clergy and was at a loss how to support his wife and children. Canisius procured for him a position as teacher in the university of Ingolstadt.

One of the most important foundations of St. Ignatius was the German College at Rome, which had been established for the purpose of sending well instructed and trained priests to Germany. After the holy founder's death, however, the institution suffered greatly from lack of funds. Canisius used the confidence with which Gregory XIII honored him to direct the Pope's attention to its precarious condition. He was not the only one that did so. But it is remarkable, that only a few months after Canisius' departure from Rome the Pope put the German College upon a sound financial basis. During the next thirty years alone, about eight hundred young Germans received in it their education for the priesthood. It has ever remained one of the exterior bonds that unite Germany with Rome, and has served as a model for similar institutions in the Eternal City and elsewhere.

Canisius had often assisted bishops and cardinals in compiling reports on the condition of Germany. One by Cardinal Truchsess has long been considered as entirely the work of Canisius. The Pope expressed the desire to have one directly from the great Jesuit. In this memorial the writer gave utterance to a wish he had been cherishing for a long time, namely, that Papal Seminaries, like the German College at Rome, be established in Germany itself. Such seminaries were eventually founded in several German cities.

One of Canisius' journeys to Rome took place while he was preacher at the court of Archduke Ferdinand at Innsbruck. When he returned he found that another court preacher had been appointed, the Franciscan John Nas. It was a keenly felt humiliation. Worst of all, good Father Nas, who was a convert and had made rather brief studies, occasionally said strange things about good works and the sacraments, and also inveighed against the Jesuits. But Canisius was far from losing his composure. The man possessed an unusual gift of popular eloquence and did an immense amount of good by his powerful if at times uncouth sermons. Only on one occasion did Saint Peter reply in his own sermon to F. Nas' invectives, and this simply by way of stating the correct Catholic teaching and proving it from Scripture and Tradition. In a kind voice he added the remark, "This is what priests mean to say on these points. Sometimes they use strong language, and people are inclined to misunderstand them. But we should always beware of imputing to them any ignorance in theological matters." His moderation was amply rewarded. The talented friar rose to important positions in his Order and in the Church, defended religion successfully by preaching and writing, and more than once spoke of the Society of Jesus in terms of high praise.

One of Saint Peter Canisius' latest biographers concludes a similar chapter with these words: "He preaches and catechises so much, that he seems to be born exclusively for the pulpit; he writes, and he promotes literary enterprises, as if there were nothing else to engage his attention; he deals with city councils, with dukes and bishops and Emperors and Popes, and advises them on the most vital interests of the Church, as if he were a professional diplomat with no other occupation."

15. LAST YEARS AND HOLY DEATH

In 1579, Pope Gregory XIII sent Bishop Bonhomini, a man filled with the spirit of love and ardent zeal, as his representative into Switzerland. While the bishop found the Canton of Freiburg still steadfastly adhering to the Catholic religion, many of its inhabitants were lukewarm in the Faith, and the Calvinism and Zwinglianism of the surrounding cantons were seriously threatening this stronghold of Catholicity. There was already a Jesuit college at Lucerne, and Bonhomini now induced the Freiburg Magistrate to invite the Order to that city also. The Upper German Province was requested to send "a man of prudence and moderation," to take the initial steps. In the beginning nobody thought of the aging Canisius. But finally it was he that was selected, and with the ready obedience that had always been so wonderfully characteristic of him he at once set out for Switzerland.

The journey through the Zwinglian Canton of Bern was not without risk. But although Bonhomini, the Papal Nuncio, was subjected to petty annoyances, nobody suspected that the modest elderly man in his company was the dreaded Canisius.

The magistrates of Freiburg profusely thanked the Provincial for having given to their city a man, "whose fame resounds in all Christendom, above all in the German nation." Father Canisius here concluded a most intimate friendship with the Reverend Provost Schnewlin, of the Church of St. Nicholas, who acted as Vicar General for the Bishop of Lausanne. The schools were eventually opened in temporary quarters. Within a few months they counted more than a hundred students, most of whom had been recalled by their parents from the Protestant schools of the neighboring French Cantons. It was only a few years, until the college building, a substantial, well-planned structure, arose. But Canisius did not live to see the splendid new college church of St. Michael the Archangel.

For several years the indefatigable preacher continued to announce the Word of God from the pulpit. Thus for the period from March 12 to May 28, 1581, no less than thirty-seven sermons are still extant in manuscript. He also explained the Christian doctrine to the children in the streets of the city. One of the results of the new efforts made at Freiburg by the Jesuits, the Franciscans, and the many zealous secular priests, was an astounding increase in the number of communions. For all the priests Canisius for many years gave conferences on Cases of Conscience, which were always well attended. But in the course of time he was obliged to confine himself to the private instruction of individuals, in particular of prospective converts, who were, for the most part, poor immigrants from Protestant Cantons.

Meanwhile he induced the ecclesiastical and secular authorities to inaugurate a crusade against heretical books, and to revive the old custom that at the beginning of Lent every citizen should publicly renew his Profession of Faith. He could no longer make extensive journeys, but the influence of his advice and direction extended over all Switzerland. St. Charles Borromeo desired to take him along as companion on a journey of visitation in the Grisons, the eastern part of the country, and as this was impossible asked him for his views on a number of practical questions. Canisius, by several letters to Rome, prevented the excellent Provost Schnewlin from resigning his office of Vicar General, and even caused him to be appointed Apostolic Visitor of the Canton, a measure which resulted in an immense amount of good. St. Francis of Sales, not as yet Bishop of Geneva, wrote to Saint Peter a very flattering letter and wished to enter into a correspondence with him.

Nor did Canisius' pen rest. He published brief biographies of Sts. Ida, Meinrad, Fridolin, Beatus, Ursus, Maurice, and of Blessed Nicholas von der Flue, all of whom had sanctified Switzerland by their holy lives. In some of these booklets he relied upon documents which later investigations have proved to be unreliable, a procedure for which it would be unfair to reproach him. A collection of *Catechism Hymns,* an Instruction for Confession, and an exposition of the Psalm "Miserere" are other fruits of his untiring apostolic zeal. A little *Catholic Manual* was thirty times reprinted and soon translated into other languages. He also composed a Latin *Prayerbook for Princes* which in handwritten copies was used by the members of the Austrian, Bavarian, and Spanish dynasties. The most extensive product of the indefatigable writer's pen was a good-sized volume of *Notes on the Gospels of Sundays and Feastdays,* printed 1593, in Latin, for the use of parish priests, to assist them in meditating and preaching. During the same period the man of labor and prayer gave the usual instructions to the members of his religious community. He also assisted in the lowly domestic occupations of the house, and might be seen washing dishes in the kitchen or sweeping the corridors.

The more he realized his increasing inability to work, the more time did he give to devotion. Here is the place to state that nothing, perhaps, is more remarkable in this great man than his continuous spirit of prayer. In spite of his restless activity, with his many and far-reaching plans, with his public career, he never neglected his own soul. He found time to make a surprisingly large number of notes concerning his spiritual progress; he jotted down his resolutions and points for meditation, drew up sets of questions for his examination of conscience, composed prayers for various occasions and intentions, wrote out lists of institutions and persons for whom he determined to pray, or litanies of Saints whom he was wont to invoke. Among them stood out prominently the Guardian Angels and heavenly Patrons of the cities and countries, for which he and his brethren had been and were laboring. He enumerated in a kind of autobiography, which he called his Testament, the many favors received from God during his long life. A very large place he gave to the veneration of the

Sacred Heart of Jesus. He had composed for himself morning and night prayers in Its honor and a short invocation to be repeated every hour.

His prayer was a real conversation with God. Once a young member of the Order thought he heard loud speaking in the room of Father Canisius which was next to his own. Fearing the good Father might be in some distress he went out and listened at the door. Saint Peter was conversing with God. He pleaded with Him, remonstrated with Him, argued with Him, sometimes raising his voice and proving to Him that certain things had to be granted. The young man at once made up his mind not to get involved in this duel between Canisius and Almighty God. "The two will soon again come to an understanding," he reflected as he retired to his own room.

The spirit of prayer is one of the great characteristics which Blessed Peter possessed in common with St. Boniface, the first Apostle of Germany. Like him, too, he possessed an unswerving attachment to the Holy See, and the conviction that only through St. Peter and his successors could salvation come to Germany. Like him, moreover, he understood the necessity of solid study and of schools for the education of the young.

Canisius had always shown great love for the members of other religious Orders. In Switzerland the Capuchins attracted his attention by their efficient work among the people. Although they possessed no house in Freiburg, he had the consolation of seeing two Capuchin priests, together with his own brethren, present at his death.

On the feast of St. Thomas the Apostle he received the Last Sacraments. To Provost Werro, the noble successor of his friend Schnewlin he recommended the Church of Freiburg. He spoke similarly to two members of the Cantonal Council. Then he took the booklet in which he had written his familiar devotions and said the prayer for a happy death. Suddenly he cried out, "Don't you see? don't you see there?" and began to say the rosary. It is presumed that he was favored by an apparition of the Blessed Virgin. The simple assurance of the Rector of the house, that his brethren were praying for him, gave him great joy. He asked that they should say the Penitential Psalms. During these prayers, about four o'clock in the afternoon, December 21, 1597, Peter Canisius closed his life of love for God and men, of prayer and penance and indefatigable labor. He was buried, amid an immense concourse of people, in the church of St. Nicholas, whence his remains were later on transferred into the church of the Jesuit college.

The news of his death reechoed far and wide. With the Catholics in the German speaking countries the veneration for him was mixed with the feeling of deep gratitude. They continued more than ever to call him Germany's second Apostle, to whom they owed the preservation of their Faith. "They have reason," says a Dutch historian, "to pronounce the names of St. Boniface and St. Peter Canisius in one breath." That there are now some thirty million German speaking Catholics is next to God principally due to him.

But his importance reaches much farther. Within a short time St. Peter's life was written and read in practically all the countries of Europe and in the foreign Missions. People at once began praying to him. In 1655, a publication, with the approval of the ecclesiastical authorities, reported in detail a large number of cases in which remarkable favors had been obtained through his intercession. About 1750, the procedure for the beatification of the Servant of God was taken up. But the storm that broke upon the Society of Jesus a little later, and the political and ecclesiastical convulsions which followed in the wake of the French Revolution caused the matter to be dropped for another hundred years. On June 24, 1864, however, Pope Pius IX proceeded to the solemn act of enrolling Peter Canisius among the Blessed. In 1897, when the third centenary of Canisius' death was celebrated in Freiburg, Pope Leo XIII granted that the relics of Blessed Peter be carried in solemn procession, a privilege ordinarly reserved to the Canonized Saints. In the Jubilee Year of 1925, on May 21, Pope Pius XI canonized him together with St. Teresa of the Child Jesus, St. Mary Madeleine Postel, St. Madeleine Sophie Barat, Foundress of the Ladies of the Sacred Heart, St. John of Ars, St. John Eudes. Each of these holy men and women has a peculiar kind of sanctity, and represents a special field of Catholic life and action. St. Peter Canisius stands before us like the Israelites of old, who with one hand worked at the construction of the temple of God, and in the other wielded the sword for its defence. As St. Cyril of Jerusalem is the prince of Oriental catechists, so St. Peter is the prince of the catechists of the West. The Pope bestowed on him the singular honor, granted only to a small number of eminent and saintly authors, of declaring him a *Doctor of the Church*. The declaration was immediately connected with his canonization, a privilege never enjoyed by any of the former Doctors. May he become the Patron Saint of all those who devote themselves to the general promotion of Catholic life and to the defence of the Church, the Sovereign Pontiffs, and of those in and out of religious Orders who make Catholic education and instruction their special occupation.*

WRITINGS ON ST. PETER CANISIUS:

BRAUNSBERGER, OTTO, S.J., "Peter Canisius," article in *Catholic Encyclopedia,* Vol. XI, pp. 756-761.

ROBERTSON, S., S.J., *Saint Peter Canisius, Priest of the Society of Jesus.* Pamphlet of the Irish Messenger Series. Office of the Irish Messenger, Dublin, Ireland, 1925.

BRODRICK, JAMES, S.J., *St. Peter Canisius.* Sheed and Ward, 63 Fifth Ave., New York.

REANY, WILLIAM, *Saint Peter Canisius, A Champion of the Church.* Benziger Brothers, New York.

(The best lives in German are those by Otto Braunsberger, S.J., and by Johannes Metzler, S.J.)

St. Peter Canisius is also very extensively dealt with in Janssen, *History of the German People,* Vols. VI-X; in Pastor, *History of the Popes,* Vols. XV-XX; and in all Church Histories.

Of his works we have *Petri Canisii Epistolae et Acta. Edidit* Otto Braunsberger, S.J., 8 vols., *Freiburg im Breisgau.—Sancti Petri Canisii Catechismi Latini et Germanici. Edidit* Fredericus Streicher, S.J., 2 vols., published by Pontificia Universitas Gregoriana, Rome.—*Bekenntnisse des hl. Petrus Canisius, S.J. Herausgegeben von Johannes Metzler, S.J.* M. Gladbach.

* *This article is a reprint of a pamphlet, "St. Peter Canisius, Doctor of the Church," published by Central Bureau of the Central Verein, St. Louis, Mo., 1927.*

PART TWO

THE SEVENTH AND EIGHTH CENTURIES

I

St. Bede the Venerable (672-735 a. d.)[1]

DOCTOR OF THE CHURCH, HISTORIAN

IN A. D. 496, the great nation of the Franks began to enter the fold of the Catholic Church. A little more than fifty years later we find St. Gregory of Tours busy writing that nation's history. When St. Gregory died in 594, the conversion of the Anglo-Saxons, the Teutonic invaders of Britain, was about to begin. In 597, St. Augustine, sent by Pope St. Gregory I, the Great, landed on the island of Tanet in the kingdom of Kent. But the Christianization of the Anglo-Saxon was attended by much greater difficulties than had been that of the Franks. The Franks had practically only one ruler, and with his baptism by St. Remigius the work was almost done. Moreover, these new Christians simply joined the existing ecclesiastical units of Gaul. The Anglo-Saxons had seven kingdoms and seven kings, and each ruler had to be won over individually. Nor could the neophytes join dioceses or parishes already formed; the very system of an ecclesiastical organization was to be created.

This process of conversion and organization took about eighty years. It was practically finished when

[1] Reprinted from *Church Historians* with the permission of P. J. Kenedy & Sons, Publishers. Several passages in this and the following articles are overlapping. They have been left unaltered, so that each article can be understood independently.

the subject of our biography, St. Bede the Venerable, was born, in 672. He was a native of the kingdom of Northumbria, and possibly his parents, certainly his grandparents, had been converted from paganism and baptized in an advanced age. When seven years old the child was entrusted to the abbot St. Benedict Biscop, who had just established the monastery of Wearmouth on the mouth of the river Wear. To this abbey the founder later on added the monastery of Jarrow on the other side of the Wear, and transferred there, with a number of monks, also our young Bede. Both monasteries were considered as one, although St. Benedict Biscop put Jarrow under the special care of St. Ceolfrid. It was to this prudent and saintly superior that Bede owed his education. Of his boyhood we know next to nothing. But Wearmouth-Jarrow must have been an abode not only of sanctity and religious regularity, but also of solid study, where the youthful inmates were schooled by expert masters in all the branches of secular as well as of sacred knowledge. When nineteen years old, St. Bede was ordained deacon. He became priest at thirty, then the canonical age.

There is little to tell about St. Bede's life beside his activity as a writer. He spent all his days—he died when sixty-two—within the precincts of his monastery. From one of his letters it appears that he visited King Wictred of Kent. Shortly before his death he traveled to York, no great distance from Jarrow, for a scientific conference with his pupil Egbert, the bishop of that city. It is also probable that he went to Lindisfarne, the famous monastery founded by St. Aidan, in order to gather material for his life of St. Cuthbert. These are few interruptions of a life which may seem monotonous to us moderns, but which was not so to him. St. Bede was heart and soul a monk, penetrated with a firm conviction of the sublimity of those exercises to which he and his devoted brethren gave a considerable part of their time.

He sums up his life in a few inimitable lines. Having been born on the territory of the monastery, "I was given at seven years of age to be educated by the most reverend Abbot Benedict, and afterward by Ceolfrid; and spending all the remaining time of my life in that monastery, I wholly applied myself to the study of Scripture, and amidst the observance of regular discipline and the daily care of the singing in the church. I always took delight in learning, teaching, and writing. . . . For the use of me and mine, I made it my business to compile out of the writings of the venerable Fathers, and to interpret and explain according to their meaning, the following pieces." Then he gives a list of the works he had finished when fifty-nine years of age. Four more years were granted to him, during which he faithfully continued in the same manner of life and labor. Very early it seems he became popularly known as "the Venerable," but it is impossible to give a satisfactory account of the origin of this epithet.

Few lives have been spent so usefully for the Church and mankind as that of St. Bede. The productions of his indefatigable pen fill six volumes of Migne's *Latin Patrology*. He was an encyclopedic writer, that is, he tried to embrace all human knowledge as far as it had been developed down to his own time in the compass of his works. His chief attention was given to the Bible. His commentaries on the Book of Books makes up something like four-fifths of his works. He also wrote much on secular matters. His writings on mathematical geography and the manner of reckoning the years, months, and days, are numerous, though not extensive.

In all his writings he almost exclusively endeavored to garner the principal and most useful doctrine of the Fathers of the Church, as also of the great secular authors of classic antiquity. However, he follows his own original method in representing what he has judiciously gleaned from his authorities. As regards geography, he stands entirely upon the ground of Pliny and St. Isidore.

He is well acquainted with the sphericity of the earth, and with the way of interpreting the movements of the heavenly bodies as set forth by the Ptolemaic system. His booklets, *De Ratione Temporum* and *De Tempore,* owe their origin in large part to his desire to teach the correct way of reckoning the date of Easter, and incidentally to justify the Roman method which had dislodged the Celtic computation in the churches of Anglo-Saxon Britain.

His explanations of the Bible are composed of sentences and statements of the Fathers. These, however, he repeats only according to sense without reproducing them literally. Like all the other teachers of the monastic and cathedral schools of his country, he was extremely careful to put forth a truly correct Catholic doctrine. Hence he never deviates from the path trodden by the great men who had gone before him. It was the best thing to do, both for himself and for his countrymen. Their land had hardly been converted, and they were wise and humble enough to see that, novices as they were, they could not think of opening new vistas and starting original investigations in any field.

By these unassuming and yet laborious efforts, St. Bede, like St. Isidore, though in a less degree, became one of the connecting links between ancient lore, secular as well as ecclesiastical, and medieval times. Later ages were right in looking back to him with gratitude, and in making extensive use of the treasures he had accumulated in his works.

Although we cannot here devote much time to the appreciation of his Biblical studies, we must duly emphasize the fact that his punctiliousness, far from detracting from his capacity as an historian, rather recommends him. He will show the same care and circumspection when he has to make historical statements. He will assert nothing without having proof of it. One of his smaller works in particular fills us with confidence in his historical methods. He had compiled an explanation of the Acts of the Apostles. But further study showed him that his comments could have been much better, had he paid more attention to the Greek text. So he issued a little volume in which he points to a number of texts in which either the Greek article, or the gender endings, or the more distinctive formation of the case endings of the Greek language, throw a clearer light upon the Latin text and show the meaning of the sacred writer more definitely. Similar remarks, referring to different Latin translations, are to be found here and there in other of his commentaries.

In his scientific books, too, while mainly endeavoring to put at the disposal of the reader the knowledge of former ages, he corrects, for instance, the misstatements of his Roman authorities concerning the ocean tides, of which they, living as they did on the Mediterranean Sea, could not have so clear an idea as one who knew from experience the proportions which the tides assume on the coasts of the British Isles.

St. Bede was essentially a textbook writer. He summarized, extracted, boiled down or expanded the information furnished him by the older authors, with an eye to making it more accessible and intelligible for his readers or rather students.[2] He could not omit grammar, Latin grammar of course, understanding the term in the wide sense it had at his time, as including the precepts of style in general. We have three books by him in this category: *De Orthographia,* a dictionary of correct Latin spelling; *De Tropis,* a treatise of metaphors and their uses; and *De Arte Metrica,* on the art of poetry.

But in the present paper we must devote our attention chiefly to St. Bede's historical works. Let us listen to his own enumeration of them:

A book on the life and passion of St. Felix I rendered in prose form from one existing in verse by Paulinus. A book on the life and passion of St. Anastatius which had been badly translated from the Greek into the Latin, and still worse improved by some ignorant person, I corrected to the best of my knowledge as the sense required. I also composed, first in meter and then in prose, the life of the holy monk and Bishop Cuthbert. I wrote the history of the abbots of this our monastery, in which I rejoice to serve the Divine Goodness, namely, of Benedict (Biscop), Ceolfrid and Huetbert; and then the Ecclesiastical History of our Island and Nation, in five books, finally a Martyrology of the feast days of the holy martyrs, in which I tried with great care to set down not only on what

---

[2] St. Bede anticipated the advice given eleven hundred years later by Pope Leo XIII concerning history. "After the production of real learned books, which will necessarily be voluminous and clad in professional language, it remains to popularize their contents by issuing summaries and schoolbooks, and other publications which will appeal to a wider public." See this volume, page 8.

day the various saints conquered the world, but also by what kind of combat and under what judge.

To this list drawn up by him in 731, we must add the remarkable letter to Egbert, written three or four years later, when the indefatigable author already suffered from the sickness which in 735 ended his most useful and saintly life.

As it appears, a large number of these works, though small in size, are biographical in character. His one strictly historical work is the *Historia Ecclesiastica Gentis Anglorum,* which, to use a business term, would make a dollar book. Concerning most of these works we must be satisfied with the description the venerable author gives of them in his own words. Anent his Martyrology, we may add, that, although based upon personal investigations, it no doubt also embodies the result of the labors of those who before his time had composed similar lists of Saints. Nevertheless, connoisseurs assure us that, as a whole, it was an original production. On account of its excellent qualities other authors took hold of it, and enlarged and altered it to such a degree, that nowadays it is impossible to tell which parts are Bede's and which were inserted by others. There is no doubt, however, that it exercised its influence upon similar works of the centuries that followed until under Pope Gregory XIII (1572-1585) the official Roman Martyrology was compiled by Cardinals Sirleto and Baronius.

The work to which St. Bede chiefly owes his well-deserved fame as historian is the *Church History of the Anglo-Saxons.* It begins with a description of the two great islands of the British archipelago, Britannia and Hibernia, and a few notes concerning their Celtic inhabitants. The southern part of Britannia, where the Britons lived, was subjugated by the Romans, became Christianized, and soon had its ecclesiastical hierarchy. At times this part of the Church was threatened by Pelagianism, Pelagius being a native of the country. But taken all in all, their doctrine remained uncontaminated. Then followed the terrible times of the invasions of the pagan Jutes, Angles, and Saxons, whose progress, though at times interrupted and retarded, continued for a century and a half. There resulted the destruction or expulsion or enslavement of the natives and the complete disappearance of Christianity in the whole eastern and central parts of the island where the barbarous invaders had settled. In 597, St. Augustine, sent by Pope St. Gregory I, the Great, began the Christianization of the Anglo-Saxons. The marriage of King Ethelbert of Kent with the Catholic princess Bertha of the Merovingian royal family of the Franks, seemed to offer an opportunity. Monastic life was to be the chief means for establishing the new religion, and the great Pope planned a hierarchy on almost the same lines on which it was eventually shaped long after his death.

St. Augustine had an interview with the bishops of the Christian Britons in the western section of the island, and tried both to gain their coöperation in his missionary work among the Anglo-Saxons, and bring them into closer union with the Roman Pontiff. The Britons flatly refused to do anything for the conversion of their hereditary foes, the Anglo-Saxons, nor would they recognize St. Augustine as the Holy Father's representative. It was a momentous decision. So far the barrier erected by the Anglo-Saxon kingdoms along the eastern coast and the disturbances on the continent had isolated the Britons, without their fault, from the main body of the Church. Now when the Church extended her hand to them, they made this isolation voluntary. On the continent the conversion of the Teutonic invaders by the old inhabitants had in many places been completed, and in others auspiciously begun. The Britons preferred to persist in their national exclusiveness, and narrow hatred of everything Anglo-Saxon. Even later on they made no difference between baptized and pagan Saxons, and their bishops refused to eat in the same house with Anglo-Saxon bishops. How different would have been the history of the next two centuries had they listened to the voice of Christian charity and to the invitation of the Supreme Shepherd at Rome.

The kingdom of Kent, however, became Catholic, and Christianity was successfully introduced in the neighboring realms. In 625, the marriage of King Edwin of Northumbria with the Kentish princess Eadberga opened the way for Christianity into the large northern kingdom. St. Paulinus, as first Bishop of York, baptized the royal family and a large number of the people. But the attack of the Christian King Cadwalla of the Britons, an ally of Penda, the pagan king of Mercia, besides causing great devastation and destruction of life, also induced very many of the newly baptized Christians to return to paganism. The result was a two years' interruption of the work of evangelizing, during which St. Paulinus with some of his companions returned to the South. But the new king of Northumbria, St. Oswald, who had made the acquaintance of the Irish monks of Iona, was no sooner firmly seated on the throne, than he requested these monks to send some of their number as missionaries to his kingdom. They sent St. Aidan as leader of a band of zealous men. St. Aidan founded an abbey on the island of Lindisfarne, and made it a center of new and vigorous apostolic effort. In Northumbria they completed the work of St. Paulinus which had been partly destroyed by the two years of devastation and confusion? The large kingdom of Mercia owes its conversion entirely to them, and the same may be said of East Anglia. The other kingdoms, too, with the exception of Kent and Sussex, felt their influence more or less strongly. St. Bede grows very eloquent in sounding the praises of these missionaries, who made up for the hostile attitude of the Britons.

It was very unfortunate that with these zealous men an element of discord came into the new Church. Cut off from actual communication with Rome by the troubles of the Migration of Nations, which upset all the conditions on the continent, and by the barrier of pagan Saxon states, which rose on the east and south of Britain, the Island Celts had adhered to a reckoning of the date of Easter which the whole Church had meanwhile abandoned. The Catholic world, with Rome at the head, followed another method. Southern Ireland had indeed adopted this Roman Easter as early as 631. But the north of the country as well as all the Irish missionaries in Scotland, headed by the great abbey of Iona, retained the Celtic reckoning, and St. Aidan and his companions and successors still adhered to it. It happened consequently, that while those converted by the Roman and other continental missionaries were celebrating Easter, those converted by the Irish were still in Lent, or the opposite. In 664, the king of Northumbria, Oswy, in whose own family the matter had become a burning question, had it discussed by learned men at Whitby, and decided that in his kingdom the Roman Easter was to be followed. His example drew with it all the other rulers and places of the Anglo-Saxon world, as far as a change was needed.

It was the only correct thing to do. It brought unity to the Anglo-Saxon Church, and prevented the confusion from assuming larger and still more threatening proportions. Although the difference was only of disciplinary character and did not touch dogma, nobody can tell to what consequences it might have led. (See next article.)

But the unity was dearly bought. For while the Anglo-Saxon clergy and many of the Irish submitted obediently to a clearly formulated and well-known regulation of Canon Law, Abbot-Bishop Colman of Lindisfarne, with a large number of his monks, refused to conform, and withdrew to the North, where at Iona the Celtic method was still kept up. With this the coming of Irish workers from those regions ceased.

This was a hard blow to the Church. St. Bede's feelings were evidently divided, when he wrote down the report of this event, which had taken place some nine years before his birth. On the one hand he wholeheartedly welcomes the achievement of complete Catholic unity and rejoiced over the victory of the Roman Easter. On the other hand, however, he greatly admired the virtue and ability of those who now left for good the country which was so deeply indebted to them, and he did not fail to give them a very sympathetic farewell.

Another outstanding event in the history of the Anglo-Saxon Church was the coming, in 669, only five years after the conference of Whitby, of St. Theodore, sent by Pope St. Vitalian. St. Theodore was the first real Archbishop of Canterbury (669-690). He ruled the new-born Church with kindness and firmness, visiting all its parts, assembling the bishops in canonical councils, circumscribing the dioceses more accurately, inaugurating and inspiring the establishment of new schools, and in every way giving new vigor to Christian life in all classes of the people. With the activity of St. Theodore the missionary period of the Anglo-Saxon Church came to an end. During his administration the kingdom of Sussex, the only one not yet converted, came into the fold by the efforts of the Northumbrian, St. Wilfrid. True, not even at St. Theodore's death was every Anglo-Saxon actually baptized. But the country was now completely organized, and the conversion of each individual was only a question of time and would be accomplished through the agencies already established. Taken as a whole, the Anglo-Saxon Church was a full-fledged member of the Catholic world.

Although each of the five books of Bede's *Ecclesiastical History* treats of a great variety of subjects, the prominent ecclesiastical fact in the first book is the coming of St. Augustine; that of the second book the appearance on the scene of the Irish monks with the progress of Christianization through the labors of both the Roman and Irish missionaries; the third book concludes with the settling of the Easter question by the conference of Whitby; the fourth is devoted to the work and times of St. Theodore. When reading the fifth book one feels that the age of storm and stress is over. The author devotes much more space to biographical notes on the lives of saints as well as to the reports of miraculous events. He recounts the efforts of Anglo-Saxon missionaries in foreign countries. Though always keeping to his strictly historical style, the author cannot conceal the joy it gives him to narrate the acceptance of the Roman Easter by a great part of the clergy in northern Ireland, by the Picts, by many of the Britons, and finally even in the very citadel of Celtic usages, the island monastery of Iona.

To say a few words on St. Bede as an historian: he evidently was a truly patriotic Anglo-Saxon, who ardently loved his country and his nation. But this never betrayed him into forgetting the historian's duty of telling the truth, the whole truth, and nothing but the truth. Where the progress of events demands it, he tells of the crimes of his countrymen, as well as of their virtues. The Irish missionaries he treats almost with distinction, and never omits stating their direct or indirect influence upon the interests of the Church. He distinguishes clearly between facts and rumors. The beautiful story of St. Gregory and the Anglo-Saxon slaves in the Roman market he expressly introduces as an opinion. In his dedicatory letter to King Ceolwulf of Northumbria, who had with great interest watched the progress of the work, and even read what we should now call the proof-sheets, the author, almost like a modern historian, gives an account of the sources on which he had drawn. Concerning the times before St. Augustine he followed, he says, other Christian writers. He does not name them, but skillful commentators have been able to trace nearly all his statements, including the less important ones, to ancient publications. The years after St. Augustine's coming were not far removed from his own; those were still living who had witnessed very many of the facts embodied in his work. He says, however, that he was careful in accepting oral testimony. He drew largely on documents found in monasteries and elsewhere. The monks of Lastingaeu furnished information as to the conversion of Mercia, and Abbot Esi about the re-Christianization of East Anglia; Bishop St. Daniel about Wessex, the Isle of Wight, and neighboring parts. But his most active helpers were Abbot Albinus of Canterbury and one of his monks, Nothelm, both of whom had been disciples of Sts. Theodore and Hadrian. Both these men went to great lengths to assist him. They not only investigated the archives of Canterbury and other places, but continued their searches when in Rome. Once Nothelm made the trip to Northumbria to bring to the writer in person documents and oral information. Concerning Northumbria, St. Bede was of course best situated. The archives gave him their treasures, the monks, the laity, the bishops and kings, communicated to him their knowledge of former days. The coöperation thus yielded to St. Bede, enabled him, among other things, to preserve for us so large a number of valuable papal and other documents, which but for him would have been lost long ago.

A very peculiar feature of St. Bede's *Ecclesiastical History* is the very large number of biographies of saints or saintly persons which are embodied in the text. They are introduced at some moment when these persons appear for the first time, or when they become more than ordinarily prominent, but chiefly when their death is reported. Sometimes their lives occupy but a few paragraphs, at other times they extend over several pages. Miracles play a rather extensive part in them, but this was according to the spirit and the views of the times. The author reports them only on good testimony, and although he styles them miracles, he evidently does not pretend to assert their truly supernatural character. He would be the last to object, if in a process of canonization some or even many of them were not accepted as genuine by the Roman Congregation of Rites. The insertion of these biographical notices is in accordance with his program. History, he tells us in the Introductory Letter, is to deter the reader from the bad and blameworthy of which he reads, and to stir him up to the zealous imitation of the good. Owing to these numerous lives of holy persons, the reading of St. Bede's history unfolds before us the picture of a country in which a truly Christian life was the rule. No doubt a nation, and so small a nation at that, which was able to produce such a galaxy of saintly men and women during so short a period has reason to feel proud. But, on the other hand, the dark spots in the beautiful pictures are by no means glossed over or explained away, though the author never indulges in bloodcurdling descriptions of misdeeds. Only the edifying traits and facts enjoy the privilege of being represented *in extenso*. We see the kings, not only like Clovis the Frank, burn what they had adored and adore what they had burned, but no less than twenty-six kings and other persons of royal lineage exchange the pomp of the court for the poverty and menial labors of the cloister. The number of monks in many monasteries ran well up into the hundreds.

Thus, while strictly historical, as historical as the most honest efforts and the most painstaking labor could make it, the *Ecclesiastical History* is a genuine *Erbauungsbuch,* a book of religious education for the

children of St. Bede's race and for all that peruse its
pages.

To some perhaps the almost countless proper names
which are scattered liberally through the whole narrative may seem bewildering. But besides testifying to
the minuteness of the author's researches they were
what many readers desired. These names were not unknown. They had been heard occasionally, some perhaps frequently. By putting them in the right setting,
by showing the connection of these persons with the
whole current of events and disclosing the causes and
effects of their deeds and misdeeds, the author clarified
confused ideas and joined together into a coherent system whatever fragmentary knowledge existed in the
minds of his readers. It is by means of these names
that the succession of bishops of these various sees
and the branching out of royal families can be reconstructed.

Next in merit after St. Bede's *Ecclesiastical History,*
though only a pamphlet in size, is the *Vita Beatorum
Benedicti, Ceolfridi, Eosterwini, Sigfridi, atque Hwae-
berhti,* commonly referred to as the *History of the
Abbots.* These were the first that ruled, though in
different capacities, the twin monastery of Wearmouth-
Jarrow, the place of the labors of St. Bede. Much of
what he wrote in this booklet the author knew from
personal observation, or by information obtained
orally from older monks. But much is derived from
smaller written sources which existed before him,
though strange to say the author takes no pain even
to refer to his sources. Probably all these particulars
were too well known to the inmates of Wearmouth-
Jarrow, for whom he wrote in the first place. One of
these written sources is preserved to us, and was the

work of an anonymous monk of the same monastery. At first sight it may look somewhat similar, especially as it is also known among historians as *History of the Abbots*. But St. Bede proceeds along different lines.

As already stated, the founder of the twin-abbey was St. Benedict Biscop, who, however, for a more efficient administration soon appointed St. Ceolfrid Abbot of Jarrow, and a little later Eosterwin Abbot of Wearmouth, retaining all the time a sort of superintendence of both institutions. Eosterwin died after four years, when St. Benedict Biscop happened to be absent on one of his six visits to Rome. The monks of Wearmouth, therefore, with the coöperation of Abbot Ceolfrid of Jarrow, elected Sigfrid Abbot, which election Benedict cheerfully ratified on his return. But both Sigfrid and Benedict Biscop himself died some three years later, leaving Ceolfrid Abbot of both monasteries. Benedict Biscop, the founder, had ruled for sixteen years, and Ceolfrid held the dignity after his death for thirty-five. These are, therefore, the first two real abbots of the institution. The anonymous writer of the older life makes it a biography of St. Ceolfrid, and brings in the lives of the other three, including the founder, only briefly and by way of further explanation. He calls his booklet expressly *Vita Sanctissimi Ceolfridi Abbatis*.

St. Bede on the contrary begins with the life and achievements of the founder, upon which he enlarges greatly. Eosterwin and Sigfrid are naturally treated much more briefly, but get their due share of consideration and praise. Ceolfrid's position and long administration again requires more space. This manner of proceeding explains why St. Bede condenses the older life of Ceolfrid, and omits many of its details, although he brings in some items not mentioned by the anonymous writer. The result is a publication of modest size, all the parts of which are well proportioned, and which, for its literary qualities, and above all for its historical perfection, may deservedly be called a gem of historical literature. We wish indeed that St. Bede had told us more of the domestic life of the inmates of these two institutions. How grateful should we be for a simple description of their daily order, or of the celebration of some great ecclesiastical festival, or the reception of new members. But those for whom the saintly author wrote in the first place, looked upon all this as ordinary, as something of which they did not need to be reminded. Unquestionably few monastic institutions of ancient date possess so authentic and attractive an account of their origin and the first decades of their existence, an account which is at the same time a precious contribution to the history and development of religious life in England and in the Church at large.

After all St. Bede wrote Church history. Secular events, it is true, are introduced extensively, yet always with the purpose of showing how they either furthered or retarded the work of religion and piety. He dwells at great length upon the lives of the saints. The unedifying, while not omitted, is kept well in the background. The *Letter to St. Egbert,* Bishop of York, however, shows St. Bede from another side. This pious writer, this retired monk, had a keen eye for the evils of his time, and not only exposed them mercilessly, but also proposed means to counteract them. Though in the form of a letter and destined for one addressee, it is rightly numbered among St. Bede's historical writings.

Egbert had been his disciple and St. Bede speaks to him with a freedom which only such a relation can excuse. The teacher first gives some private admonitions to his former pupil. Then he pictures in a language not free from indignation, several national and local failings and is evidently glad to have a chance of airing his mind on the subject. There were bishops, let us hope not many, who exacted the usual tribute from every place in their diocese, even from those remote villages which had not seen the bishop for many years, nay, which had not even a priest to instruct them. Some bishoprics were evidently too large, and should, with the help of the king, have been split into several dioceses. To provide the new episcopal sees with revenue, the bishops might be made abbots of some of the rich monasteries. There were nobles who in order to avoid the tribute due the king, would establish sham monasteries and become abbots of them, without caring in the least for monastic life. Thus, adds the author with the foresight of the statesman, even the country's defensive power was being weakened, because these sham abbots were no longer bound to go to war, or to furnish troops to the king.

Such language one is not accustomed to find in Bede's works. It is his swan song. He wrote this letter less than a year before his death.

Had he been in some highly responsible and influential position, he would no doubt have made his mark in the Anglo-Saxon world, either in Church or State. But such dignities were not in the divine plan of his life. He loved to be praying and studying, teaching and writing. We can hardly doubt that as monk and scholar, teacher and writer, he has done more for the kingdoms of the Anglo-Saxons and for the Church at large than he could have achieved in any other position. What a gap would there be in ecclesiastical literature if we had no Bede. What services to the education of later centuries would have been impossible had the schools not possessed his works. We need not go into more remote centuries. St. Bede had been Egbert's instructor. St. Egbert in turn established at York a famous school of learning with a still more famous library. One of the fruits of this institution was the great Alcuin, friend, adviser, and practically minister of instruction, of Charlemagne, the man, who through the power and far-sightedness of his illustrious pupil became one of the most prominent in the literary and scientific life of the Middle Ages. Thus in a twofold way, namely through his books and his school, did St. Bede become a most influential man, not only in England, but on the Continent also, and as far as ecclesiastical learning extends over the globe.

It is not necessary to dwell on the eminent service St. Bede rendered to historical science by producing those excellent works which later writers, often unconsciously, have taken and are taking as their model; works from which they will ever derive encouragement in their vocation.

One point must not be left unmentioned, namely, his eminent service to chronology. The Christian era, that is, the counting of the years from the birth of Christ, had been devised nearly two hundred years before his time. But its adoption was very slow. With the Roman missionaries, St. Augustine and his companions, it is supposed to have been introduced in Britain, and some instances are quoted, though not without misgivings as to their genuineness, which would show that it was used by King Ethelbert of Kent as early as 605 and by others on later occasions during the seventh century. Whatever authority these instances may have, it is certain that St. Bede, when writing his *De Temporibus* and *De Temporum Ratione,* supposes this reckoning to be generally known among the Anglo-Saxons. And the fact that he employed it throughout in his *Ecclesiastical History* helped greatly to make its hold upon the nation still more secure. From his time on it was an established element in the dating of charters. On the Continent, however, it was not known, at any rate not practised, at this time. But through the spread of St. Bede's books it gained admittance first in the Frankish Kingdom and Empire and thereby gradually came to be generally used. That his authority and example had a far-reaching influence on the spread of the "Christian Era" is unhesitatingly admitted by historians.

St. Bede writes an easy fluent Latin, which, with some few peculiarities, is a successful imitation of the language of the later classic period. His narrative runs on quietly, placidly, like a little brook, whose limpid waters hardly begin to foam when they run over the rocks. He simply relates the facts, and leaves it to the reader to feel and express the emotions which they may provoke.

St. Bede is not only the sole source of history of the Anglo-Saxon lands, but he is also the organizer of this history. It was a difficult task to arrange in one continued narrative the many bits of information which were submitted to him concerning a subject which none as yet had attempted to embrace in one work. He had no predecessor in the field to point him the way; no one to furnish the outlines along which he could proceed. He had to draft the outlines himself. But he knew how to place himself upon a pin-

nacle so high that he was able to survey the whole
of the Anglo-Saxon world; nay, his horizon was even
wide enough to include the principal events of the
nations which surrounded that world and came into
contact with it. The very fact that such a history was
conceived and planned, throws favorable light upon
the intellectuality of all the persons concerned, the
author himself as well as those who suggested, encouraged, promoted and appreciated an enterprise of this
kind. St. Bede's work is a monumental proof of the
elevating effect Christianity had had upon the minds
of the Anglo-Saxons.

His *Church History* is one of several works which
profess to be histories of Germanic races. Two of
these were produced in the sixth century. Cassiodorus,
who died about 578 in Italy, wrote a *History of the
Goths,* which unfortunately has come to us only in a
rather inferior summary made by Jordanis. His contemporary, St. Gregory of Tours, who went to his
reward seventeen years later, is the author of the ten
books of the *History of the Franks.* This work perhaps was not without influence in encouraging Bede to
resolve upon composing a history of his own Anglo-
Saxons. But he surpasses St. Gregory in the succinct-
ness of his plan. He does not begin like Gregory with
the creation of the world, but with the land which
was the scene of the events he was going to record;
nor does he draw into the compass of his work any
but those nations which were in immediate contact with
his own. Critics moreover agree that he commands a
more genuinely historical style and shows greater skill
in handling his material. During St. Bede's later years
there was born in Northern Italy the Lombard Paul
Warnefried, afterwards called the Deacon, a Bene-

dictine monk, more brilliantly gifted than Bede, but directing his attention more to the events of a secular nature. To him we owe a *History of the Lombards*. But he too interrupts his narrative by digressions into the history of other lands, especially that of the Franks.

Here again we should not omit noticing the effect of the Church's educational methods. Cassiodorus, the historian of the Ostrogoths, was no Goth himself, but the scion of an old Roman family. St. Gregory, the author of the *History of the Franks,* was no Frank, but a Gallo-Roman. These men lived in the sixth century. The seventh century passed, and the educational agencies of the Church, the bishops and the monks, kept faithfully at their task. The next national historians, St. Bede and Paul the Deacon, were sons of their own peoples, whose facts and fates they immortalized in their books. These nations had not sat in vain at the feet of their ecclesiastical teachers.

In thus concluding our brief study on St. Bede, the historian, let us offer our congratulations to the English nation, and in particular to the English Catholics, for possessing so excellent an account of the origin and growth of their Church and its organization, as also such precious notes even on their secular institutions. But we should extend our felicitations to the Church at large, and even beyond it to the whole of mankind. St. Bede has enriched Catholic literature by contributions, such as few others have been able to offer. Although his *Ecclesiastical History* does not command the popularity his other books enjoy, the large number of manuscripts of this history that have come down to our times, bears witness to the wide interest which it provoked in and out of England. His works form an essential part of historical lore, not only of the Catholic Church, but of the civilized world as well. We can only wish, though in vain, that we possessed similar accounts of the beginnings and vicissitudes of many other nations.

A word for us Americans. St. Bede wrote his history of the Anglo-Saxon Church before it was too late; before all the documents referring to these times had perished; before all those had died who could assist him by their word-of-mouth contributions. We of America are not much farther removed from the beginnings of the Catholic Church in this country than he was from those of his. We should now write our history. A good beginning has been made. But we need more than one Bede. Our country and our church offer too great a variety of facts to be happily consolidated by any one man. God grant that St. Bede multiply himself in our midst.

We have the same wish for the Church at large and for all mankind. God grant that we find men like him working in all parts of the wide field of history; men who produce books equally truthful, equally useful; men of whom is true what no less an historian than Theodore Mommsen says of St. Bede the Venerable: "He calls himself a *verax historicus,* a truth-loving historian, and he has a right to do so. Those who have followed him up will testify that few authors when representing the facts have proceeded with the same degree of accurateness."

BIBLIOGRAPHY

A. *Biography:*

There is no good medieval life of Bede. Apart from the two anonymous biographical accounts in the *Vita quorundam*

Anglo-Saxonum, edited by J. A. GILES (London, 1854), there is no worthy attempt before the work of KARL WERNER, *Beda der Ehwurdige und seine Zeit* (Vienna, 1875). This is the only serious life up to our time. RAWNSLEY, *The Venerable Bede* (Sunderland, 1903), is a superficial sketch. BROWNE, *The Venerable Bede: his Life and Writings* (New York, 1919), is written from the Anglican viewpoint and is not free from historical inaccuracy. Numerous sketches appear in various dictionaries, as for example, HUNT in the *Dictionary of National Biography,* and THURSTON in the *Catholic Encyclopedia.*

B. *General Works on Bede and His Writings:*

The classic edition of Bede's works is that by CHARLES PLUMMER, *Venerabilis Baedae Historiam Ecclesiasticam Gentis Anglorum, Historiam, Epistolam ad Egbertum, una cum Historia Abbatum Auctore Anonymo Ad Fidem Codicum Manuscriptorum Denuo Recognovit, Commentario tam Critico quam Historica Instruxit Carolus Plummer, A.M., Colegii Corporis Christi Socius et Capellanus Tomus Prior, Prolegomena et Textum Continens. Tomus Posterior, Commentarium et Indices Continens.* Oxford, Clarendon Press, 1896. This is an admirable work. The text has been reconstructed with an incredible amount of patience and labor. The commentary and notes have been composed with a loving care that does not forget the smallest detail, and with that far-sightedness which sees connections with numerous other literary productions. If anyone wishes to make a study on some detailed topic of these works of Bede, let him first turn to Plummer. It will save him a great deal of useless trouble. WERNER gives a thorough appreciation of all of St. Bede's works. Cf. also *The Venerable Bede's Ecclesiastical History of England,* also the *Anglo-Saxon Chronicle* (London, 1900); F. RUHL, *Chronologie des Mittelalters unt der Neuzeit* (Berlin, 1897); REGINALD POOLE, *Medieval Reckonings of Time* (London, 1922); LINGARD, *The Antiquities of the Anglo-Saxon Church* (London, 1848).

The best bibliography on Bede's works and commentaries thereon will be found in PLUMMER, *op. cit.,* Vol. I.

II

THE ISLAND CELTS ADOPT THE ROMAN EASTER CALCULATION [1]

INTRODUCTION

I. *The Island Celts.* By Island Celts we understand those Celts that were living in the British Isles,
in opposition to the continental Celts in Gaul, Spain,
etc., who by the time we have in view were completely
Romanized and had also received among themselves
a sprinkling of Germans. All Britain was originally
inhabited by various races of Celts. The inroads of
the Angles, Saxons, and Jutes during the fifth century,
however, confined these old inhabitants to the western
peninsulas of Cornwall, Wales, and Strathclyde. Here
alone they preserved their identity and also some civic
organization.

The Jutes, Angles, and Saxons established themselves, by successive invasions, during the course of
about a hundred and fifty years in the entire East and
center of the island and formed seven states, called
the *Anglo-Saxon Heptarchy.* The northernmost of
their states and one of the mightiest was *Northumbria.*
The Anglo-Saxons destroyed every vestige of Christianity, and left hardly any trace of the former Celto-
Roman civilization. As far as occupied by the Anglo-

[1] Paper read at the Convention of the Jesuit Historical Association, August, 1928. Printed in *Catholic Historical Review* (1928-
1929), pp. 485-499.

Saxons the land needed a new conversion to Christianity.

Some twenty years before this devastation of the largest part of Britain began, St. Patrick had started, in 432, the conversion of the Celts in Ireland, which was practically finished by the end of the fifth century. Ireland had become intensely Christian, filled with numerous monasteries, which soon began to send out zealous monks into other countries to preach the doctrines of Christianity by word and example. One of their greatest fields of apostolic activity was the northern part of Britain, now called Scotland, inhabited like Ireland by a Celtic population. St. Columba (Columbkille, died 597) became the organizer of these missionary efforts. In 564, he established the great monastery of Hii (Hy, Hi) or *Iona*, which was destined to be the center of those apostolic labors, and the ecclesiastical capital of Scotland. Its abbot was never a bishop himself. Episcopal functions were performed by several of his subjects who had received episcopal consecration. He exercised ecclesiastical jurisdiction over the whole country. A number of abbeys in the opposite parts of Ireland, too, were under his sway.

It should be well known, however, that the name of Scots, *Scoti,* and Scotia at that time was applied exclusively to the inhabitants and the country of Ireland. These names travelled across the North Channel at a much later date.

When St. Columbkille had nearly finished his great task and when monastic and apostolic life was in full development in what is now called Scotland, St. Gregory the Great dispatched forty Benedictine monks under the leadership of St. Augustine to the lands of the Anglo-Saxons. They began their missionary activity in the kingdom of Kent and won several other kingdoms for the Gospel. In 625, one of his disciples, St. Paulinus, began the conversion of the northern Kingdom of Northumbria. But in 629, a fierce persecution forced him to flee back to the South. His deacon James remained in the land and as best he could continued Paulinus' work, but was unable to prevent the apostasy of the bulk of the converts. It was under these circumstances that the Irish monks from Iona appeared in Northumbria, 625 A.D., with a new Bishop Aidan. St. Aidan established a monastery on the Island of Lindisfarne, and began with his monks a zealous missionary activity which was blessed with much success. Lindisfarne founded other monasteries in Northumbria and on many occasions extended its influence to other Anglo-Saxon kingdoms. Northumbria, however, remained the principal scene of their edifying life and missionary successes.

II. *The Easter Controversy.* In determining the date for the Easter festival the Celts followed a method which had been widely, though not generally, in vogue on the continent at the time when St. Patrick began his apostolate among them. The Council of Nicaea, in 325, had prescribed a certain calculation for this purpose, but the application of its rules did not at once produce general unity. Several ways were put into practice. As late as 525, i.e., two hundred years after the great Council, the Italian monk Dionysius Exiguus, devised a method which seemed to be fully satisfactory.[2] It was officially adopted by Rome, and rapidly gained ground on the continent. But meanwhile the Island Celts had been practically cut off from

[2] It was on this occasion that Dionysius introduced the counting of the years from the Birth of Christ.

communication with Rome by the turmoil of the Migration of Nations. Hence they continued to employ the calculation which their first Apostle had brought to them in 432. They went by an eighty-four year cycle, according to which after each eighty-four years the dates of Easter would again follow in exactly the same succession. This cycle had originated in Asia Minor. The Roman calculation supposed another cycle. It is often called a nineteen year cycle, and in fact it is based on such a cycle which had been devised in Alexandria. In reality the Roman cycle ran 532 years.[3]

It is not the purpose of this paper to enter into all the intricacies of the two calculations and their history, since we are concerned only with the manner in which one of the two finally gave way to the other. But it will help to clear up the situation if we bring out two of the chief differences. *First,* both parties held that Easter was to fall on the first Sunday after the first full moon of Spring. But the Romans considered the twenty-first of March as the beginning of Spring; the Celts the twenty-fifth of that month. If therefore a full moon fell between these dates, the Romans accepted it as the first full moon of Spring, and celebrated their Easter on the succeeding Sunday. The Celts waited a whole month for the next full moon. In the year 604, for instance, the Roman Easter was on the twenty-second of March; the Celtic on the nineteenth of April. *Second.* If the first full moon of spring fell on a Sunday, the Romans placed their Eas-

---

[3] The literature which, from the earliest times of Christianity, had grown up around the controversy of the several Easter reckonings is copious, and still more copious are the elucubrations of later scholars on that subject. We refer the reader to an article by Charles W. Jones, "The Victorian and Dionysiac Paschal Tables in the West," in *Speculum*, Vol. IX (Oct., 1934), pp. 408-421, which is furnished with numerous references.

ter on the Sunday following; the Celts chose that very date of the full moon. Hence it could happen, that the two Easters were just one week apart, the Celtic being the first.

Rome had adopted the Dionysian calculation and certainly wanted it to be introduced everywhere. But it does not seem that any formal law or decree or Canon to that effect was issued, or that a definite penalty was threatened for not following the lead of Rome. Had this been the case, the advocates of the Roman Easter would not have failed to quote it. Although they advanced the will of the Sovereign Pontiff and laid great stress upon it in their writings and addresses, they gave much more space to what they thought were the merits of the Dionysian reckoning. The Celts proceeded in a similar manner. Theological and mystic reasons were put forward, authorities appealed to, and on the side of the Celts national considerations were not lacking. They erroneously derived their eighty-four year cycle of Easter dates from St. John the Apostle. The Romans equally erroneously claimed St. Peter as the originator of their system. We may say, however, that whenever later on the Celts abandoned their own Easter calculations, it was felt to be an act of submission to the Holy See and the Prince of the Apostles. Indeed the order of the Pope is the only peremptory reason for the date of Easter and any other feast. He possesses the supreme power to regulate all public worship, and his decisions must be accepted by all who wish to call themselves true members of the Church of Christ.

THE CESSATION OF THE CELTIC EASTER CALCULATION

The Paschal calculation of the Island Celts did not come to an end in all parts of the Celtic world at one time. It disappeared at various times in the various parts in the course of some one hundred and twenty years. Nor were the districts which successively abandoned it geographically contiguous. Almost the only source for our knowledge of these events is the *Ecclesiastical History of England by the Venerable Bede*,[4] though here and there other historical documents must be consulted.

A very prominent, nay a decisive role in several cases is played by some learned and unselfish personages. As on so many other occasions of history God here also bestows his blessings through the instrumentality of men, just as He often permits great evils to come through the activity of evil-minded or ill-instructed persons.

I. *Southern Ireland, about 630.* Concerning the South of Ireland St. Bede is not any too definite. Pope Honorius, he says (Book II, Chap. 19), wrote a letter to the nation of the *Scoti* (i.e., the Irish in Ireland), whom he had heard to err in the celebration of Easter, to induce them to adopt the right method. Pope Honorius I ruled the Church 625-638. St. Bede gives no year for his letter. It was probably addressed to the northern as well as the southern Irish. But it was the southern *Scoti* who benefited by it, as we see from the following quotation. When speaking of the coming of St. Aidan, 635, St. Bede adds, that

by this time those of the *Scoti* who live in the southern parts of Ireland had long ago, by the admonitions of the

4 See Bibliography of preceding article.

Bishop of the Apostolic See, learned the celebration of Easter according to the canonical rule. (Book III, Chap. 3.)

In a passage referring to the year 664, relating to the appointment of Tuda as Bishop of Lindisfarne, he brings us back to about the same time. Tuda, he says,

had been educated among the southern Irish, had the ecclesiastical tonsure, and followed the Catholic rule in keeping Easter. (Book III, Chap. 26.)

If Tuda was old enough to become bishop in 664, the Roman calculation of Easter to which he had been accustomed as part of his education must have been in vogue in southern Ireland some thirty years before.

There can, therefore, be no doubt that about 630 A.D. the southern Irish had conformed to the Roman Easter calculation. How far the district of southern Ireland then extended we do not know in detail.

Charles Plummer, author of the latest edition of St. Bede's historical works, draws also on other sources. He harmonizes all the facts he thinks are of importance in the following way, dating the actual adoption, however, somewhat later.

In 631 delegates from a South Irish synod were at Rome having been sent to consult the Roman Church on the Easter question. While there, they had an opportunity of seeing with their own eyes how widely their own use might diverge from that of the rest of the Western Church, for in that year there was a difference of a month between the Roman and Celtic Easters. Probably these men brought back with them the letter of Honorius I. On their return another synod was apparently held, and the Roman Easter adopted. This must have been in 632 or 633. (Vol. II, p. 125.)

II. *Northumbria, 664.* There had not been any special occasion in southern Ireland for the change except the desire to conform in all things with Rome. It was different in Northumbria, the great northernmost kingdom of the Anglo-Saxon Heptarchy. (Book III, Chap. 25 and 26.) Here the two Easters literally clashed. Missionaries originally sent from Rome adhered to the Roman method. The zealous Irish monks who had come from Iona and had converted the greater part of the kingdom, followed the eighty-four years cycle. The discord entered the royal family. King Oswiu siding with the Irish, his wife, Queen Eanfled and her chaplain Romanus adhering to the Roman reckoning.

To settle this dissension King Oswiu, in 664, summoned an assembly of the great men of his realm to meet at Whitby,[5] where the bishops and priests were to discuss the matter. Colman, then successor of St. Aidan in the see of Lindisfarne, defended the Celts, while Wilfrid, Abbot of Ripon and intimate friend of the king's son Alchfrid, spoke for the Roman view. When Wilfrid stated that the Roman calculation was derived from St. Peter, the king declared he was going to follow St. Peter, because "he is the doorkeeper, lest perhaps when I arrive at the gate of the Kingdom of Heaven, there might be none to open it for me." Unwittingly he thereby gave the only reason for the Roman calculation, namely, the authority of the Sovereign Pontiff. In spite of his great veneration for Bishop Colman he let it be known that he would not tolerate in his kingdom any ecclesiastics who refused to conform to Rome. Hence Colman with some thirty Irish and Anglo-Saxon monks left the country, and went to Iona, whence they returned to Ireland. The departure of these otherwise excellent men was a considerable loss for religion in Northumbria, which was

[5] See next article.

made up for only by the great advantage of complete disciplinary unity, an advantage most important in a land where nearly all Christians were converts and necessarily imperfectly instructed in their religion. No Irish missionaries arrived any longer from Scotland or the North of Ireland, though the intercourse between the Anglo-Saxon lands and Southern Ireland went on uninterruptedly.

Concluding from the way in which St. Bede treats of the matter, there do not seem to have been great difficulties in other Anglo-Saxon kingdoms. At any rate they must have disappeared in consequence of the victory of the Roman Easter in the Kingdom of Northumbria by the decision at Whitby. In 669, St. Theodore, sent by the Pope, arrived in Britain as Archbishop of Canterbury and Primate of England. He traveled much in the various states and dioceses, and everywhere sought to confirm or introduce the observance of the laws of the Church. He does not seem to have encountered any difference in the celebration of Easter. St. Bede, at any rate, who otherwise lays the greatest stress on this point, does not mention it. To secure the existing correct practice, however, Canon I of the National Council of Heresford, in 763, again emphasizes the observance of the Roman Easter. It is the last and only time after Whitby, that the controversy is alluded to by the national historian of England in connection with the Anglo-Saxon states and bishoprics.

III. *Many of the Northern Irish and Northern Britons.* As early as A.D. 640, i.e., twenty-four years before the meeting of Whitby, Pope John IV had addressed an epistle on the celebration of Easter to some bishops of Northern Ireland, which, however, cannot have produced great results. (Book II, Chap. 19; and Plummer II, p. 112.) It was much later, about the year 686, that St. Adamnan, the great Irish scholar, at that time Abbot of Iona, had more success. In that year he went as ambassador to Aldfrid, King of Bernicia (the northern half of Northumbria), to ask for the return of Irish captives, whom according to an ancient Irish source he was able to send back to Ireland. But being received with great kindness by Aldfrid, he tarried a long time among the Anglo-Saxons and conversed with the learned ecclesiastics of the country. He also paid a visit to the monastery of Wearmouth-Jarrow. He became fully convinced of the correctness of their Easter calculation. Upon his return to Iona he made every possible effort to induce his monks to abandon the Celtic Easter cycle. But his endeavors were in vain. The monks refused to obey their own venerable abbot and stuck to their peculiarities. Adamnan then sailed over to northern Ireland. Here he was much more fortunate. By his kind instructions he persuaded a large number of Irish institutions to conform to the rest of the Church. But those monasteries which were under the power of Iona imitated the mother house and retained their Celtic Easter. (Book V, Chap. XV.)

When mentioning Adamnan's success in Northern Ireland St. Bede adds that also some part of the Britons was won over. He can refer only to the northernmost of them, the Strathclyde Britons, since he represents this also in connection with the endeavors of Adamnan. It is indeed natural to think that, as he had to pass through the territory of Strathclyde, he improved the opportunity by speaking on the same subject to their ecclesiastics. Here, too, he succeeded to a

considerable extent. A number of them abandoned the
Celtic calculation and adopted that of Rome.

This conversion of these northern Irish, if we may
call it so, and the Strathclyde Britons must have taken
place about 690. After his frustrated attempt to win
over his own monastery, Adamnan stayed in Ireland
among those who had listened to his words. When an
old man of nearly eighty years he returned another
time to Iona to make a last effort. It was equally
fruitless as the first. He died there in the first months
of the next year, before the difference between him
and his stubborn monks became practical. Divine
Providence, says St. Bede, took him away, lest the
quarrel with them should become aggravated by the
actual presence of the two Easter dates. The year of
his death is variously given, 703, 704, 705. The following consideration, closely connected with our subject, seems to speak for 704. The two Easter dates
for those three years, the Roman and the Celtic respectively, are these:

> 703, April 8 and April 1;
> 704, March 30 and April 20;
> 705, April 19 and April 12.

In 703 as well as in 705, the Roman Easter was a
week after the Celtic.[6] In these years the monks would
simply have smiled at St. Adamnan (and his companions) when he continued his fast a week longer.
But it would have roused their anger to the utmost,
if in 704 he had celebrated his Roman Easter while
they were in the middle of Lent. It would have caused
a regular uproar among them. Hence the year 704

[6] On this and similar questions, cf. Franz Ruehl, *Chronologie des
Mittelalters und der Neuzeit*. Berlin, 1897.

seems to be much more adapted to show in his earlier death a special act of Divine Providence.

From the few other facts I have had the time to gather concerning the life of St. Adamnan it appears to me that he was a highly educated man, a man who bent to reason, a mild and lovable character who endeavored to reach his end by means of kind instruction, and who was at the same time, and in a much nobler way than his Iona monks, tenacious of his purpose. It rouses our admiration to see how this great man after being practically exiled from his own home by his indocile and recalcitrant subjects, and with one foot in the grave, tries another time with his dying breath to reduce them to reason.

IV. *Many of the Cornish Britons*. St. Adamnan had made the beginning of the propagation of the Roman Paschal computation among the Britons. He gained those of Strathclyde, or at least many of them. These Britons were under the political control of Northumbria. In the South the Kingdom of Wessex had conquered another part of British territory, namely, Cornwall. At this time the great St. Aldhelm was abbot of Malmsbury, which under him became a very flourishing institution. (He was afterwards made bishop of the new diocese of Sherborne.) By his Latin writings Aldhelm contributed efficiently to the spread of Roman education, having himself been for years disciple of Archbishop Theodore of Canterbury. St. Bede states that while abbot of Malmsbury St. Aldhelm by order of a synod of his people wrote a lengthy letter to the Cornwall Britons concerning the celebration of Easter and other Celtic peculiarities. The letter was addressed to a King Geraint whom St. Bede calls Gerontius. (Book V, p. 18.) A large number of the Cornish

Britons accepted the Roman Easter, though we do not know whether King Gerontius was among them. It does not seem that either here or in Strathclyde, any pressure was exercised by the Anglo-Saxon kings, who evidently hoped to gain the Britons over by peaceful persuasion. This letter of Aldhelm must have been written between 675 and 705, because it was during these years that he was abbot of Malmsbury. Plummer (Vol. II, p. XXVIII) places it in 705. It was, therefore, about this year, that many of those Cornish Britons who were subject to Wessex accepted the Roman Easter calculation.[7]

Thus the Roman Easter had extended to both the northern and the southern peninsula of the Britons. The center part, Wales, was to give way last of all. The next Celtic land to which we have now to turn is the Kingdom of the Picts (in present Scotland).

V. *The Kingdom of the Picts.* As the Picts had been Christianized chiefly by monks from Iona and were under their spiritual care, they of course celebrated Easter according to the Celtic custom. But the controversy was transferred to them from the neighboring Northumbria, where since 664 the Roman Easter was observed. To decide the question King Naiton (Nechtan) of the Picts sent to the famous twin monastery of Wearmouth-Jarrow to ask for information. Abbot Ceolfrid answered the inquiry. In a long letter—it covers nearly twelve pages in Bede—he set forth the theoretical reasons for the Roman calculation. He also mentioned the visit of St. Adamnan to his monastery and recounted how this eminent scholar had become convinced of the necessity of a change. King

---

[7] The text of St. Aldhelm's letter is found in Migne, *Latin Fathers,* Vol. 89, Col. 87-92.

Naiton, who seriously doubted the correctness of the national custom, was won over completely. When the letter was read to him in a solemn gathering, which must have been of the nature of the assembly at Whitby, he rose from his seat, and on bended knee gave thanks to God for having received such a precious gift from the land of the Angles. "And I declare here solemnly before all here present, that I want this date of Easter to be observed by my whole nation." Without delay notifications were sent out throughout the kingdom, and with them the Roman Easter tables, to be copied, studied, and observed everywhere.[8] On this occasion St. Bede mentions also the Celtic tonsure more explicitly than in any other place. "All the ministers of the altar and the monks," he says, "received the crown-shaped tonsure. The whole nation rejoiced to have entered as it were into a new allegiance to the Prince of the Apostles and to possess a new claim to his protection." (Book V, Chap. 21.)

Another ancient source, the annals of Tighernach, reports under the year 717: "The communities of the Iona monks were expelled across the mountains." King Naiton was in earnest. After means of kindness, which we must suppose were employed first, had not produced the desired result, he acted as King Oswiu of Northumbria had done, and expelled those who refused to conform. We need not take this too tragically, however. St. Bede expressly states, that ALL accepted the Roman tonsure. Hence the number of those who preferred exile can have been only a small fraction.[9]

[8] Bede here speaks of the Roman cycle as of nineteen years. In reality the Roman cycle was of 532 years, and Bede himself has worked it out entirely. See p. 213 above.

[9] The Annals of Tighernach are here quoted from Plummer, II, 331. If the statement is correct, a difficulty arises from the other

VI. *Iona.* We now approach the introduction of the
Roman Easter into the very citadel of hereditary Iro-
Celtic usages, the mighty Abbey of Iona, the backbone
of most of the resistance offered in other places to the
champions of the Dionysian computation. Adamnan,
its own abbot, one of the greatest men of his time,
had seen his efforts frustrated by the stubborn par-
ticularism of the monks. The submission of Iona is
connected with another prominent name, that of St.
Egbert. This Saint was the scion of a Northumbria
family of high nobility. In his youth he went to Ireland
for the sake of study and the practice of piety. While
there he was seized by a contagious disease, which
swept the whole island. He vowed that if God would
grant him more time for penance, he would never return to his native land, and devote his years to severe
austerities. He recovered and conscientiously carried
out his vow. But the voluntary banishment from his
beloved land did not dull his supernatural love for
the welfare of his race. He decided to sail over to
the continent, and preach the Gospel to his pagan
kinsmen, the Frisians and Saxons. He had already won
able companions and gathered provisions for the long
trip, when a young monk informed him of a vision
he had had the preceding night. The young monk's
teacher, Boisil, had appeared to him and ordered him
to tell Egbert that the proposed undertaking would not
be carried out. Instead of going to the Frisians, Egbert
was to go to Iona and preach to the monks there.
Egbert took no notice of this message, and bade the
young messenger to keep it a secret, since the whole

statement, made by St. Bede, that Iona gave up the Celtic computation in 716, a year after St. Egbert arrived in that monastery.
However, Plummer rightly remarks (II, page 335) that Egbert may
have taken his time in carrying out his plan.

might be merely an ordinary dream. Secretly, however, he feared the vision might be genuine. After a few days the young man returned. Boisil had appeared to him again, and reproached him for not speaking to Egbert forcibly enough. "Go now," he said, "and tell him he must go to the monasteries of Columbkil (i.e., Iona and the institutions dependent on it), whether he likes it or not, *because their ploughs do not go straight.* He must direct them into the straight line." Egbert evidently feared a mission to Iona and its dependent convents more than a trip to the wild and far-off Frisians. Though he could no longer doubt the genuinity, he made an attempt, as once the Prophet Jonas did, to escape the hand of God. He had all his provisions and other things which were destined for the voyage put into the boat, and only waited for a favorable wind. But one night a terrible storm arose, threw the vessel on the shore, and destroyed part of its lading. Then at last he resolved to give up the undertaking. He sent, however, several Anglo-Saxons, who had received their education in Ireland, to Frisia, among them St. Willibrord, the Apostle of the Netherlands and fatherly friend of St. Boniface.

St. Egbert, says Bede, was a most amiable teacher, who carried out by his example what he taught by words, and was therefore gladly listened to by everybody. He began his mission by winning over the convents in northern Ireland, which were subject to Iona, and after some eleven or twelve years ventured the dreaded journey to the head monastery itself. He was received with great honor and joy by the monks. A change of mind had evidently taken place at Iona since the days of Adamnan. Possibly the defection of their monasteries in Ireland, and the catastrophe among the

Picts, together with the renown of sanctity and learning which had preceded his arrival had made them
more pliable. Moreover, their position among the
Irish themselves was now completely altered. The
whole Irish nation had become Roman. The Iona
monks were holding out not only against the Church
of the continent but also against their own kinsmen.
Could they afford to be more Irish than the Irish?

St. Egbert came to Iona in 715. Though he was received so cheerfully, the change does not seem to have
taken place at once, because according to the Annals of
Tighernach the refugees from Pictland arrived in
717. Had Iona accepted the Roman Easter in 716,
the fact no doubt would have become known in the
neighboring country in the institutions depending on
Iona. Probably all the Iona monks among the Picts
would have followed their example. At any rate they
would not have gone to Iona had they known such an
action concerning Easter. It would, however, have been
quite in keeping with the mild character of Egbert,
that although the soil appeared to be pretty well prepared he did not urge the matter unduly. For some
time even two Easters may have been celebrated at
Iona. The text of St. Bede, however, rather strongly
suggests, though not in so many words, that such a
period of transition, if it existed at all, could not have
lasted very long. Iona gave up its separatistic and now
completely isolated position.

The man who had conquered this last stronghold remained in Iona for the rest of his long life, and continued his practices of prayer and penance. During
these years Easter was celebrated on the Roman date
which was always different from the Celtic. In 729,
the ninetieth of St. Egbert's life, Easter fell on April

24, a date on which it could never have fallen according to the discarded reckoning, which permitted no Easter after April 22. On April 24, the venerable old man celebrated the solemn High Mass, and died the same afternoon. The monks saw in this coincidence a divine approbation of the step the Saint had so ably advocated and which they had taken some twelve years before.[10]

VII. *The Britons of Wales.* We have still to see how the Easter controversy came to an end in the center portion of the land of the Britons, i.e., in Wales. St. Bede closed his busy life in 735. The introduction of the Roman Pasch in Iona was one of the very last events he was able to report to posterity in his *Ecclesiastical History.* The Britons of Wales remained much longer in their particularistic attitude.[11] The sources to which we must turn concerning this point give us very scant information. We have only a few entries in the *Annales Cambrenses.* Under the year 755 they tell us that North Wales accepted the Roman Easter upon the urgings of Bishop Elvod (Elfod) of Bangor, but that the other bishops (those of South Wales are meant) did not concur therein. In 777, however, South Wales also conformed. But this did not finish the matter. Bishop Elvod lived to a very old age. When he died, in 809, the chronist says, "a great tumult occurred among the ecclesiastics on account of Easter, because the Bishops of Llandaff and Menevia (in

[10] Wm. Bright, in *Chapters of Early English Church History,* p. 469, asserts, without giving authority, that "a section of the monks set up a new abbot, and this schism lasted for nearly sixty years."
[11] From this time dates a letter written by Pope Gregory III to the bishops of Bavaria and Alemannia, warning them against British priests. *"Gentilitatis ritum et doctrinam vel venientium Brittonum vel falsorum sacerdotum . . . renuentes ac prohibentes abjiciatis."* Tangl, *Die Briefe des heiligen Bonifatius und Lullus,* p. 71.

South Wales) would not succumb to the Archbishop of North Wales (i.e., Bangor), being themselves archbishops of older privilege." [12] How long this controversy, which evidently received much of its acrimoniousness from getting mixed up with a question of jurisdiction, may have lasted, our sources do not disclose. In later centuries no difference between the Britons and their eastern and western neighbors in the point of the date of Easter is mentioned again.

CONCERNING THE TONSURE: The shape of the tonsure was another point of difference which disappeared with the Celtic Easter. The Celtic priests and monks would shear the front part of the head to a line from ear to ear. The Romans left a crown of hair around the upper part of the head and shaved away all the rest. (This latter tonsure is still worn in Catholic lands by the members of certain religious Orders.) Each party adduced theoretical and ascetical considerations in favor of its tonsure. The advocates of the Roman method held theirs was St. Peter's tonsure and maintained that the Celtic tonsure was that of Simon Magus. In the meeting at Whitby there was a separate and it seems rather heated discussion about the tonsure (*quaestio non minima*). But the impression one gains from St. Bede's report is that it was looked upon as of much less importance. In the assembly of the Picts it is also brought up explicitly, but dismissed very briefly. The Roman tonsure was accepted with the Roman Easter.

Conclusion. We may be tempted to consider this whole question as of little importance. What does it matter on what date Easter is celebrated as long as it is kept with that devotion and solemnity which befits so great a festival, and as long as every Christian guides himself by Christian laws and precepts? Yet we should consider how serious this question was taken

---

[12] For these entries see Haddan and Stubbs, *Councils and Ecclesiastical Documents relating to Great Britain and Ireland*, Vol. I, p. 204.

by all the great men of the time. More than one Pope thought it necessary to write peremptory letters on this point to the Celts. Sts. Adamnan and Egbert almost devoted their lives to the settling of this question. St. Bede himself, to whom we chiefly owe our knowledge of these struggles, looks upon the particularistic tendencies as a great calamity.

It was, indeed, objectively speaking, a standing disobedience towards the supreme authority of the Church, and although we need not enter into an investigation concerning subjective good will or malice, it was by way of fact a rift which might have widened in the course of longer altercation. The constant appeal to theoretical, mystic, and ascetical considerations was a permanent danger for dogmatic questions to be dragged into the controversy and might have opened the door for the gradual introduction of incorrect, perhaps even heretical views. The Easter question had been very briskly agitated in the first three centuries of Christianity. When the Council of Nicaea had prescribed a certain calculation, one part of the opponents, the *Quarto-decimani*, refused to submit and actually fell away from the Church.

For the Anglo-Saxons of that time the double Easter was especially dangerous. They were new in the Faith. They attached great consequence to external things. That the two Easters should stand for two different religions was a conclusion which must have appeared rather obvious to these children of nature. And though in itself less important the double form of the tonsure no doubt caused this impression to appear still more plausible. On the other hand the unity in the celebration of the Easter festivities helped to preserve and foment ecclesiastical unity among the several Anglo-Saxon realms as well as with the body of Christianity on the continent, a double unity without which there could have been no wholesome development of the young Church of England. This spiritual bond was at the same time one of the various elements which later on brought about the political unification of the country under King Egbert.

As for the Celtic communities, they had by adopting the Easter calculation of Rome given another tangible proof that in spite of their local remoteness from the rest of the Catholic Church they did not mean to set themselves up as a separate religious entity. In his article on Whitby,[13] Father Herbert Thurston, S.J., speaks of the Irish Church as "declining." We cannot share this view. St. Bede's reference to that Church certainly give us a different idea. When reporting the end of the Whitby conference, in consequence of which those who refused to conform were obliged to leave Northumbria, he pays a high tribute to their virtues and abilities. "Their whole endeavor," he says, "was to serve God and not the world. Hence there was in those days the greatest reverence for the monastic habit. Wherever a monk showed himself, he was received with joy as a servant of God. If a priest happened to come into a village, the villagers would flock around him to hear the word of Life. For the monks had no other purpose in coming into any village but to preach, baptize or visit the sick." (Book III, Chap. 27.) Such activity is not the sign of decline. Nor were the monasteries and groups of monasteries in which men like St. Adamnan and St. Egbert moved and prayed declining institutions. It is worth remarking that outside of Northumbria and the land of the Picts

[13] *Catholic Encyclopedia*, Vol. XV, p. 610.

the whole momentous change took place without any political pressure, and that the Roman Easter was accepted solely for spiritual motives, which brought no sort of temporal advantage and averted no disadvantage. Nor were the motives different in the minds of those who at Whitby and in the assembly of the Picts resolved to pass over to the Roman Easter. Far from being declining all the communities concerned showed by the very act of transition that there was reigning in them a vigorous Christian spirit. For many it meant a real sacrifice to discard the old hereditary method, but the sacrifice was made.

The Roman Easter came to the Celts greatly through the instrumentality of Anglo-Saxons. St. Bede finds a special act of divine Providence in it that that race which had gladly and unstintingly assisted in communicating to the Saxons the heavenly doctrine, was itself brought by the Saxons who owed it so much to the full practice of Catholic life. Unquestioningly now that the Celtic Churches were in full union with the center and heart of Christianity, the life blood of the Church flowed still more freely and invigoratingly through the veins of the fervent communities of the Island Celts.

III

THE MEETING AT WHITBY, 664 A. D.[1]

I. THE TRANSACTIONS

IN the year 664, a meeting of bishops, kings, and other prominent personages took place in the noble monastery of Whitby in the Kingdom of Northumbria. Its purpose was to decide the controversy which had been discussed for three decades and which had gradually assumed the character of a burning question. There had been no unity in fixing the date of the greatest feast of Christianity. Easter was celebrated by two parties according to different calculations. The cause of the difference has been made clear in the preceding article, and we shall here see more in detail how the matter was settled at Whitby for the Kingdom of Northumbria. (Book III, Chap. 25.) There will be added, by way of supplement, a short discussion of the character of the Whitby meeting.

When Irish monks from Iona, under the leadership of St. Aidan, entered the Anglo-Saxon mission field, they brought with them their eighty-four year Cycle, and taught it the converts. The two methods thus entered into the same region. The Roman missionaries calculated the Easter date according to the Roman, the Irish according to their own manner. And since missionaries of both classes were present in some other

---

[1] Address delivered at the Convention of the Jesuit Historical Association, Aug., 1927, Chicago, Ill. Printed in *Catholic Historical Review*, Vol. VII (1927-1928), pp. 620-629.

Anglo-Saxon kingdoms as well, this necessarily led to bewilderment and confusion in many places.

It was above all in Northumbria, the northernmost kingdom, that the two systems were bound to collide. Here the Irish monks had begun their work, having been invited by King Oswald. Here they had established their central monastery, Lindisfarne, which was to be another Iona. Very many, probably most, of the Christian Northumbrians, including the royal family, were their spiritual children. At the same time the Roman Easter had its representatives. When St. Paulinus, the first Apostle of Northumbria, was forced to flee and when so many of his converts relapsed into heathenism, his deacon James had remained at York and continued his missionary activity, adhering of course to the Roman Easter. Travelers returned from the continent with the news that the whole world celebrated Easter according to a different computation. In particular an Irish priest is named, Ronan, who visited Rome and came back as an ardent advocate of the Roman method of calculation. Though his efforts had only a limited amount of success with his countrymen, they served to increase the desire for unity, and to encourage a deeper study of the question. Very great was the influence of St. Wilfrid, an Anglo-Saxon, at that time Abbot of Ripon. After being educated by the *Scoti* at Lindisfarne a long sojourn on the continent had changed him like Ronan into a determined champion of the Roman custom. More than all this, the royal family was now divided into two camps. King Oswiu adhered to the Irish method. Queen Eanfleda, who had been born and educated in strictly Roman Kent and had brought with her as chaplain a priest Romanus, celebrated Easter on the Roman date.

Alchfrid, the royal heir, assumed by Oswiu as co-regent, followed the example of his mother, and was strongly encouraged by Abbot Wilfrid, his intimate friend.

How confusing the matter had become will best be seen by a glance at the list of the actual Easter dates. The Irish missionaries had come in 635. Between that date and 664, the date which interests us, Easter had been celebrated every year on two different dates, with the exception of only three years, 638, 655, and 658. As a rule the Celtic Easter was a week earlier, but four times it fell several weeks later than the Roman. Practically, therefore, during this quarter of a century one party was still observing Lent while the other sang the Easter Alleluja. It is somewhat amusing to think of the conditions in the royal kitchen, where the Easter banquet had to be prepared for one party while the other demanded Lenten fare.[2] The different Easter dates affected the whole of Lent including Holy Week, and the feasts of Ascension and Pentecost.

The Roman Easter seems to have been gaining ground. Its chief champion was St. Wilfrid. To him is probably due the determined stand made by the Roman party in the King's family. King Oswiu's implicit confidence in the correctness of his beloved Irish teachers had become shaky. He wanted the matter decided.

So an assembly was called to meet at the famous monastery of Whitby, over which presided the abbess Hilda, a lady distinguished by royal family connections, exemplary virtue, and practical wisdom. The most prominent personages in the gathering were the fol-

[2] The Sundays in Lent then were days of abstinence.

lowing: On the side of the Irish King Oswiu (himself), Abbot-Bishop Colman of Lindisfarne with a
number of his clerics, Hilda the abbess, and Cedd,
Bishop of Essex, himself a Saxon, but trained by the
Irish and adhering to their customs. The side of the
Romans was represented by young King Alchfrid,
James the Deacon, Wilfrid the Abbot of Ripon with
one of his priests by the name of Agatho, and Agilbert,
the Bishop of Wessex, a Frank, who happened to be
the guest of King Oswiu. Queen Eanfleda does not
seem to have been present. Bishop Cedd, well versed in
both the Irish and Anglo-Saxon languages, acted as
official interpreter.

It is impossible to reproduce in detail the lengthy
speeches by which each party tried to establish the
claims of its Easter calculation. They may be read in
St. Bede's *Historia Ecclesiastica*.

King Oswiu opened the meeting by a short address.
Those who serve one God, he said, should also be
guided by one rule of life. There should be no discrep-
ancy in celebrating the heavenly mysteries among those
who hope for the one heavenly kingdom. Let there be
an investigation as to which tradition is supported by
the better reasons, and let that tradition be followed
by all.

The speakers were practically only Colman, the
Abbot-Bishop of Lindisfarne, and Wilfrid, Abbot of
Ripon. Colman appealed to the authority of St. John
the Apostle, who he said had established the calculation followed by the Irish. Wilfrid replied, that the
Scoti in reality do not follow St. John. This great
Apostle celebrated Easter always on a certain date
according to the Jewish Calendar, no matter whether
it was a Sunday or not. The *Scoti* always choose a

Sunday. Besides St. Peter was greater than St. John, and he was the author of the calculation adopted by the Romans. Colman then advanced the authority of St. Anatolius, to whom in reality is due the eighty-four year cycle, which the *Scoti* had adopted and retained. He also claimed that the injunctions of St. Columba, the founder of Iona and Apostle of Scotland, ought not to be disregarded. Wilfrid pointed out that the *Scoti* did not follow Anatolius, because they sometimes celebrated Easter when Anatolius' rules would require another date. St. Columba, however, he said, had never had any opportunity to learn about the Roman Easter. But Colman and his adherents knew the decrees of the Apostolic See, and yet they refused to conform. Our Lord never said to St. Columba what He had said to St. Peter: "Thou art Peter, and upon this rock I shall build My Church, and the gates of hell shall not prevail against it. And to thee I will give the keys of the Kingdom of Heaven."

At this point King Oswiu in a rather dramatic way concluded the discussion. "Is it true, Colman," he said, "that these words were spoken to Peter by Our Lord?" "That is so," replied Colman. "And can you advance anything like it that was addressed to St. Columba?" "Nothing." "Do then both of you grant without any hesitation that these words were said to Peter, and that the keys of the Kingdom of Heaven were given to him?" And both said yes. Thereupon the king declared: "And I tell you, that I do not want to contradict him who is the Keeper of the Gate. As far as I understand the matter and am able to act, I wish to obey his rule in all things; lest perhaps, when I arrive at the gate of the Kingdom of Heaven, there might be none to open it for me, since he is the one in whose power are the keys."

The King's words were received with applause by all the members of the Assembly, high and low. This was the end of the separate Easter for the Kingdom of Northumbria. Cedd, the Bishop of Essex, too, returned to the South as an adherent of the Roman calculation.

As stated in the preceding article, page 216, the acceptance of the Roman Easter in Northumbria meant its ascendancy or permanence in all the other Anglo-Saxon realms.

The unity, badly needed, was, however, dearly bought. While the Anglo-Saxon clergy and many of the *Scoti* obediently submitted to the Roman law, Abbot-Bishop Colman of Lindisfarne with a large number of monks, chiefly but not exclusively Irish, refused to conform, and withdrew to the North, where at Iona and the institutions dependent on it the Celtic method of calculation was still kept up. No more Irish workers came to the Anglo-Saxon lands from those quarters. Though rejoicing over the victory of the Roman Easter, St. Bede does not fail to express his admiration for the virtue and ability of those who now left for good the country which was so deeply indebted to them, and to give them a very sympathetic farewell.[3]

In order to appreciate the Easter Question correctly we may say that both the Celts and the Romans were wrong in appealing to an Apostle, the Celts to St. John, the Romans to St. Peter, as authors of their calculations. The eighty-four year cycle used by the

---

[3] Irish missionaries continued to come from the South of Ireland, because that part of the Celtic world had accepted the Roman Easter some thirty years before Whitby.

Celts was not in existence at the time of St. John. It was not even supported, in all its details, by the authority of Anatolius. This Cycle was tried out on the continent but found wanting in several points. On the other hand, it is sure that St. Peter, too, did not leave any regulation as to the date on which Easter was to be celebrated. The Romans had no more reason to appeal to his authority than the Celts had to appeal to St. John. The Council of Nicaea had laid down the chief features of the Easter calculation, but the details had caused a wavering attitude, a tentative admission and rejection of several modifications for a period of two hundred years. As late as 525 A.D., as remarked before, did Dionysius Exiguus end the troubles by devising a satisfactory method of calculation.

In all discussions concerning the merits of the Celtic and the Roman Easter calculations much was made of reasons taken from the Old and New Law, and of mystical and symbolic considerations. There was in reality only one peremptory reason for the Roman Easter, alluded to by St. Wilfrid when he reminded Colman that now the Celtic world was no longer in ignorance as to the will of the Roman Pontiffs. It was the will of the Popes that made the method of Dionysius Exiguus the Roman method. We may find that same reason expressed in the concluding words of King Oswiu, who declared that he accepted the Roman Easter in order not to displease St. Peter, the Keeper of the Keys of the Heavenly Kingdom.

2. CHARACTER OF THE MEETING AT WHITBY

What was the Character of the Meeting at Whitby? The Rev. G. Stebbing, in his *Story of the Catholic*

Church, calls it a synod, meaning evidently an ecclesiastical Council. Hilaire Belloc, too, in his new *History of England,* Vol. I, speaks of it as the first English
Council (contradicting himself a few pages later where
he mentions the Council of Heresford as the first).
Other works employ the same appellation.

To decide this question we must first consider the
persons who composed this meeting. There were present the two kings, Oswiu and Alchfrid; three bishops,
Colman, Cedd, and Agilbert, a number of priests who
had come with Colman from Lindisfarne, the priests
Wilfrid, Agatho, and Romanus, and the deacon James.
There was finally the Abbess Hilda *cum suis,* which
probably means both nuns and clerics. Besides these
there must have been, however, a considerable multi-
tude of other participants. St. Bede's report concludes,
*Haec dicente rege faverunt adsidentes quique sive
adstantes, majores cum mediocribus,* "the king's words
were received with applause, as well by those who
were seated as by those who were standing, the prominent ones and those less important." Evidently the
number of bishops, priests and other clerics was small
in proportion to the rest of the Assembly. This is certainly not the composition of an ecclesiastical Council.

Secondly, it is decidedly the king who presides over
the meeting and directs its proceedings. King Oswiu
makes the opening address. He gives the floor first to
Bishop Colman, and then expressly to Bishop Agilbert. The latter asks that Wilfrid speak in his stead,
since he himself is not sufficiently familiar with the
Anglo-Saxon tongue. Wilfrid does so, but *jubente rege,*
called upon by the king. Finally no vote is taken by
either bishops or priests. The king himself cuts off all
further disputation by the declaration that he will

adhere to the practice ascribed to St. Peter. If there is any vote at all, it is the applause of the *adsidentes* and *adstantes,* the *majores cum mediocribus.* That these were not the clergy is evident. Two of the three bishops present, Colman and Cedd, advocated the Celtic Easter. Only three of the priests, Agatho, Romanus, and Wilfrid, and Deacon James championed the Roman method. Far greater was the number of those who had come with Bishop Colman from Lindisfarne or belonged to the train of Abbess Hilda. None of these would have concurred in a vote for the Romans. The *adsidentes* and *adstantes,* who applauded the king's resolution can only have been the lay participants of the meeting, the great men of the kingdom, who according to their rank were either seated or standing. *So the meeting of Whitby, consisting overwhelmingly of lay members, presided over by the king, and deciding by a vote of laymen, was no ecclesiastical gathering, was no Council.* It was in all probability nothing but the regular national gatherings of the Northumbrians, a *Witenagemot* or *Witan,* summoned for the special purpose of coming to a conclusion in a matter which had caused much confusion for many years.

It would seem at first sight, that an assembly of this character was incompetent to render any verdict in such a question. But the members were perfectly in their right. In fact, they rendered no verdict at all. They did not pass on doctrines of Faith, nor did they attempt to force a new law upon the Church of their land. They did on a smaller scale what their ancestors had done thirty-seven years earlier, in 627 A.D. In that year the assembly of Northumbria with their King

Edwin had decided to accept Christianity. In the Whitby assembly the members had gathered for the purpose of finding out what was, in one particular point, the law of the religion they had adopted. They assembled not with the will to dictate to the Church, but to obey her laws in all points.

IV

St. Boniface and St. Virgil

A Study from the Original Sources of Two Supposed Conflicts

I. SAINT BONIFACE [1]

A CENTURY had elapsed since St. Augustine, the Benedictine monk, sent by Pope St. Gregory the Great, himself a Benedictine, had arrived on the shores of Britain to commence the evangelization of the Anglo-Saxons. That century had wrought great changes. The country had become Catholic. It was ruled over by a well-organized hierarchy of bishops. A large number of monasteries harbored devoted monks and nuns, who

---

[1] BIBLIOGRAPHICAL NOTE

As stated on pages 247, 269 and 282, the author confines himself strictly to the original sources, which are principally two letters of Pope St. Zachary to St. Boniface. Letters of Popes St. Gregory II and St. Gregory III will also be utilized. These letters are found in Migne's *Patrologia Latina,* Vol. 89, where they are grouped with other letters of these Popes. A recent edition of these letters, also in Latin, and furnished with critical notes, has been issued by Michael Tangl, *Die Briefe des heiligen Bonifatius und Lullus,* Berlin, 1916, which is Vol. I of a special section of the *Monumenta Germaniae Historica, Epistolae Selectae.* (On this collection of sources see *Catholic Historical Review,* Vol. IV, (1924-1925) pp. 202 ff.) All these documents are accepted by historians as undoubtedly genuine.

Here might also be mentioned G. Kurth, *St. Boniface,* translated from the French by Monsignor Victor Day. The Bruce Publishing Co., Milwaukee, Wis., 1936. This is the first and only Life of St. Boniface by a Catholic author in the English language.

served God in the retirement of the cloister, and by
their example, prayer, and preaching supported and
strengthened the Christian life of the laity high and
low. The monasteries were the homes of flourishing
schools. Prominent men traveling to the continent
brought the books which nourished the desire for
knowledge in teachers and students. The school of
Malmsbury had reached its zenith under the Abbot-
Bishop St. Aldhelm. In the far north St. Bede the
Venerable studied and taught indefatigably, and composed his immortal books in the Abbey of Jarrow.
Canterbury cherished the learned traditions of Sts.
Augustine, Theodore, and Adrian. Numerous students,
too, crossed the Irish Sea and enjoyed the instruction
and hospitality of the famous monastic schools of the
Green Isle.

The spot which attracts our attention is the Abbey
of Nutscelle (Nutshalling, Nursling) in the diocese of
Bishop St. Daniel of Winchester. The Abbot of Nutscelle, St. Wynbrecht, had held the position of chancellor at the court of the Kings of Wessex, before he
joined that Benedictine community, and was favorably
known as a scholar and a teacher. His community enjoyed the reputation of sanctity and learning. One of
his monks, *Winfrid,* later called *Boniface,* had acquired such renown for sacred and profane knowledge,
that the neighboring communities vied with one another in welcoming him to their homes in order to
benefit by his teaching. Bishop and king had successfully employed him on important missions. But his
desires were not confined to abbey or schoolroom, nor
were they satisfied with the brilliant career in Church,
and State which evidently lay open to him. Once al-

ready had he made the trip to the continent to work as missionary, but had been forced by untoward circumstances to return home. Upon the death of the beloved Wynbrecht there was no doubt as to who would be the next abbot. But through the mediation of Bishop Daniel the future apostle begged off. His heart was beyond the seas, with the Germans who still sat in the darkness and shadow of death. This time he wished to start his work in a different manner. He wanted to go to Rome, to obtain the apostolic mission from the successor of St. Peter, and be guided by his directions.

At an unknown date in the fall of A. D. 718, Winfrid knelt at the feet of Pope St. Gregory II, and expressed to the Holy Father his desire to preach the Gospel to the pagan Germans on the east side of the Rhine. When asked for his credentials he produced the sealed letter he had received from his bishop, Daniel of Winchester. The text of this letter is not extant, but we can well guess what it contained. Bishop Daniel no doubt informed the Sovereign Pontiff that the bearer of the communication, Winfrid by name, a monk of the Abbey of Nutscelle, was an ornament both of his Order and of the diocese of Winchester; that he had for many years been a successful teacher and preacher, and had shown considerable ability in the settlement of difficulties which had arisen in the diocese; that, however, his bishop and his brethren had made the sacrifice of parting with so promising a man in the conviction that God's Providence would use him as a fit instrument for the enlargement of Christ's Kingdom on earth.

Upon perusing this letter St. Gregory ordered Winfrid to remain in Rome, and had numerous conversations with him during the succeeding winter. He imposed upon him the Roman name of Boniface, officially declared him a papal and apostolic missionary, and on May 19, 719, dismissed him to the nation of which he was destined to become the Apostle.

God indeed blessed the work of the Roman missionary. Three years later, when receiving from him the report of his successes, St. Gregory II summoned him to Rome, and himself ordained him bishop of the regions gained by him for Christ. According to the pope's testimony, the conversion of a hundred thousand idolaters was the result of the first ten years of his activity. The next Pope, St. Gregory III, in 739, made Boniface Archbishop and ordered him to establish bishoprics wherever he should see fit. Soon the same Pope named him papal legate for all the countries north of the Alps, with power to convoke councils of the bishops and to preside over them as the representative of the Sovereign Pontiff.

His original field of action was what is now called Central and Southern Germany. He never penetrated into the North, where his kinsmen, the pagan Saxons, allowed no missionary of the Cross to enter. During the first period of his activity, when he was missionary in the strict sense of the word, he was exposed to the greatest physical hardships. Later on, when by his elevation to the position of archbishop and apostolic legate the field of his jurisdiction had greatly widened, he met with other troubles in the regions already partly converted. Many of the priests, or so-called priests, caused him much grief and sorrow by their immoral lives, by their obstinacy, and by their doubtful or heretical teaching. But when, as an old man "with white hair and bent with age," he traveled down the Rhine to finish the conversion of the Frisians; and when his head was cleft by the ax of the infuriated pagans: Germany had ceased to be a missionary country, and had taken its rank upon the same level with the rest of Christianity. Christian life in the whole Frankish realm, too, had been renewed; and without ever meddling in politics, St. Boniface had established a close union between the Holy See and the mighty kingdom of the Franks, a union which was destined to be of the greatest consequences, long after the saint's martyrdom.

In the person of St. Boniface, therefore, we have before us a really great man. Now, great men, saints included, can make mistakes; and Catholic historians are fully prepared to admit that some saints did not excel in learning, even concerning points in which we should suppose them to be well informed; that they betrayed weakness in pursuing their aims; or that they misjudged conditions and took ill-advised measures. No historian, however, will admit such shortcomings unless they are proved by incontestable evidence.

As to St. Boniface there are two flaws on his fair renown, the only ones so far as I can see, but pointed out by both Catholics and Protestants alike. His theological training, we are told, was rather elementary, because he ordered the Sacrament of Baptism to be repeated without reason; and he denounced Virgil, a learned Irishman, who he heard taught the sphericity of the earth and the existence of antipodes, to the Pope as a heretic.

In view of the position held by St. Boniface before he started out on his missionary career, it is indeed

very improbable that charges like these should have
been founded on facts. They have nevertheless been
made persistently. With some modifications they have
been passing from book to book. They are encountered
in our Church histories—even in tiny grammar school
manuals; in the lives of the saints; and under various
captions in encyclopedias of all shades and sizes. Some
of these works express themselves very respectfully as
to St. Boniface, giving him due credit for personal
sanctity and admirable organizing ability. Others speak
sneeringly of the semi-educated and narrow-minded
Boniface. During the period of the Prussian Kultur-
kampf a number of Protestants found the Virgil affair
a powerful weapon for their contention that the whole
activity of St. Boniface consisted merely in destroying
a flourishing Christianity of Celtic origin and subject-
ing the converts to the sway of the Roman Pope.

It is the purpose of these pages to investigate this
question in the way recommended by Pope Leo XIII,
and demanded by sound historiography, namely *adeundis rerum fontibus*—by going directly to the sources.
We shall not seek information from modern authors,
either Catholic or Protestant, nor shall we be satisfied by their assurance that they base their representations upon the sources. We shall approach the documents themselves. We shall read them, and read them
entirely; not omitting anything that may bear upon our
subject, and drawing only those conclusions which the
facts we glean from them will suggest. On the other
hand, we shall affirm nothing that is not borne out by
the sources. We shall not proceed from any preconceived view, but shall take the documents as our starting point, and shall try to discover what they have to
communicate, what message they have to convey to us.

To have a solid foundation for the question of the alleged teaching of the sphericity of the earth and the existence of antipodes, a preliminary study will be necessary. We must know exactly whether or not there was in the eighth century any knowledge of these geographical theories. On this point the present writer has made an independent investigation. He has himself examined a goodly number of those authors that could come under consideration. He knew very well that he was not the first to do so, but he did not wish to base his deductions upon the results of the researches of others. This preliminary study is the subject of the next chapter.

It will also be a natural introduction to the dispute between Boniface and Virgil concerning the sphericity of the earth. Chronologically indeed this discussion should come later. The controversy about the repetition of baptism took place in or about A.D. 746; whereas the clash about the shape of the earth was one or perhaps two years later, in 747. But not to interrupt the line of thought started in our next Section II, we shall treat of the latter question right after our investigation concerning the transmission of the early knowledge of the shape of the earth in Western Europe. Incidentally Chapters II and III will also be a modest contribution to the history of mathematical geography.[1]

II. EARLY KNOWLEDGE OF THE SPHERICITY OF THE EARTH

It is a recognized fact that when the intellectual life of the Middle Ages was at its height, the sphericity

[1] See Appendix Q.

of the earth was well known, at least to the whole educated world. But was it known as early as the eighth century? To answer this question nothing will be more satisfactory than to follow that theory from its earliest recorded beginnings through the subsequent centuries, and thus to ascertain whether the Christian writers were acquainted with it, and if so what was their attitude towards it. In the first place we must briefly sum up the knowledge possessed by those who preceded the Christian era, the Greeks and the Romans. We shall thus gain a starting point for our investigation concerning the views held by the Christian authors.

Eratosthenes, an Alexandrian Greek who died in 194 B. C., is considered by many as the founder of mathematical geography. For him the earth was a globe. He distinguished between geographical longitude and latitude, spoke of the poles and the equator, of parallels and meridians. He calculated the length of the thirty-sixth parallel which passes between Greece and the island of Crete. The length which he gave to it would suppose the equator to be 28,500 miles long. As the actual length of the equator is now known to be 24,500 miles, his calculation is certainly not discreditable, considering the fact that he had very few data and practically no instruments.

Strabo, a contemporary of Christ, was so convinced of the globular shape of the earth as to state, fifteen centuries before Columbus, that, were not the extent of the ocean an unsurmountable obstacle, one could reach India by sailing in a western direction from Spain.[2]

Concerning the relative motion of earth and stars there was no unity among the older Greek scholars. The Pythagoreans held that the earth itself by its rotation produces the difference between day and night. But the number of those who believed that the earth stands still and the heavens revolve around it was greater. About the middle of the second century after Christ, Claudius Ptolemy, of Alexandria, who was great as

[2] Botsford, *Source Book of Ancient History*, p. 307.

astronomer, mathematician, and geographer, summed up what
he thought were the genuine results of the labors of his predecessors, and he decided, after long and arduous studies, to
follow the opinion that the earth is a globe, that it stands
motionless in the middle of the universe, and that sun, moon,
and stars daily revolve around it. This is the fundamental
feature of the system which makes the earth the center of the
world, and is called after him the *Ptolemaic Theory*. It should
be remarked that Ptolemy was not the first to outline this system. It was the common possession of most of the Greek
astronomers centuries before him, and it had even been adopted
and set forth, as we are going to see, by a goodly number of
Latin writers in Italy. But Ptolemy worked it out more consistently. After him and under his name it dominated the
world of scholars until the time of Copernicus.

In our investigations we shall refer to this fundamental
feature only, because it has direct bearing upon the shape
of the earth. Ptolemy's ingenious doctrine concerning the paths
of the planets we can afford to leave aside. Nor is it necessary
to enter upon a discussion of the proofs for the sphericity of the
earth. Suffice it to say that the arguments advanced by the
ancients, in particular the fact that in the case of a ship sailing
away the lower parts of buildings and elevations first disappear
from view, are still found in present-day textbooks of mathematical geography.

The practical-minded Romans, more bent on conquering the
earth than on speculating about its shape, have not furnished
a single man who by observation or study enlarged the realm
of astronomy. But after they had once submitted to the sway
of the Greek genius and had themselves embarked upon literary
and philosophical pursuits, many, probably most, of their leading writers adopted the views of their masters and believed
that the earth is a globe. We must not be misled, however,
by the phrase *orbis terrarum,* which occurs so frequently in
classic literature. The word *orbis* commonly means a circle
or a disc. Its use in connection with *terra* dates from the time
when the Romans still thought of the earth as a plane. In the
term *orbis terrarum,* there was no reference to the sphericity
of the earth. Even a part of the earth's surface might be called
orbis, as, *orbis Romanus,* the Roman world. And there is still

extant a gold medal struck in B.C. 22, which represents the three continents, Europe, Asia, and Africa as three circles.[3] The term *orbis terrarum,* therefore, cannot serve us in our investigations, unless as is sometimes the case, the context shows that the word *orbis* is meant to denote a globe.

Happily the number of Roman writers, of the late republican and the imperial periods, who speak of the earth as a globe in the most unmistakable terms, is not small. I mention in the first place, *Publius Ovidius Naso,* the boyhood friend of many of us. When describing, in the beginning of his *Metamorphoses,* the chaotic state of things at the creation, he says:

> No sun, as yet, threw light upon the world;
> Nor did a moon its blunted horns renew;
> Nor did the earth, by its own burden poised,
> Suspended hang, encased in floating air.
>
> (Book I, 10-13.)

Then divine interference brought order into this chaos, and the poet continues:

> When thus the god, whatever god he was,
> Had disentangled all, and into members
> Had shaped the elements; he first took care
> *To mould the earth into a spacious round,*
> And make it equal from whatever side.
>
> (32-35.)

Ovid also knows the five zones of the earth:

> And as five zones do cross the heaven above,
> Two on the right, two on the left, one hotter,
> So also was the *weighty globe beneath,*
> By heaven enclosed, divided in five zones.
> Unfit to dwell in is the middle zone
> For boundless heat; deep snow forever shrouds
> The outer two; but two betwixt the three,
> Heat mingling with the cold, are temperate.
>
> (45-51.)

Evidently, Ovid had learned his elementary astronomy or mathematical geography. In a similar strain writes a less-known poet, Marcus Manilius, Ovid's contemporary.

---

[3] Miller, *Mappae Mundi,* Heft 3, p. 129.

The philosopher Seneca, for a time the friend and adviser of Emperor Nero, expressly states that the ocean participates in the rotundity of the earth.[4] The mountains, he says, do not change the sphericity of the earth any more than the seams of a toy ball change the ball's roundness. The question whether it is the earth or the universe that moves every day he does not venture to decide.

In A.D. 79, Mount Vesuvius gave to the world the first recorded spectacle of a terrific eruption. The commander of the Roman fleet, which was stationed nearby, climbed up the trembling mountain to observe the event more closely, but was killed in consequence of his daring. This man was Cajus Plinius Secundus, called the Elder, to distinguish him from his famous nephew, Cajus Plinius Caecilius Secundus, called Pliny the Younger. Pliny the Elder is a typical Roman scientist. The main part of his time was devoted to affairs of the state, since under several emperors he held important civil and military positions. Science could not be more than an amateur occupation, to which, as he says himself, he gave his spare moments and *nocturna tempora,* hours of the night. The indefatigable man boiled down the contents of some two thousand works into his *Historia Naturalis,* a large collection of sixty-five books.

While Pliny is reproached for superficiality in selecting and editing his material, he is very clear and explicit when speaking of the shape of our planet. He evidently had grasped the main features of the astronomic system as developed by the easterners and adopted by educated Romans. He thinks indeed that the mountains made the shape of the earth somewhat irregular, but all in all it is a perfect globe. (Chap. 64, 1.) The night is brought about by the shade of the earth, the same which causes the eclipse of the moon, while the eclipse of the sun occurs when the moon stands between it and the earth. (Chap. 7.) The author also discusses the ocean tides and attributes them to the influence of the moon. He considers them another proof for the roundness of the earth. (Chap. 99.) The stars and the sun move around the earth, and pass the earth's other side in exactly the same way as they pass the side which we ourselves inhabit.

[4] *Naturales Quaestiones,* Lib. III, Chap. 28, 4.

This leads him to a related question. If the earth is round, are there men on its other side? Are there *antipodes?* The educated, he says, hold that men are on all sides on the earth, and that the feet of those on one side are turned against the feet of those on the other side. The common people ask why those on the other side do not fall off, "as if there were not the same reason, to ask how it is that we ourselves do not fall off."

Pliny also touches upon another question, which has vexed thinking minds before and after him: *How is the earth supported.* But he conceives the universe as something massive and solid, which presses upon the earth and by its constant whirling motion not only grinds the earth into a globular shape but also keeps it in its place. Besides, he says, nature has not provided any place into which the earth could fall. According to him the seat of fire is in fire, that of air in air, that of water in water, and so there is no place for the earth except the earth itself. While this explanation is far from satisfying present-day science, it no doubt shows that even great theoretical difficulties did not deter Pliny from holding to his conviction of the rotundity of our planet. (Chap. 65.)

It would lead too far to enter upon a passage of the *Agricola* of Cornelius Tacitus (Chap. 12) which seems to refer to the form of the earth. Tacitus tries to give an explanation of the shortness of the summer nights in Britannia. The passage at first sight undoubtedly looks like a denial of the sphericity of the earth. At best it shows that the great historian had a rather hazy idea of mathematical geography, or that he was very unfortunate in the choice of his expressions.

For our purpose it will suffice to have mentioned the foregoing authors. Although, as Pliny the Elder states, the common people were not inclined to favor the correct view concerning the shape of the earth, and although even such lights as Cornelius Tacitus do not seem to have shown much interest in the question, the rotundity of our planet was well known to the Romans, and was not at all confined to the sacred circles of those who of set purpose busied themselves with scientific investigations.

The Romans were, however, as already pointed out, not productive in mathematical geography. Their field was geography only as far as it served practical purposes. They wished to know how to get from one place to another, and thus they produced their admirable *Itineraries,* in the form of books or inscriptions or maps. The *Itineraries* are the peculiar Roman contribution to geography. The production of really scientific maps, such as we have today was not in their line.[5]

If we have dwelt so long upon the geographical views of the pagan period of Latin literature, it was for two reasons: first, because we had to find out how far the belief in the sphericity of the earth extended, when Christianity was allowed to come out into the open and when the great Christian writers began to dominate the field of literature; secondly, because we shall have to deal with the Christian productions of Western Europe, which were much more of Roman than of Greek ancestry.

The great authors, who shed so brilliant a light upon the next centuries, were first and foremost theologians, and the overwhelming number of them never adverted to secular science at all. Nevertheless, we are able to show that the correct knowledge of the shape of the earth did not lack advocates in the Christian camp.

Unfortunately the first one whom we are obliged to mention Lucius Caecilius Firminianus Lactantius, called the Christian Cicero on account of the brilliancy of his style, is strongly opposed to the sphericity of the earth. Lactantius had witnessed the fierce persecution under Diocletian, and was resolved to attack heathenism with the same fierceness in the intellectual field. He takes to task the pagan philosophers, and endeavors to show, on several instances, how God abandoned them to their own folly after they had swerved from the way of truth. One of these points, in his opinion, is the question of the shape of the earth and the existence of antipodes. This brief passage is cer-

[5] See *Catholic Historical Review,* 1921, pp. 296 ff.; and the article on Ptolemy in this vol., pp. 28-38.

tainly not to his credit. The reasons which he adduces
against the existence and possibility of antipodes are
simply the talk of the masses, to which Pliny the Elder
alludes: "Is anybody so foolish as to believe that there
are men who have their feet above their heads? that
grain and trees grow downward? that rain and snow
fall upward?" (*Divinarum Institutionum Libri Sep-
tem.*, Book V, Chapter 24).[6] He has not the time,
he says, to enter upon what they call their arguments:
but these arguments really prove nothing. We can only
regret that he did not take the little time and trouble
of examining the *proofs* of the Greek scholars. If we
did not know more of him than this one passage, we
certainly should not look upon him as one of the
greater minds of his century.

But in this point Lactantius was by no means the
spokesman of Christian scholarship. His contemporary,
St. Hilary of Poitiers, the indomitable champion of
orthodoxy against Arianism, the Athanasius of the
West, speaks very differently. In his treatise on Psalm
105 [7] he says: "By suspending the earth in the middle
and fastening it He (God) determined its place in
such a way that it holds the central position in the
circle which surrounds it at equal distances from all
sides."

St. Hilary is firmly convinced that there must be
men on the other side of the globe, and he even endeavors to prove this from the Bible. "We learn this,"
he says, "from the Apocalypse (V. 3, 4) which tells
us that no man, either in heaven or upon the earth,
or below the earth, was found worthy to open the

---

[6] The quotations from the Latin Fathers employed in this discussion are taken from Migne's *Patrologia Latina*.
[7] Migne Lat., Vol. 9, p. 774.

sealed book. Now, the phrase 'below the earth' cannot denote those that are buried in the earth, because those spoken of in this passage are not said to be *in* the earth, but *below* it; and not those who are dead, but those who live can have any interest to unseal the book." (Migne Lat., Vol. 9, 280, 281.) We need not approve of this argument, which would almost declare the existence of antipodes an article of Faith, but it certainly leaves no doubt as to St. Hilary's opinion concerning the shape of the earth.

Let us now turn to St. Ambrose, the renowned Bishop of Milan, who was born in the same year in which Lactantius died, and himself died in 397, that is, thirty years later than St. Hilary. When explaining Psalm 118 (Migne Lat., Vol. 15, 1438) he almost goes out of his way to express his opinion on our subject. "The earth, therefore, is as it were the foundation on which we stand. Philosophy teaches that it is in the middle of the cycle of heaven; and Holy Scriptures, too, seems to indicate the same, since Job says of God that He suspends the earth in nothing.[8] Consequently the earth is surrounded by the heavenly sphere, and this is the reason why the sun is not visible during the night, because in completing its orbit it is in the lower part of the sphere." We should have liked the Saint to tell us a little more of his view, but he remembers that he is preaching, and suddenly breaks off with the remark that saints give their attention to spiritual things only, and delight in either teaching or learning what will bear fruit for eternal life.

By his eloquent sermons St. Ambrose was instrumental in bringing about the conversion of Aurelius Augustinus, then a celebrated teacher of oratory, and

---

[8] Job, XVI, 7.

in thus giving to the Church one of her most saintly sons and most prominent doctors. When the Roman world lay prostrate under the first blows of the invading Teutonic nations and many at the sight of so much destruction and depravity began to despair of Divine Providence, St. Augustine composed one of his most celebrated works, the *City of God,* which represents a magnificent Christian philosophy of history. After refuting the claims of paganism he enters upon a description of the course which the City of God on earth took among the existing nations. Soon the question turns up, should he include the antipodes in his considerations? He comes to the conclusion that he can safely ignore them. The passage (Book XVI, Chap. 9), is too important not to be translated in full.

But if some authors talk of the fabulous existence of antipodes, that is to say of men living on the opposite side of the earth where the sun rises when it sets for us; men whose feet are turned against ours: that is by no means to be believed. And indeed they do not make this assertion on the ground of any positive testimony (*historica cognitio*). They rely on a sort of scientific conjecture (*ratiocinando conjectant*), which they base on the theory that the earth is suspended in the concavity of heaven, and that it (*mundus*) holds a place which is at once the lowest and located in the center. (See Appendix A.) From this they presume that the other part of the earth, which is below, cannot be without inhabitants. They overlook that, although the earth (*mundus*—see Appendix B) be supposed to be round and spherical—for which view there may even be some scientific argument—it does not follow that the other side of the earth be bare of water; nor if it be bare, that it should be inhabited. For Holy Scripture, which proves the truth of its historical statements by the accomplishment of prophecies, gives no false information. And it is too absurd to hold that some men should have been able to cross in boats the immense ocean and safely arrive on the other side, so that even there a human race descending from the first man should have been established. Let us, therefore, look for the City of God, which here on earth is leading a pilgrim life, among the tribes of men which were divided into seventy-two nations and as many languages.

Let us note above all the quiet, serene tone in this passage. The saint is not bent on rejection or condemnation; but his guiding star is his imperturbable Faith. He does not antagonize those who hold that the earth is round. On the contrary, he grants that there are reasons for their opinion; but this point does not engage his attention, except in so far as it is necessarily connected with the antipodian theory. His work is of an historico-religious character, not a textbook of science, as are those of several great men with whose writings we shall make acquaintance later on. But he makes it clear enough that in the idea of the sphericity of the earth he does not in any way see a danger for Christian dogma and the purity of the Faith.

It is different concerning the existence of antipodes. No Columbus or Vasco da Gama or Magellan had as yet returned with the news that the ocean was by no means impassable, and that there were actually men on its other shore. He was fully justified in rejecting that idea as a fact, as long as no positive proof was forthcoming. But his main reasons were of a higher nature. As long as it was not demonstrated that men can traverse the ocean, it was impossible to assume that there should be any men there, because, according to Holy Scripture, all men must have descended from Adam, and the progenitor of the human race must have lived on our side of the great barrier. To assume that there are men beyond the impassable ocean, would mean to admit the existence of a human race independent of

Adam, and would consequently amount to a denial of
the unity of mankind, the denial of the dogmas of
original sin and general necessity of redemption. Had
St. Augustine lived to see the discoveries of later ages,
he would without hesitation have given up his opposition, because they furnished exactly what he demanded,
the *historica cognito*. Nor would he thereby have given
up one iota of his theological principles.[9]

In their famous edition of this work of St. Augustine, the Maurist Fathers call attention to the great
difference between the attitude of Lactantius and that
of St. Augustine towards the antipodes. Unlike Lactantius, St. Augustine does not deny the sphericity of
the earth, nor the *possibility* of men living on the other
side. He merely insists, and rightly so, that there has
not been brought forward any conclusive proof for
their actual existence. The fact that if there were antipodes, their feet would be turned towards ours, does
not frighten him; nor does he believe that the antipodes walk with heads downward; or that rain and
snow fall upward. His counter-reasons, which he wants
to see removed before he admits the existence of men
on the other side of the globe, are such as suggest
themselves to a mind accustomed to cool, sound reason-
ing, a mind which does not for a moment lose sight of
anything worthy of consideration.[10]

This sober view, however, contrasts remarkably with
the assurance, nay enthusiasm, with which St. Hilary
defends what is almost the contrary. Needless to say,
St. Hilary, though not mentioning it expressly, sup-

---

[9] See Appendix C.
[10] Beazley therefore, in his great work, *Dawn of Modern Geography* (Vol. I, p. 274 ff.) is incorrect in stating that St. Augustine
simply repeats Lactantius' objections, though in more measured language.

poses his antipodes to be descendants of Adam, but the difficulty of how they could have crossed the ocean, in whose existence no doubt he too believed, did not occur to him.

The Migration of Nations, meanwhile, ran its course. New kingdoms arose, sometimes ruled for short periods by brilliant leaders. Sixty years after the death of St. Augustine, Theodoric the Great founded the kingdom of the Ostrogoths in Italy and succeeded in drawing to his court many of the noblest and ablest Romans. Among these was Magnus Aurelius Cassiodorus, also called *Senator*. For a long time he was the soul of Theodoric's excellent administration, and he remained practically at the head of affairs for fifteen years after Theodoric's death. In 540 A.D. he withdrew from the court, to devote the rest of his life to the practice of piety and study. He founded a large monastery, Vivarium, in which he himself undertook the direction of the monks. But according to his idea the monk was to be a thoroughly educated man. Cassiodorus would have welcomed the establishment in the Western world of some kind of a university such as the East possessed at that time, but circumstances were too unfavorable. Italy was suffering under the ravages of the Twenty Years' War, which was to end in the expulsion of the Ostrogoths from the peninsula. Cassiodorus did what he could do. He composed two treatises, which were to serve as a program of studies, one on the sacred sciences, another—which will concern us here—on the liberal arts, *De Artibus et Disciplinis Liberalium Literarum.** One section of it is devoted to astronomy. It is a very brief and indeed sketchy summary of the Ptolemaic System.

* Migne Lat., Vol. 70, 1216 ff.

There is no express statement in the book to the effect that the earth is a globe. But the fact that Cassiodorus recommends most earnestly and most unreservedly the works of Ptolemy to the study of his monks, leaves no doubt as to his own conviction; and as he explains the eclipse of sun and moon in almost the same words as Pliny, he cannot have differed from this author's teaching as to the shape of our planet. In the much-troubled times of the sixth century, we therefore find another witness to the belief in the sphericity of the earth, a witness who is a monk by profession.

While Cassiodorus thus spent the last fifteen of the nearly hundred years of his useful life in Italy, Spain saw the boyhood of one of her greatest sons, St. Isidore of Seville. By the time that St. Isidore had succeeded his brother, St. Leander, in the bishopric of Seville, the fury of the Migration of Nations had mostly spent itself, and the foundations of the more prominent of the later European states had been laid. But a great deal of the old Roman civilization had already perished, and still more was fast disappearing. St. Isidore was above all a bishop. As a theologian of the first rank, he most vigorously defended Catholic doctrine against all enemies, and his unflinching attitude won him the fullest confidence of St. Gregory the Great. But this was not enough for him. He deliberately set himself to save as much from the wreck of Roman culture as was possible. He was less concerned with fresh researches than with the garnering of the scientific inheritance of his intellectual ancestors, and he excluded nothing worth knowing from his indefatigable zeal. One of his principal productions is the work called *Etymologiae*,* a collection of all kinds of information on the secular sciences.

Let us listen to some of his many utterances concerning the earth and its position in the universe:

The sphere of heaven, that is the universe, is a thing round in shape, the center of which is the earth, which is by it surrounded on all sides at an equal distance. (Therefore the earth too must be a sphere.)

The heavenly sphere moves from the east to the west during a day and a night in the space of 24 hours, during which time the sun finishes its course above the earth and below it. (Book IX, Chap. 34.)

There is an eclipse of the sun, when the moon, on the thirtieth day of its course, crosses the same line upon which the rays of the sun travel, and throwing itself in the way of the sun renders it invisible. For the sun gives us the impression of disappearing as long as the orb of the moon stands in front of it. (Book III, Chap. 52.)

There is an eclipse of the moon, when it runs into the shade of the earth. For the moon is believed not to have its own light but to be illumined by the sun, wherefore it fails when the earth comes between it and the sun. (Book III, Chap. 59.)

The stars are immovable, and are carried, fixed in the heavens, in an uninterrupted course. They do not fall down during the day, but are obscured by the splendor of the sun. (Book III, Chap. 62.)

The cause that makes either day or night is the sun being either above or below the earth. (Book V, Chap. 30.)

This is as faithful a representation of the main tenets of Ptolemy's theory, with the round earth in the center of the universe, as can be desired.

Cassiodorus, whose views are considered before, does not allude to the antipodes at all. It is quite possible that he was deterred from giving an opinion by the

* Migne Lat., Vol. 85, 73-727.

manner in which St. Augustine, who was one of his
favorite authors, deals with this subject. St. Isidore,
however, expressly takes an attitude similar to that of
St. Augustine. There is, he says, no experimental proof
for the existence of antipodes, who are merely a creation of poetical imagination. He omits the theological
reason which prompted St. Augustine, but adds another one of his own, the meaning of which it is hard
to grasp. He thinks that neither the solidity of the
earth nor its center would allow men to subsist on the
other side.

That the Spanish scholar has in view the verdict
of St. Augustine is clear from three phrases which are
taken literally from that author: *"Nulla ratione cre-
dendum est,"* (it must by no means be believed);
"Historica cognitio," (experimental proof), and
"quasi ratiocinando conjectant," (they surmise by way
of conjecture).

Upon what does the round earth rest? Pliny the
Elder, as we have seen, thinks that there is simply
no place into which it could fall; so it must needs
remain immovable. St. Isidore touches upon this problem in several passages. In what is perhaps the clearest
of them (in another work *De Rerum Natura,** Chap.
45) he first quotes approvingly the words of St. Ambrose referring to the Bible text that God suspended
the earth in nothing. "The philosophers," St. Isidore
continues, "utter similar opinions, namely, that the
earth is suspended in dense air; that like a sponge (in
water) it is hanging immovable by its own weight;
and that in consequence of an equal pressure from all
sides, and as if propped by wings, it rests perfectly
balanced and cannot incline to either side."

* Migne Lat., Vol. 83, pp. 965-1048.

For the purpose of our investigation the question of how the earth is supported is of no importance, and it ought not to disconcert us in the least if concerning it we find a certain wavering in the notes of St. Isidore. In spite of his several answers it remained for him an unsolved riddle. In one place he peremptorily states that this is a point which "none of us mortals is permitted to know; nor ought anybody inquire into this work of the Most High, as long as it is clear that by Divine ordination the earth rests immovably either upon waters or upon clouds." [11]

We may not like this *verboten* placarded up against any attempt at further inquiry, but whether it was pronounced or not, the effect was the same. It is certainly not wrong to say that at that time the world was not yet able to proceed any further. And if we ourselves, since the days of Newton, speak of *gravity* as the cause of both the stability and the motion of the earth and other heavenly bodies, do we really say so much more? We know the effect of that mysterious power, but its nature is as much a secret to us as was for the ancients the nature of the support on which they thought the globe of the earth was resting. Although in this particular point St. Isidore confesses his helplessness, his works abundantly prove that the shape of the earth itself is in no way a matter of dispute.

St. Hilary of Poitiers died in 366; St. Ambrose of Milan in 397; St. Augustine in 430; Cassiodorus in 575; and St. Isidore in 636. We have therefore at least one witness in every century to the tradition of the sphericity of the earth. Cassiodorus and St. Isidore were indeed more than witnesses; they were promoters of the idea. Let us add, for the eighth century, St.

[11] See Appendix D.

Bede the Venerable, one of the most brilliant lights of the Church. Unlike Cassiodorus and St. Isidore, St. Bede never stood on the high pedestal of ecclesiastical or secular dignity, not even within the precincts of the Abbey of Jarrow in England, of which he was the most illustrious member. He held the position of teacher of his younger brethren, and he says of himself that he ever delighted in studying, teaching, and writing. He never left, for any length of time, the territory of his abbey, but he was well supplied with books. His abbot several times journeyed to the continent, and never returned without a large number of manuscripts. "Whatever in literature and art the abbeys of Italy and Gaul could furnish was secured up in the North, near the boundary of Scotland, and there it flourished in a new bloom." [12] Like Cassiodorus and Isidore, St. Bede was an encyclopedic writer, but he was above all a schoolmaster. He produced a number of treatises for the use of his scholars. St. Bede is the Patron Saint of textbook writers. His "textbooks" were the fruit of painstaking study and mature deliberation.

It is particularly his work *De Rerum Natura* * to which we turn. St. Bede clearly and unmistakably adheres to the Ptolemaic system, though he says somewhere that his chief authority is Pliny the Elder. As far as I can see he makes no express mention of *antipodes*. Probably the attitude taken by St. Augustine and St. Isidore deterred him from doing so. In fact, since there was at his time no more positive proof for their existence than in former centuries, he may have thought that he could well pass them over

---

[12] Baumgartner, *Geschichte der Weltliteratur*, Vol. V, p. 277.
* Migne Lat., Vol. 90.

completely. His view concerning them could not have been different from that of those two great masters.

But he puts beyond all doubt what he holds concerning the *shape of the earth*:

The world, consisting of heaven and earth, he says, is the entirety of all things. The world is shaped into a perfect globe by the four elements, the fire, by which the stars shine; the air, by which all living creatures breathe; the water which communicates with the earth by surrounding and penetrating it; and the earth itself, which, being in the middle of the world and the lowest part of it, is suspended immovably, being poised by its rotating surroundings. (Chap. III.)

We call the earth a globe, not as if the shape of a sphere were expressed in the diversity of plains and mountains, but because, if all things (terrestrial) are included in the outline, the earth's circumference will represent the figure of a perfect globe. Hence it is that the stars of the northern hemisphere appear to us, but never those of the southern; while on the other hand, the people who live on the southern part of the earth cannot see our stars, because the globe obstructs their view. (Chap. XLVI.)

The firmament is the heaven which is of subtle and fiery nature; it is spherical, and equally distant on all sides from the center of the earth. (Chap. V.)

The numerous passages in which St. Bede accounts for the eclipses and the difference between day and night are the same as those found in Pliny the Elder, Cassiodorus, and St. Isidore, and given almost in the same words. St. Bede the Venerable concluded his life in the year 735, three years after Charles Martel had driven the Mohammedans back across the Pyrenees, and at the time when Bede's great countryman and brother in religion, St. Boniface, was founding and organizing the Church of Germany.

Let us now briefly review the results of our investigations. At the time of St. Augustine the first terrible signs of the end of the existing social order began to appear. The progressive destruction of the admirable Roman civilization had gone very far, when Cassiodorus retired from a torn and distressed world to give his life as a monk entirely to religion and science. Still more had perished when St. Isidore rose into well-deserved prominence on the Spanish peninsula. St. Augustine's works, above all his *City of God,* were among the most read books of the next centuries. Cassiodorus urgently recommends its perusal: *Infastidibili sedulitate percurramus* (Let us never weary of reading it continuously). We have already seen how much St. Isidore is influenced by the *City of God.*

The *City of God* is an encyclopedic work of its own kind. The author enlists all there is of divine and human knowledge, but he draws on human knowledge only as far as it serves his purpose of setting forth and vindicating the existence of the Kingdom of Heaven and God's undying providence concerning it. The three other authors, Cassiodorus, St. Isidore, and Bede, really go out of their way, and for the moment become secular teachers of secular knowledge in order to encourage the study of secular branches among others, in particular to inmates of monasteries. Their works were like a program, those of Cassiodorus being expressly meant to give an "idea of a University"; and the "suggestions of St. Isidore," says F. Baumgartner (in the work quoted above), "if carried out consistently would have led not only to a general university education, but also to the establishment of polytechnical institutions, extensive libraries, botanical gardens, anatomical and chemical laboratories, and all kinds of scientific collections."

As to his influence upon later times, let us quote the words of Professor Rand of Harvard: [13]

It is sometimes stated that the Middle Ages had no interest in the natural sciences, and that philosophy in that period meant the application of formal logic to mendacious assumptions. Critics who make such statements had better read St. Isidore. In fact, one of the most useful rules I know for guiding the investigator in medieval fields is to inquire first, "what does St. Isidore say about it?" It will really save one time to begin by looking him up.

It must have become clear, too, that there has never been, on the part of the Church, any opposition to the doctrine holding the sphericity of the earth, least of all any official antagonism against that belief. As to the existence of antipodes, it was denied by St. Augustine because no facts were known which might have proved it; and the imperfect geographical knowledge of the time furnished no means to harmonize this assumption with the dogma of the unity of mankind, the universality of original sin, and the general necessity of redemption. St. Isidore, while denying the existence of a human population on the other side of the earth for lack of experimental proof, seems to make an attempt at demonstrating its physical impossibility. Cassiodorus and St. Bede ignore the question. But the attitude of St. Hilary of Poitiers shows that other minds were fully convinced of the reconcilability of this theory with faith. The Popes were not likely to take an official stand in the matter, unless the theory were proposed in such terms as to be positively inconsistent with Christian dogma.

With St. Bede we have reached the eighth century, the age of St. Boniface, a contemporary of the Monk

[13] *Philological Quarterly* of 1922, p. 274.

of Jarrow. The shape of the earth was evidently
known. In the monastic schools of England the *City
of God* and the writings of St. Isidore were now ably
seconded by those of their own countryman, St. Bede
the Venerable.*

It goes without saying that alongside of this enlight-
ened knowledge of the earth's shape there remained
the "popular" idea of the flatness of our planet. It is
quite possible, also, that erratic minds here and there
tried to startle their fellow men by phantastic concoc-
tions about earth and sky. But what interests us is that
unbroken line of intelligent tradition which had passed
through all the vicissitudes of civilization and now had
reached the period which will occupy us in some of its
details.

For our particular purpose it is not necessary to
follow this tradition any further. Nor need we worry
about its permanence and increase. With the books of
Augustine, Cassiodorus, Isidore, and Bede it had taken
possession of the then existing educational centers, the
monasteries, both in England and on the continent.
The activity of St. Boniface and above all the reign of
Charlemagne which was close at hand was to usher in
a period more propitious for the retention and widen-
ing of human knowledge.

III. "ANOTHER WORLD AND OTHER MEN"

1. *The Documentary Evidence.* In A.D. 748, St.
Boniface sent a long report on the conditions of the
Church in Germany to Pope St. Zachary. He had it
presented to the Holy Father by St. Burchard, Bishop
of Würzburg. This document is lost. But we have the
reply to it in the shape of an extensive letter of the

* See Appendix E.

Pope, in which St. Boniface's communication is answered. In another chapter we shall have to study this papal epistle in detail. For the present we are interested in one of its weighty paragraphs, which counts about one hundred and fifty words in the Latin original. It runs thus in English:

Thy brotherly holiness has also communicated to us, that a certain Virgil, whether he is said to be a priest we do not know, is maligning thee, because to his shame he was convicted by thee to be guilty of an error against Catholic doctrine; that he talks disparagingly about thee to Otilo [14] the Duke of Bavaria, in order to cause enmity between thee and him, and this for the purpose of obtaining the diocese of a deceased bishop, one of the four thy fraternity established in that region (Bavaria); and he even maintains to have received a recommendation directly from ourselves. But this is by no means true. Iniquity hath lied to itself.[15] But as to the perverse and iniquitous doctrine, which he uttered against God and his own soul: if he is found to hold that there is below the earth another world and other men or sun and moon; call a council, deprive him of the honor of the priesthood, and expel him from the Church. We ourselves, however, are writing to the aforesaid duke concerning the above-mentioned Virgil, that he be presented to us, in order that, if after a close investigation he appears to be in error, he be condemned according to the canons of the Church.[16]

This is all we possess of historical sources referring directly to this controversy. Says Rohrbacher in his *Histoire Universelle de L'Église Catholique*: "We do not know of any other ancient document which speaks of it; or any author of the time by whom it is men-

[14] This name is variously spelled, Odilo and Otilo. The scholarly "Lexikon für Theologie und Kirche" uses Otilo but treats of this duke under Oatilo.

[15] See Appendices F and I.

[16] Migne Lat., Vol. 89, pp. 943 ff.; Tangl, *op. cit.*, pp. 172 ff. For Latin text see Appendix K (I).

tioned." [17] Nor have I myself ever found that in modern literature any other source is referred to as authority. We may therefore make no statement on this point that is not warranted by these one hundred and fifty Latin words.

This passage conveys to us the following facts:

1 : There was one, named Virgil whom in a personal dispute Boniface had shown to hold an erroneous doctrine.[18]

2 : After this defeat, and on account of it, the same Virgil endeavored to prepossess Duke Otilo of Bavaria against St. Boniface, who up to this time, much to the advantage of the Church, had enjoyed the good will and friendship of that prince. Some nine years before the date of this letter, St. Boniface, in the capacity of apostolic legate, and with the duke's hearty coöperation, had given a stable organization to the Bavarian Church, dividing it into four bishoprics.

3 : Virgil aspired to one of those four bishoprics, which was now vacant, but saw himself rejected by St. Boniface. It was with the view of gaining his end over the head of the apostolic legate by the influence of the secular authority, that he began to sow enmity between the legate and the duke.[19]

4 : He even went so far as to maintain that the Pope himself had given him permission to accept the vacant diocese, an assertion which the Pope emphatically denies.

[17] Nous ne connaissons aucun monument ancien, dans lequel il en soit parlé; aucun auteur du temps, qui en aie fait mention.

[18] That this was done in a personal interview can hardly be doubted. The Latin original has, *Virgilius . . . malignatur adversum te pro eo quod confundebatur a te erroneum se esse a catholica doctrina,* which cannot well be understood to refer to a dispute carried on by third persons or by writing.

[19] See Appendix O.

5 : The fact that Virgil aspired to a bishopric would indicate, though by no means with certainty, that he was a priest. He may have posed as one. The Pope says expressly, he did not know whether Virgil was a priest.

6 : Virgil's doctrine was, "that there is another world and other men below the earth or another sun and moon," which we shall discuss later on in detail.

7 : As one of the steps to be taken against Virgil, St. Boniface is to call a provincial council, and to investigate the matter again. If the man persists in his opinion, solemn excommunication and expulsion from the Church will be the penalty. In case he poses as a priest or really is one, he will at the same time be deprived of all sacerdotal honors.

8 : Pope St. Zachary, however, takes up the matter immediately. He writes to Duke Otilo requesting him to have Virgil sent to Rome for an investigation at the papal court. It is not clear in what relation the two processes are to stand toward one another. Probably the second one is threatened only conditionally—namely, in case Virgil should refuse to submit to the verdict of the German synod. No doubt the people of the time understood the meaning of the Pope's words better than we do. Besides Bishop St. Burchard, who had brought St. Boniface's letter to the Pope and was to take the Pope's reply back to Germany, could orally give more detailed explanations. This is all the positive information we can gather from this passage.

Among the many things which these one hundred and fifty words do NOT disclose, and which we are unable to ascertain from any other sources, are in particular the following: (*a*) We do not know whether that synod in Germany was ever held, and what steps

were actually taken concerning Virgil. Seeing, however, that St. Boniface made it a special point of his
policy to carry out papal orders, it is safe to conclude
that it was held, and that the injunctions given to
St. Zachary were executed. The fact, known from
Frankish and Bavarian history, that Duke Otilo died
in 748, the same year in which the letter was written,
may not have remained without effect upon the further
development of the case. If indeed, as is not impossible,
Virgil to some extent enjoyed the duke's favor, the
latter's death may have deprived him of an influential
protector, and St. Boniface may have been at greater
liberty to deal with him as the welfare of the Church
demanded. (*b*) The assertion, given as a matter of
course by some authors, that Pope St. Zachary later
on changed his attitude and amicably composed the
difference between Virgil and St. Boniface, is without
the slightest foundation. (*c*) We learn nothing of the
nationality of Virgil. He may have been a native
Bavarian, or an Italian, or an Irishman, or a Frank,
or an Anglo-Saxon—or a Chinese for that matter.
(*d*) By countless authors it is taken for granted that
this Virgil was identical with the Irish St. Virgil,
Bishop of Salzburg and Apostle of Carinthia, and
with Virgil, the Baptizer. Our passage, the only one
that can come into consideration, contains no proof
for this assumption, but as we shall see, offers a very
strong argument for the contrary. (*e*) This text does
not allow us to charge either St. Boniface or Pope
St. Zachary with having been ignorant of the sphericity
of the earth, much less with having considered it an
heretical tenet. We shall have to return to this feature,
after speaking of the error itself.

2. *Virgil's Teaching.* The doctrine of Virgil, on account of which he had his clash with St. Boniface, and in which so many writers find a cause to extol him as a wonder of learning, is the very heart of the controversy. What did he really teach? The Pope's words are:

> Concerning the perverse and iniquitous doctrine, which he has uttered against God and his own soul: If he is found to hold that there is below the earth another world and other men or sun and moon, summon a council, etc.

Before examining these words we should remember that Pope St. Zachary had before him an official report of St. Boniface. This saint had been working in Germany since 719 with wonderful success. For years he had held the office of apostolic legate with power to watch over the purity of faith and morals, to establish bishoprics, and to convoke provincial councils; and the letters of three Popes are full of praise for the zeal and prudence he had displayed. He was the man to know what he was writing about. In this particular case he most probably did not base his statements upon information obtained from other reliable parties but upon personal interviews with the man whom he denounced to the Holy See. Moreover, should anything have been less clear in his letter, there was the distinguished messenger who had brought it to Rome, Bishop St. Burchard of Würzburg, who was well able to give all the additional information the Holy Father might desire. Now if the communications of ambassadors are always received with implicit credence, the Pope in this case certainly was sufficiently acquainted with the actual teachings of Virgil.

The phrase which naturally will strike us first as

most incongruous is the assertion that there are below
the earth "another sun and moon." [20] What sort of
an idea must Virgil have had of the earth and the
world below it, if he could make such a statement?
That the sun and the moon which shine on the opposite
side of the earth are exactly the same as those which
give light to us, is one of the most essential elements
of the belief in the sphericity of the earth. One who
denies the identity of sun and moon for both hemi-
spheres cannot suppose that the earth is a globe. These
two words give us a perfect right to deny that Virgil
had any inkling of the real shape of the earth. The
ease with which he duplicates sun and moon shows
that he had no idea at all of the important position
these luminaries hold in the Ptolemaic system. It is,
however, evident that had this astronomical or cos-
mographical view been Virgil's only blunder, neither
the Pope nor St. Boniface would have thought of
taking any notice of him and his dreams.

The principal point of his error is the doctrine that
"there is below the earth another world and other
men" (*quod alius mundus et alii homines sub terra
sint*). If this sentence is to express the fact that there
are antipodes, the terms could not be worse chosen.
The other side of the earth is not another world, but
simply an extension of that part which we inhabit.
If by "other men" were meant negroes or pigmies or
giants, or the monsters which St. Augustine speaks of,
the matter would not have been new or alarming for
St. Boniface or the Pope. Such men were known or
fabled about for centuries and had never caused any

---

[20] The genuineness of these words cannot be doubted. They are
found in all the manuscripts of this letter, from the earliest times
on—and one of the most reliable manuscripts even puts it more
clearly by saying "AND another sun and moon." (Tangl.)

apprehension to Church authorities. But they were not conceived as "other men," except by their color or other accidental differences. By his "other world and other men" Virgil can only have meant a completely different race, which had nothing in common with our own, a race not descending from Adam, and consequently not subject to original sin and not in need of redemption; a race which was not obliged to receive the sacrament of baptism. If taken in this sense, and it is the only sense in which it can be taken, it accounts for the indignation which speaks from the words of St. Zachary, and for the severe measures to be resorted to in the case of Virgil.

Nor was such a doctrine too odd, too monstrous, for the time of St. Boniface. The lands under his jurisiction were rife with errors concerning baptism. Bold innovators even denied the necessity of the first of the sacraments. These errors were in the air in more or less dangerous forms. The long papal letter, of which only one paragraph concerns us here directly, deals very largely with just such heresies. The assertion that there is "another world and other men below the earth," fits very well into that chaos of rude superstitions and monstrous doctrinal aberrations which is depicted in this papal document. Our paragraph of one hundred and fifty words is fully in keeping with the rest of the letter. This will become clearer in the next chapter.

It is evident that Virgil had never read what Christian writers state about the shape of the earth and its relation to sun and moon. They say clearly that the earth is round, situated in the center of the heavenly sphere; that the sun, the same sun, rises there when it sets for us; that the difference between day and night is brought about by the sun's being either above our horizon or being hidden by the earth. It is impossible that a man with average intelligence should have perused these passages and then come and talk of "another world, or another sun and moon." A grade school pupil who has received the ordinary instruction in geography can talk more intelligently about earth and sun and moon than this Virgil.

Nor can Virgil be said to have been a great theologian. He was no theologian at all. Since, however, he was bold enough to engage with St. Boniface in a doctrinal dispute, he certainly considered himself a divine, and possibly had some smattering of sacred knowledge. But this cannot have amounted to much, or he would himself have noticed the bearings of his doctrine of the "other world and other men." Not much theology is required to see that this doctrine undermines the very foundations of Christianity. That little amount of theology Virgil did not possess.

While it is difficult to advance any definite explanation of Virgil's paradoxical system, if it deserves the name of a system, we may be permitted to point to the peculiar cosmography of Cosmas Indicopleustes, a native of Alexandria, who lived in the sixth century. Cosmas had traveled much, and he left a valuable description of the lands and cities and peoples of the eastern world. But he tried his hand also at cosmography and constructed a universe of quite a unique character. According to him, the earth is flat; at one end there rises a huge conical mountain, around which the heavenly bodies revolve at different heights, thus producing days and nights of varying duration.[21] If we suppose that Virgil accepted this theory and, for

[21] See John Fiske, *The Discovery of America*, Vol. I, pp. 265 ff.

reasons known to him alone, duplicated this world below the earth, perhaps in the opposite direction, we really have another world, other men, and another sun and moon. Whether this was really his idea we cannot tell; but the words of Pope St. Zachary much better suit such an absurd cosmography than the theory of the sphericity of the earth.

3. *St. Boniface and Pope St. Zachary.* But after all, might not St. Boniface have misunderstood or misinterpreted his antagonist? Indeed many of the authors who wrote on this subject take it for granted that he possessed no knowledge of the rotundity of the earth; that consequently he was unable to grasp the learned discourses of Virgil; and that he was even rude and uncultured enough not to understand the matter when it was explained to him in personal interview. Some take this for granted, though there are plenty of sources to know the past of the Apostle, while we know absolutely nothing of the kind of schooling received by Virgil. St. Boniface had been an ardent student all his life. The monastery of Nutscelle, in which he spent the greater part of his youth, was known for the excellence of its school and the scholarly attainments of its abbot and members.

For some fifteen years before he set out for Germany, he had enjoyed the renown of being a very learned teacher, whose services were much in demand by the monastic schools of the neighborhood. He was a contemporary and personal acquaintance of the great St. Aldhelm, who had sat at the feet of Irish and Roman teachers, and who had been in close contact with the Greek Theodore, the sainted Archbishop of Canterbury. Astronomy is expressly mentioned as one of the branches of science which Aldhelm communi-

cated to others. The time which St. Boniface spent in
Anglo-Saxon England was a period of education and
serious scholarly endeavors, the time when St. Bede
the Venerable wrote his immortal works on all the
branches of secular and sacred learning. Sixteen years
before the Apostle of Germany left his native country,
St. Bede had finished his treatise *De Rerum Natura,*
in which the rotundity of the earth is stated in so
many words. (See page 266.) Besides it is highly
improbable that so studious a reader as St. Boniface
should not have known the most popular book of
these centuries, the *City of God* of St. Augustine. (See
pages 256-259.) There was, certainly, no intellectual
narrowness in the circles in which he moved during the
first forty years of his life. It would need very strong,
positive arguments to prove that he did not know the
real shape of the earth. And if he did not actually
know it, he was certainly advanced enough in the
teachings of the Church to tell a geographical opinion
from a theological issue.

Nor can we suppose that Pope St. Zachary misunderstood the case. St. Zachary, a Greek though born
in Italy, was known for his learning and practical
wisdom. It would not have been difficult for him to
discover from St. Boniface's report and from the explanations given by Bishop St. Burchard, whether perhaps St. Boniface was scared by an unusual but very
harmless assertion of Virgil concerning some merely
geographical or astronomical theory.

It is impossible, therefore, to have recourse to ignorance or misunderstanding on the part of either St.
Boniface or of St. Zachary. Nothing remains but to
take the Pope's words as giving the main features of
the opinion held by Virgil. But a man that holds and

preaches that there is another world and other men
below the earth does not stand on Christian ground
any longer. No wonder that St. Boniface saw fit to
report him to the Pope. Any bishop would be obliged
to do the same, if similar views were propagated in
his diocese. In the case of Virgil the matter was the
more urgent, as probably the favor of the Bavarian
duke enabled him to spread this and perhaps other
errors widely among the people of Germany, who were
just making their first steps in Christian and secular
education.

Virgil's case is hopeless. He cannot be named among
the champions of science. It is impossible to say that
he taught or even knew the sphericity of the earth,
while in theology his doctrine was clearly heretical.
Only those can continue holding him up to admiration,
who completely disregard the sources and do not shrink
from making assertions which they are utterly unable
to substantiate.[22]

4. *Virgil the Man.* We must now briefly view Virgil
as a man, in his moral qualities. We need only recapitu-
late a few of the facts we gathered from Pope St.
Zachary's letter.

Until the coming of Virgil St. Boniface had possessed the unlimited favor of Duke Otilo, and had thus
been enabled to accomplish great things for the Church
in Bavaria. As far as it lay in the power of Virgil,
this friendship between the two men was now to come
to an end, not because the welfare of the Church demanded such a change, but simply because it so suited
a man who thereby hoped to gain a bishopric. Virgil
knew very well that St. Boniface had been the right
hand of three successive pontiffs; that he had under the

[22] See Appendix G.

greatest hardships labored for the German Church for
thirty years. To oppose such a man for merely personal reasons which were not of the noblest kind required indeed a great deal of audacity and quite an
unusual degree of meanness. Although not without
obstruction on the part of the Frankish government in
the appointment of archbishops, St. Boniface had been
relatively free from his influence in the selection of
bishops for the sees he had founded himself. Virgil's
endeavors to win a bishopric over the head of the apostolic legate by enlisting the support of a secular prince
is the first known instance of extending state influence
to these new bishoprics also. It is a sad honor for him.
*By his intrigues he contributed his share to enhance
that Byzantinism which eventually grew into a veritable curse of the European courts, and which it took
all the energy and drastic measures of Popes like St.
Gregory VII to eradicate.* Virgil even resorted to the
bare-faced lie that he had been recommended by the
Holy See for this bishopric. For these reasons, all of
which are guaranteed by our source, we are obliged
to set down Virgil as an unscrupulous ecclesiastico-
political wire puller, who selfishly put his own private
interests above the laws and the welfare of the Church.

It is impossible to explain why this side of the question has been so entirely neglected by many authors
who occupied themselves with Virgil. Some take no
notice of it at all. Some unhesitatingly lay the whole
blame at the door of St. Boniface, and accuse him of
theological and scientific ignorance. Others even charge
him with wilful misrepresentation of truth out of petty
jealousy and selfish ambition. In other words, they
ascribe to him exactly those blameworthy actions

of which our source shows Virgil to be guilty. We know indeed quite a number of facts of the previous life of St. Boniface, all of which show him to have been a man of high intellectual standing with the inclinations and aspirations of a scholar. History guarantees us nothing concerning the previous life of Virgil. He steps out of the German forests as a perfect stranger gifted with nothing but his pseudo-science and an unscrupulous ambition. But many authors make him at once an unrivalled scientist and a man worthy of the honors of the altar. This is possible only by a most superficial reading of the sources.

IV. THE REPETITION OF BAPTISM

1. *The Charge Against St. Boniface.* We now approach the other accusation against St. Boniface, namely that he ordered the repetition of baptism upon insufficient reason. As remarked on page 248 this affair began chronologically two years before the dispute of Boniface with Virgil the Pseudo-Astronomer. The letter of Pope St. Zachary written to St. Boniface in 748, from which we drew the knowledge of that dispute, will very largely serve to settle the baptismal controversy also. But this controversy did not begin with it. It started by a rather short communication of the same Pope dated 746. We shall reproduce this letter in full:

Virgil and Sidonius, two pious men in the province of the Bavarians, have sent us a letter and intimated that thy venerable fraternity orders Christians to be rebaptized. This intelligence has troubled us very much and caused us to wonder whether this be really so as it is related. They reported that there was a priest in the same region, who was entirely ignorant of the Latin language, and in baptizing, being unable to pronounce correctly, enunciated in broken Latin: "Baptizo te in nomine Patria et Filia et Spiritus Sancti;" and for this reason, thy venerable fraternity thought it necessary to rebaptize. But, most holy brother, if he who baptized did not introduce any error or heresy, but out of ignorance of the Roman tongue merely pronounced the baptismal formula in this faulty way, as we said before, we cannot consent to rebaptism—because as thy holy fraternity is well aware, whosoever is baptized by heretics in the name of the Father and the Son and the Holy Ghost must not be rebaptized, but merely reconciled by the laying on of hands. Therefore, most holy brother, if it is as related to us, let no longer such things be told to them by thee, but what the holy fathers teach, that thy holiness may endeavor to preserve. May God keep thee in His protection, most holy brother." [23]

According to an eminent authority on St. Boniface, Professor Tangl of Berlin, this letter was written on July 1, 746.[24]

This papal letter warrants the following historical facts:

(1) Two men, evidently priests, accused St. Boniface of having ordered the repetition of baptism *for the sole reason* of the faulty pronunciation of the baptismal formula. (2) Pope Zachary is worried and surprised at this charge, which he finds it hard to believe. (3) He makes no statement as to the actual facts in the case. He uses the conditional form all through the letter. He evidently does not consider the matter as settled.

As long, therefore, as we have nothing but this letter to go by, we are not allowed to say that St. Boniface really enjoined the sacrament of baptism to be repeated for no other reason than the mispronun-

[23] Appendix H.
[24] Migne Lat., Vol. 89, p. 929; Tangl, *op. cit.*, p. 141.

ciation of the baptismal formula. But this unwarranted step has really been taken by many authors. Without adducing any other proof, they jump to the conclusion that St. Boniface committed this fault. We cannot but deplore this proceeding as running counter to the simplest rules of historical criticism. Some writers even go farther, and accuse St. Boniface of having ordered rebaptism because he erroneously deemed baptism administered by heretics to be invalid. The letter does not contain the slightest hint that would justify the charge of so colossal an ignorance. When referring to baptism by heretics the Pope expressly adds, "as thy holy fraternity is well aware," etc.[25]

Although it does not bear upon our subject, we may here again call attention to the complete absence of any indication as to the *nationality* of the two priests. It is merely the identity of the name which has seduced many authors [26] to suppose that this Virgil is the same as the later Irish Saint Virgil, the Bishop of Salzburg and Apostle of Carinthia. And let it be stated right here, that the Virgil who is said to have taught the sphericity of the earth and the existence of antipodes, is not identical with either of the two. We shall return to this question on another occasion.

Let us now suppose for a moment that the corrupted formula alone really induced St. Boniface to proceed to rebaptism—would that be such a bad reason? I dare say that many a Catholic priest, if present at a baptism administered in this slovenly manner, would be seized with the gravest doubts as to its validity. Nor do I think that anyone knowing that he himself had been baptized by such an ignorant man

[25] Appendix I.
[26] See Appendix P.

would feel quite at ease concerning the state of his soul. And probably every bishop would be inclined to demand a conditional repetition of the sacrament, were he to admit a young man so baptized to ordination. The fact that after more than eleven hundred years this controversy is still alluded to in the dogmatic and moral instruction of our own days, shows how well founded such doubts really were.

Of course we know now authoritatively from Pope St. Zachary's letter, that even if the baptismal formula be expressed in this sort of kitchen Latin, it does not invalidate the sacrament. Many a scrupulous priest may have felt reassured by the Pope's definite declaration—because, though he may think he did not pronounce those important words quite correctly, he certainly knows that he was not guilty of so glaring a corruption.

All this supposes, however, and the Pope makes it clear enough, that the mispronunciation is the *only* *flaw* in the administration of the sacrament of baptism. If there are other deficiencies, the aspect may change essentially, and as we shall see, in the case of St. Boniface there were other deficiencies of the most serious nature.

One such deficiency suggests itself if we consider these very words a little more accurately. Is there not an essential and objective difference between *pater* and *patria* (father and fatherland), and between *filius* and *filia* (son and daughter)? Do these words objectively, considered in themselves, still express the mystery of the Blessed Trinity? True, the priest himself, with his total ignorance of the Latin language, may not have perceived any difference. But St. Boniface may have had other reasons, just on account of this egregious ignorance, to fear that the man did not mean to baptize in the name of the Father and the Son and the Holy Ghost, or that he not even intended to do what Christ has ordained—a presumption not at all unlikely, in view of the confusion then prevailing in the countries under St. Boniface's care.

St. Boniface, however, does not seem to have been in a hurry to exculpate himself to the Sovereign Pontiff. He was too busy. The letter reached him just in the midst of his greatest activity as reformer of the Frankish Church, when in the Pope's name and supported by the Frankish mayors of the palace, he celebrated that series of councils, about ten in number, partly provincial, partly national, which were to purify the religious life of Frankland. He sent to Rome the decrees of these important assemblies, and received the Pope's joyful approbation. He asked for information on a great variety of subjects, and we know the Holy Father's replies. When Pepin the Short, the great Frankish mayor of the palace, had requested the Pope's directions concerning twenty-seven points relating to the conduct of priests and faithful, St. Zachary sent the answers not only to Pepin, but also to St. Boniface, the apostolic legate, with the order to publish and enforce them as laws of the Church.

2. *The Papal Verdict on St. Boniface.* It was not before the end of A.D. 747 that St. Boniface saw fit to refer to the accusation brought against him by Virgil and Sidonius. He laid before the Pope the entire problem of rebaptism, not only in theory but also in practice—that is, as it confronted him under the concrete circumstances which existed in the field of his activity. The letter in which he did so is lost, but as in

so many other cases it can be reconstructed from the Pope's answer. In this particular case, the recapitulation by the Pope of St. Boniface's missive is even remarkably extensive and complete. The Holy Father evidently was eager to show how fully he realized the attitude taken by his legate. We know already that paragraph of this letter which is the basis of all our knowledge concerning Virgil the Pseudo-Astronomer. As remarked before, the letter dates of A.D. 748. We now proceed to examine it in its entirety to see the bearing of its contents upon the baptismal controversy.[27]

We learn from the Holy Father's reply that St. Boniface had first stated from what sources he had received his own theological knowledge concerning the sacrament of baptism. He adhered, he said, simply to the doctrine which had been preached and practiced by the great Roman missionaries sent by St. Gregory I to the Anglo-Saxons, and which had been confirmed afterwards by St. Theodore, whom the Apostolic See had deputed to regulate ecclesiastical matters after the seven kingdoms were converted. According to that doctrine, whosoever was baptized without the invocation of the Blessed Trinity, or with the omission of one of the Three Divine Persons, "did not possess (i.e., receive) the sacrament of regeneration." On the other hand, a heretic or schismatic will baptize validly, if he performs the act in the name of the Father and the Son and the Holy Ghost, while the most saintly and orthodox man who does not so baptize will not confer the sacrament. The Pope concludes this part of his recapitulation by stating explicitly: *"It is therefore well known to thy fraternity, what the sacred canons deter-*

[27] Migne Lat., Vol. 89, pp. 943 ff.; Tangl, *op. cit.,* pp. 172 ff.

mine about all this, and we exhort thee to hold to it firmly."

But this was not all. In his own letter, St. Boniface had mentioned another most important source of his knowledge. When he left his Anglo-Saxon home, he first directed his steps to the Eternal City, to receive his canonical mission from the successor of St. Peter. During the winter of 718 to 719, Pope St. Gregory II had almost daily conversations with him. In this familiar intercourse, however, no subject seems to have been so thoroughly discussed as the sacrament of baptism. We conclude this from the fact that in the letter of appointment, with which St. Boniface was finally dismissed to the field of his labor, the correct administration of baptism is expressly insisted on, and it is the only point of doctrine mentioned in the document.[28] The new apostolic missionary is told by Gregory II always to follow the "prescriptions and customs of the Apostolic See, in which thou hast been instructed." It is no wonder that St. Zachary could only repeat this admonition. "Hold fast, brother," he says, "to what thou hast learned from our predecessor of holy memory, Gregory (II), Bishop of this Apostolic See."

St. Boniface could hardly have expected a more explicit testimony to the correctness of his theological views. And if historians, Catholic as well as Protestant, assert that Virgil and Sidonius were much his superiors in theological knowledge, they evidently have not read this letter.

After thus recognizing the orthodoxy of his legate,

[28] See Migne Lat., Vol. 89, p. 495; Tangl, *op. cit.,* p. 17.

Pope St. Zachary goes on to summarize the next part of St. Boniface's letter. It is the description of the conditions existing in Germany, which had induced St. Boniface to order the repetition of baptism. This is just the feature which so many writers lose sight of entirely. A perusal of the exposition of the affair as given by these writers, leaves the impression that real causes for rebaptism did not exist, except in the erroneous opinion of St. Boniface. These writers want us to suppose that everything was going on smoothly in the newly founded and organized Church of Germany; that among the clergy there was practically only one black sheep—that ignorant priest, and he was not so very black after all. The papal legate, poorly instructed as he was, took alarm at the way this priest pronounced the baptismal formula, and without listening to the advice of men who knew better, he peremptorily ordered that all those to whom the good man had administered the sacrament be rebaptized. Was it any wonder that the theological conscience of Virgil and Sidonius revolted against such an unwarranted procedure? This is the picture frequently drawn of the dissension between St. Boniface on the one side and the two priests on the other. But this picture is far from reflecting the reality. Things were not thus plain and simple; and those who represent them so, would have known better had they attentively read the papal letter which we are examining.

"According to your letter," says the Pope, "there were in Germany priests who offered sacrifices to the pagan gods, participated in abominable banquets, and led the lives of adulterers. They are now dead, and it cannot be found out whether or not these men in baptizing pronounced the Persons of the Blessed Trinity. Consequently, those baptized by them greatly fear that the sacrament has not been conferred validly. In response to the wishes of these persons, you gavest orders that they all should be baptized (again)."

This was not the worst, however. There were men, the Pope learns from St. Boniface's letter, who passed themselves off as bishops though they had never received Holy Orders, and usurped the ministrations of the Church, while they committed all imaginable kinds of excesses. There were also run-away slaves posing as priests. All these fought shy of the real bishops, but some had powerful secular protectors. They assembled credulous crowds in the forests and in the dwellings of rustics. They did not preach the Christian Faith, nor did they have the right Faith themselves. When baptizing adults, they did not care to ascertain whether the latter knew those prayers (*verba solemnia*), which every Christian must know by heart and understand; nor did they put those questions, "Dost thou renounce Satan, etc.," nor did they teach the belief in one God and the Blessed Trinity.

"These men," continues the Pope, "must be deprived of all sacerdotal honor, and must spend the rest of their lives under monastic discipline and in penance, that by this temporal affliction they may some day return to the path of righteousness. But if they do not repent, you wilt have your consolation in the approval of the Apostles. On the other hand, give every kind of encouragement to the orthodox bishops, priests, and other clerics who are so dear to us; and to the most glorious dukes and all the nobles who observe Christ's law, that they may be our helpers in the struggle against the enemies of the Catholic Faith.

"You also write that you have found a priest, named Samson, who goes so far in his error as to maintain that one can become a Christian without any baptism at all, by the mere imposition of a bishop's hands.[29] Take care that a man who preaches such an abominable doctrine be condemned and ejected from the Church."

Upon the sombre background thus painted by the letter of St. Boniface, how insignificant and small appears the charge of Virgil and Sidonius. There were most weighty reasons for St. Boniface to doubt the validity of countless baptisms, reasons far greater than mere grammatical correctness or alphabetical integrity, reasons so important that in this whole part of his letter, the Pope does not think any more of the petty charges of the two fault-finders. While it may have happened, nay while it is very probable that one or even several of those ignorant priests actually mispronounced the baptismal formula, this was not St. Boniface's motive when he ordered the repetition of the most necessary sacrament.

Pope St. Zachary winds up this part of the letter by *expressing his unqualified approval of the policy of his legate in the matter of baptism,* and positively orders St. Boniface to continue doing as he had done so far. If there is any doubt, he writes, whether those baptized by heretics are really baptized in the name of the Father and of the Son and of the Holy Ghost, and if an investigation does not remove the uncertainty, "do not fail to have the defect supplied, according to the direction given thee by Gregory, our predecessor of good memory, and by the sacred canons, lest those souls perish eternally." [30] This is the pope's final verdict in the matter of the repetition of

[29] The pope calls this Samson a *presbyter.* Most probably the man feigned to be a bishop, because apparently he claimed episcopal powers.

[30] See Appendix J.

baptism. It is the most glorious and unreserved vindication of St. Boniface's theological knowledge, and the pastoral method followed by him in his missionary activity.

There had been two enclosures in St. Boniface's communication, each of which provoked unstinted praise from the Sovereign Pontiff. The first was a kind of encyclical written by St. Boniface as apostolic legate to all the bishops and clergy under his jurisdiction. The second was a joint profession by the Frankish bishops of the unity of the Catholic Faith and of their filial devotion to the Holy See: "In our name, dearest brother, greet them all in the kiss of the peace of Christ." The saint had asked, moreover, that some special delegate be sent by the pope to preside in the provincial and national councils of the Frankish bishops. This the Pope peremptorily refuses: "As long as thy brotherly holiness is alive and represents the Apostolic See and ourselves in those countries, it is not necessary to depute anybody else. Thou wilt send able and well-instructed men to places selected for the preaching of the Word of Salvation, and thou wilt have the bishops assemble in councils when and where it seems good to thyself."

3. *The Papal Verdict on Virgil and Sidonius.* As already remarked, by far the greater part of this papal letter is devoted to recapitulating St. Boniface's communication. Nor does the Pope in any way allude to the repetition of baptism upon the mere ground of faulty pronunciation of the baptismal formula. But towards the end of the long letter, the Holy Father expressly refers to the two priests. This passage deserves a closer inspection, because it reveals new

features of the affair. We find out what kind of characters the two "pious men" really were.[31]

"But concerning Sidonius, above mentioned,[32] and Virgil, the priests; we have taken notice of what thy holiness writes. We have written to them a threatening letter as was meet, and more credence is given to thy holiness than to them. If it pleases God and we live long enough, we shall summon them by Apostolic letter to this Holy See, as it is preferable; for thou hast instructed them, and they have not accepted thy words. It has happened with them as it is written, 'he that teaches a fool is like one that glueth pot sherds together. Sand and salt and a mass of iron is easier to bear than a man without sense, that is both foolish and wicked.' (Ecc. xxii, 7-18.) Therefore brother, let not thy heart be provoked to anger; but where thou findest such persons, admonish, beseech and chide them, that they may turn from error to the way of truth. If they become converted, thou hast saved their souls; if they remain hardened, thou wilt not lose the reward of thy efforts. But avoid them according to the Apostle's words."

This passage which evidently refers to the same men who had complained to Pope St. Zachary about St. Boniface, furnishes evidence for the following facts: (1) St. Boniface had written a letter explaining the matter from his own standpoint, and the Pope implicitly believes him. (2) The mutilated formula of baptism is no longer mentioned. (3) The two men are severely reproached; they have already received a threatening letter, and may even be summoned to Rome. (4) Yet the Pope does not despair of them; they are to be admonished, besought, chided, and they may possibly

[31] For the Latin text see Appendix K (II).

[32] As a matter of fact, Sidonius' name had not been "mentioned above" in the whole letter. The phrase, *pro Sidonio autem supra dicto, et Virgilio, presbyteris,* refers in a general way to the first part of the letter, where the matter concerning which both had complained is extensively discussed and disposed of.

become converted. (5) But if they do not amend their ways, they will have to be avoided as excommunicated.

We ask what may have been the cause of the reprimand and the threats of sterner measures. Certainly not the mere fact that they had reported about the apostolic legate. To do so was the right of every priest. They must, therefore, have committed other transgressions, which, we conclude from the whole context, consisted in the refusal of canonical obedience. They must have continued during the two years which had elapsed since the writing of the first papal letter in 746 to disregard the legate's injunctions, and there must have been, no doubt, every probability that they would persist in their refractory behavior. Hence the threat of severer penalties. They evidently belonged to the number of those whom St. Boniface has in view when he writes to his friends in England, that he suffered more from those within the fold who ought to assist him than from the outside enemies of the Faith.

It was, we said, within the right of the two "pious men," to complain to the Holy See concerning the mode of action chosen by St. Boniface. Yet here we are confronted with a dilemma: if they really possessed the knowledge we give them credit for, they must have been able to evaluate the situation in Germany and to see the absolute necessity of wholesale repetition of the sacrament of baptism. They must have known that the mispronunciation of the baptismal formula was by no means the real cause. But, if they knew this, how could they represent things to the Pope the way they actually did? They must have been wilful calumniators, bearing false testimony against the representative of the Holy See—or they had not the elementary theological knowledge we grant they have possessed. Are we wrong if we call them intriguers?— men who had not the welfare of the Church in view nor the salvation of souls, but some other selfish purpose? St. Boniface, we have learned, from Pope St. Zachary's letter, requested to be relieved from the duty of presiding in councils. This was no doubt in consequence of difficulties put in his way by enemies. Whether there existed an organized opposition against him, and whether or not Virgil and Sidonius were members of the clique, we are unable to tell.

It is indeed surprising that many of the writers who expatiated upon the subject of rebaptism under St. Boniface, have either paid little or no attention to the second letter, or have failed to take due notice of its first part; or if they adverted to the passage we are just through examining, found in it a condemnation of St. Boniface, or at any rate entirely overlooked the moral characteristics of Virgil and Sidonius.

4. *Previous Papal Utterances.* We remarked above that St. Boniface was in no hurry to answer the charge of the two "pious men" because he was too busy. There was no need either. The whole matter concerning the administration and repetition of the Sacrament of Baptism had been settled by papal decisions ten years before. It was St. Boniface's custom to ask the Holy Father for instructions and directions not only when new or complicated matters occurred, but also when it was clear to him what answer he would receive. He wished to be backed by a higher authority, because he had to deal with many recalcitrant characters, who would not bend to his own commands, but needed a higher power to curb them. We do not know how many of the letters of St. Boniface to the Roman pontiff and

how many papal communications addressed to him are lost; but enough remains to show that there had been a correspondence between Germany and Rome under Gregory II and Gregory III concerning baptism and its repetition. Gregory II states that baptism must not be renewed if only the questions, "Dost thou renounce Satan?" etc., and "Dost thou believe in God the Father Almighty?" etc., have been omitted. For this case, he emphasizes the duty to instruct persons so baptized more carefully afterwards. (He does not speak of supplying these or other ceremonies.) But if no certainty be obtainable whether grown persons had been baptized as children, he wants the sacrament administered.[33] His successor, Gregory III, categorically orders that all those baptized by pagans or by such priests as also offered to the pagan gods, should be rebaptized—as well as those who did not feel sure that they had received the sacrament.[34] These papal utterances are more than a hint that the whole subject of baptism had been thoroughly discussed between St. Boniface and the Roman Pontiff. Had St. Boniface not known the theology of the first of the sacraments before, he certainly now possessed all the knowledge, theoretical and practical, required of a man of his station—and that by authoritative decisions of the supreme head of the Church.

One of these apostolical replies deserves a special mention. It is found in a letter of Gregory III written October 29, 739:

Those who have been baptized according to the different case endings of the pagan tongues, since they have anyhow been baptized in the name of the Trinity, must (simply) be con-

[33] Migne Lat., Vol. 98, p. 525; Tangl, *op. cit.,* p. 46.
[34] Tangl, *op. cit.,* pp. 50-51; Migne Lat., Vol. 98, p. 577.

firmed by the imposition of hands and the anointing with holy chrism.[35]

It certainly looks more than probable that this covers just the case referred to by the two "pious men"; in other words, even this particular case had already been discussed and decided by the Apostolic See. St. Boniface, therefore, had been for seven years in possession of directions for this eventuality also, namely, that no rebaptism was to take place. Now for St. Boniface to be aware of the Holy Father's view and not to put it into practice was a complete impossibility. Friends and enemies alike agree that devotion to the Apostolic See was one of the most strongly marked traits in his character, so much so that non-Catholics occasionally reproach him for it. We may therefore rest assured that at least after the receipt of this letter St. Boniface did not think of ordering the rebaptizing of persons if the sacred formula had been pronounced incorrectly, as long as there were no other grave reasons besides. The more unwarranted and inexcusable appears the charge raised against him seven years later by Virgil and Sidonius.

By these authoritative decisions St. Boniface guided himself during the years following their reception. As the matter was clear, we do not find any such questions alluded to in the later correspondence between him and Gregory III. Nor was anything of the kind mentioned in the first years of the new Pope, St. Zachary. St. Zachary, while receiving from the papal legate the decrees of councils, and giving them his supreme sanc-

[35] "Illi quippe, qui baptizati sunt per diversitatem et declinationem linguarum gentilitatis, tamen, quod in nomine Trinitatis baptizati sunt, oportet eos per manus impositionem et sacri chrismatis unctionem confirmari." (See Appendix L.)

tion, does not seem to have been sufficiently acquainted with the difficulties as to baptism which had confronted, and were still confronting the German missionaries.

It is well to remember this; it gives us a clue to the explanation of some features in the letter written in response to the complaints of Virgil and Sidonius. After a silence of seven and more years on rebaptism, this letter of Pope St. Zachary comes almost like a bolt from the blue. But the august writer did not know the conditions in Germany. He indeed speaks to St. Boniface with the same fatherly love and respect which is noticeable in all the papal letters addressed to the Apostle of the Germans; he is careful to show that he does in no way side with the accusers; yet he does not fail to state how this news worries him. He even shows a certain haste in answering, this being the only letter in which not more than one matter is treated, while in all other cases the Pope waits until several questions accumulate, which he answers in one reply.

St. Boniface meanwhile did not see how this letter could alter his mode of procedure. For years he had possessed the papal approval of his method in black and white. It is possible that when the two "pious men" observed no change in his attitude, they wrote a second time to Rome, and that the Holy Father simply urged his legate to report also. This supposition, which, however, is by no means necessary, would explain why St. Boniface waited several years before he sent his answer to Rome. It was then that the Holy Father received a detailed description of the conditions in Germany, which St. Boniface encountered as soon as his activity extended farther than his first mission field, conditions

which embittered his life and retarded the progress of
his work during the duration of the reigns of three
successive Popes. When he described these conditions
in his letter they no doubt were disappearing. His own
energetic and unceasing endeavors to clean up the vineyard of the Lord, the appointment of able bishops with
well-circumscribed dioceses, the provincial and national
councils celebrated by him and inspired by his wisdom
and zeal; the assistance of the secular power granted
to a large extent by Pepin the Short—all this cannot
have remained without effect in the long years that the
indomitable Anglo-Saxon represented the person of the
successor of St. Peter in the countries north of the
Alps.

The documents at our disposal do not warrant the
assertion that Virgil and Sidonius were better versed in
dogmatic and moral theology than St. Boniface. The
same documents show them up as intriguers, who did
not stop short of misrepresentations in order to further
their own selfish ends. While probably newcomers
themselves, they tried to undermine the renown, and
arrest the success, of a man who had been in the field
for a quarter of a century and had borne the full
weight of the privations and disappointments which
are the common lot of missionaries. All that can be
said in their favor is, that while their insubordinate
behavior caused trouble enough to St. Boniface, he
seems to have felt that they would not take sides with
outspoken heretics. Their subsequent fates do not interest us here. With Sidonius we part entirely. (See,
however, Appendix M.) To this Virgil we shall refer
as "the Baptizer" to distinguish him from Virgil "the
Pseudo-Astronomer,"

V. THE THREE VIRGILS

As already indicated, the number of authors is not small who treat it as a matter of course that Virgil the Baptizer, Virgil the Pseudo-Astronomer, and Virgil the Irish Saint, the Bishop of Salzburg, are one and the same personality. Several writers, however, distinguish two Virgils. The Right Rev. Horace Mann [36] is the first, as far as I can see, to state that the sources really speak of three Virgils. So let us return to our sources and examine them with this point in view. They are indeed remarkably explicit.

We first investigate whether Virgil the Baptizer and Virgil the Pseudo-Astronomer are identical. The documents that bear on this question are chiefly the passage in Pope Zachary's long letter, where he settles the affair of Virgil the Pseudo-Astronomer; and, immediately following this, the paragraph in which he gives his final verdict on Virgil the Baptizer and Sidonius. [37]

No one who reads these passages with even superficial attention will fail to notice that they differ widely in tone. While severity and indignation, nay exasperation, speak from the lines of the one which refers to Virgil the Pseudo-Astronomer, there is a considerable amount of mildness and forbearance in the other, in which the Pope deals with Virgil the Baptizer and Sidonius. The Pseudo-Astronomer does not seem to have had any accomplices. He is sternly reprimanded, and is actually summoned to Rome, besides being tried in a provincial synod. Virgil the Baptizer's name is al-

[36] Mann, *Lives of the Popes,* St. Louis, 1922, Vol. I, part II, page 248, note.
[37] See above, pages 270 and 293 respectively. For the Latin text, see Appendix K (I and II).

ways coupled with that of Sidonius. These two men also have received a letter of reprimand, but no actual and immediate summons to Rome, nor is their case to be submitted to a local council. Both are expressly called priests, while the Pope states just as explicitly that he does not know whether Virgil the Pseudo-Astronomer is a priest. Besides, if these two Virgils were one person, the pope would not have started the second paragraph the way he does. He would have used some phrase as, *idem Virgilius* (the same Virgil), or he would have omitted the name of Virgil altogether. Instead of doing so, he begins the new paragraph with the name of Sidonius and adds *Virgilius* to him, inserting the particle *autem* (but). It is therefore evident that in these two passages of the Pope's letter the name of Virgil stands for two different persons, who are guilty of different transgressions, and to whom are meted out different kinds of penalties.

But in what relation is Virgil the Saint to them? Since Virgil the Baptizer and Virgil the Pseudo-Astronomer are two different persons, Virgil the Saint cannot be identical with both of them together. It is sure that Virgil the Saint received episcopal consecration in 767, but it is also sure that he was administrator of the Diocese of Salzburg several years before that date, and that during these years he had the episcopal functions performed by a companion who was a bishop. He was meanwhile abbot of the monastery of St. Peter's, Salzburg—a position which had more than once been combined with that of the bishop. The sources leave us in the lurch as to the duration of this kind of preliminary period of the saint's life. Some investigators think that he began the administration of the bishopric in 745. In that case he cannot have been

identical with either of the two other Virgils, who had
no episcopal position when the pope wrote his letter of
748. Others hold that he became abbot-bishop in 757
or 758—and still others place that event in 765. The
latter date seems to us the more probable one.[38] It
makes no difference, however, for our considerations,
whether the postponement of consecration lasted two
years or twenty. It is most unlikely that either of the
other Virgils should have waited that long. Both lacked
the virtue which no doubt prompted the saint to refuse
consecration, namely, humility. The Pseudo-Astronomer, in particular, was too eager to become bishop.
Both would rather have hastened the day of their consecration, to rise as soon as possible and as fully as
possible, to the episcopal dignity, and to make its possession more sure against attacks.[39]

This leads us to their moral character. All those
authors who advocate, or rather suppose, the identity
of the two with Virgil the Saint, do so because they
mean to bestow an honor upon the saint, by imagining
erroneously that thereby they make him a better theologian than St. Boniface, and a champion of science in
a dark age. They forget that they must take the transgressions of the other Virgils into the bargain. They
must be prepared to allow that their saint, as Virgil
the Baptizer, for several years refused canonical obedience to his superiors; and that as Virgil the Pseudo-
Astronomer he showed the greatest ignorance both in
theology and science; and that he obtained, or was at
least fully determined to obtain, his bishopric by curry-
ing the favor of a secular ruler, by opposing a papal
legate, and by falsely asserting to possess a papal

[38] See Appendix M.
[39] See Appendix O.

recommendation. It is evident, too, that the Pseudo-Astronomer completely lacked the necessary theological training, while the Baptizer rendered useless whatever knowledge he had by his continued obstinacy.

Of course, a man may change from sinner to saint. But this is not the rule in human affairs, especially not in persons that are past the formative period of their lives. In our case it is still less likely in view of the outspoken selfishness and the intriguing character of the two Virgils, who in so glaring a manner subordinated the welfare of the Church to their own personal interests, and brought upon themselves such severe reprimands from the head of Christianity. Had both men been faithful workers in the Lord's vineyard, satisfied with their station, and loyal to their superiors, the common name might suggest the query whether or not both or one of them was the Saint of Salzburg. And even then historians would notice the absence of positive proof. Seeing, however, the character of the two Virgils, the question whether one or each of them became a saintly bishop should indeed not be raised at all. Neither of them was on the way to sainthood. Nor were they fit subjects for the exalted office of bishop. In our own days certainly nobody would have the audacity to propose men like them for a vacant diocese in any part of the world.[40, 41]

40 Appendices N and P.
41 When the present elucubration had appeared in pamphlet form, one reviewer objected to the last sentence. In our days, he said, such men would indeed not come into consideration for a bishopric, but it was different in the Middle Ages, when princely favor often raised unworthy men to high ecclesiastical dignities. As a general statement this objection may pass, though it does not do away with any of the arguments adduced before. But in our specific case it meets another obstruction. The princes that might have any influence were either Duke Otilo or his successor Thassilo. Both were ecclesiastical-minded men (whatever their political aspirations). Otilo, be-

VI. CONCLUSION

As long as our sources remain what they are now—
and there is no prospect of their ever being supplanted
or supplemented by other reliable evidence—so long
neither of these Virgils can claim a niche in the hall of
fame. We remarked in its place that the documents do
not give us the slightest clue as to their nationality. As
a matter of fact, both are most commonly saddled
upon the Irish race. But such were not the graduates
turned out by the schools of the Isle of Saints and
Scholars. *If* these men were really born in Ireland, they
certainly never saw the inside of any of those Irish
institutions of learning and sanctity, which are the
cause of Ireland's undying glory. The less said of them
the better.

On the other hand St. Boniface, the Apostle of the
Germans, renowned for learning before he set out upon
his missionary journeys, and ever a lover of books and
an ardent student, cannot be accused of ignorance in
either sacred or secular science. We observe him as the
watchful shepherd of the flock entrusted to his care by
the successor of St. Peter. The dangers threatening the
welfare of his spiritual children did not escape his unerring eye, and his keen and well-trained mind discovered the dogmatic consequences of fantastic theories
that claimed to be science. He stands before us not
only as the indefatigable missionary but also as the
great papal legate to the peoples beyond the Alps,
invested by the Head of the Church with almost un-

sides, died in 748, the year in which this papal letter was written,
and could hardly have taken any step. And that Thassilo should
have gone against such a document as the papal legate received from
beyond the Alps is very improbable.

limited power and enjoying an unbounded confidence
—a power which he knew how to employ, and a confidence which he well deserved.

As to Virgil, the Bishop of Salzburg, this Irish Saint
(Fergil, Fearghil) was indeed a conspicuous figure in
his time.[42] He gave himself up whole-heartedly to the
duties of his exalted office. He kept his diocese in perfect order, and looked carefully after the welfare of
its religious institutions. He rebuilt the cathedral of
Salzburg, and transferred thereto the remains of St.
Ruprecht, a former bishop, and apostle of the region.
A flourishing school arose in connection with the cathedral. By sending out missionaries and directing their
work, he was able to extend his activity to the neighboring countries, and, though never leaving his diocese,
to become the Apostle of Carinthia. After his death
the learned Alcuin celebrated his praises in an elegant
poem. St. Virgil remained a favorite saint of the people of Salzburg and was widely venerated throughout
Germany.

St. Virgil cannot be identical with the two men of
the same name referred to by Pope St. Zachary; he
was never reported to Rome for doubtful teaching or
uncanonical behavior, and never was at variance with
either St. Boniface or the Sovereign Pontiff.

[42] St. Virgil should not be called archbishop. Salzburg became an
archbishopric in 798—that is, fifteen years after his death.

APPENDICES

Eundemque locum mundus habeat et infimum et medium.
This clause may seem difficult to understand—but the terms belong to the astronomical parlance of the time. The place of the earth is *infimus* (the lowest) and according to the limited knowledge of that age, all things fall towards it. The place of the earth is at the same time *medius* (central), because it is on all sides surrounded by the *convexa coeli* (the concavity of the heavens). St. Augustine here uses exactly the same phraseology which we find in Cicero's *De Re Publica* (17): *Nam ea quae est media et nona, tellus, neque movetur et infima est: Et in eam feruntur omnia motu suo pondera.* "The earth which is located in the center and the ninth (sphere in rank), does not rotate and is the lowest (point of the whole system); and all masses tend to it by reason of their gravity." It is therefore incorrect to translate St. Augustine's clause by "that it has as much room on the one side of it as it has on the other." (Marcus Dods, *The Works of Aurelius Augustinus.*) The point to be made is not that the "upper and lower" parts of the earth are of equal size, but that being affected in the same manner by the heavens around them, both must have the same qualities, and be equally fit to be inhabited. So far the advocates of the antipodian theory may be right. But they are decidedly wrong in jumping to the conclusion that the other side is also actually peopled, an assumption which needs new positive proofs.

The translation of *mundus* by "earth" should cause no surprise. According to good dictionaries, *mundus* was used in this meaning during and after the time of Augustus. (Heinichen, 1909.) But even the very context here demands this rendering. The sentence *Eundem locum mundus habeat et infimum et medium,* gives no sense if we substitute the translation "universe," because the universe can in no way hold a place

307

which is *infimus et medius*. The universe is the whole in regard to which other things may be said to hold such a position. Besides, a comparison with the sentence of Cicero as quoted in the preceding appendix, which St. Augustine evidently had in mind, confirms this—since *tellus* is never the universe. When referring to the universe a few lines before, the author employs the unmistakable phrase *concava coeli*. Furthermore, in the sentence to which this note refers, *mundus* cannot signify the universe. That the universe was round nobody in those days doubted or denied, while the sphericity of the earth was unknown to all but the educated. If St. Augustine had meant the universe, there would not have been any reason for granting that there are some grounds for asserting that it is spherical. Hence in this passage he evidently uses *terra* and *mundus* promiscuously in the same meaning. This is indeed the impression which his words make when read in the context of the whole paragraph.

APPENDIX C—PAGE 259

St. Augustine refused to accept the existence of antipodes because he demanded some *historica cognitio,* some positive proof. In our days we can say that we know the earth rather perfectly. Its whole surface lies charted before us. But how do matters actually stand according to our present knowledge? If we examine the globe, we find that with the exception of Spain, all Europe and Northern Africa, the land where St. Augustine lived and wrote, really have no antipodes. Diametrically opposite to them is the sea which extends in a southeastern direction from Australia.

APPENDIX D—PAGE 264

Anent Isidor's wavering attitude in this question, it may be well to remember a warning given by Dr. Bardenhewer in his *Patrology:* "Very little has hitherto been accomplished for the textual criticism of this much used and variously altered and corrupted work." (English edition by Bishop Shahan, p. 662.) May not perhaps just the passages referring to the point here under consideration have undergone alterations for which the author is not responsible?

APPENDIX E—PAGE 269

We should not make the mistake to believe that this preservation of a precious heirloom of better times was in any way due to contact with Arabian scientists. No Arabian literature which might have influenced the Christians existed in the eighth century. It was only during this century that the Mohammedans in the East slowly began to take to the works of the Greek philosophers and scientists which Syrian Christians translated for them; and not before the middle of the ninth century did the study of those works approach any extent and intensity. The Arabians adopted and ever retained the Ptolemaic system, though they enriched astronomy by new observations. Their intercommunications with Christian scholars, chiefly by way of Spain and Sicily, set in at a still later date.

Nor should we make it an indictment of the ages we have gone through that though retentive of the knowledge of former times, they were unproductive themselves. This whole period, filled almost entirely with the Migrations of Nations and their sad effects, was in no way fit for any new undertakings in the intellectual field. Besides, the imperiled interests of the Christian religion, partly also the extension of the Faith among barbarous nations, demanded whatever talents might otherwise have been available for the increase of science. We should rather give our unstinted admiration to those men, who while acting as the defenders of their Church, proved able, amid the confusion which surrounded them, to appreciate the importance of secular learning, and broadmindedly to sacrifice time and efforts to its perpetuation.

APPENDIX F—PAGE 270

The phrase, *Quod et a nobis esset absolutus unius defuncti* (scil. *episcopi*) *diocesim obtinere,* causes some difficulty. Pagi in his Notes to Baronius' *Annales Ecclesiastici* (*ad Annum* 746) thinks the word *absolutus* is the same as *dimissus* (dismissed)—namely, from Rome; and Pagi consequently presumes that Virgil had been in Rome. But this is impossible, because the pope speaks of him as a completely unknown personage, and does not even know whether or not Virgil is a priest. Külb, in *Sämmtliche Schriften des heiligen Bonifatius* (Vol. I, p. 234) understands it literally and translates, "that he was absolved by us," of course from some kind of censure. This, too, would rather suppose that Virgil had been in Rome, than that he should have been absolved through somebody else. We prefer to follow Dr. Lanigan's explanation, who says in his *Ecclesiastical History of Ireland* (Vol. III, p. 184, note 134) that it is a phrase not unfrequently used for, "to be empowered, authorized." "Thus we find *absolutio* used for power, liberty, license; and *absolutionem facere* for granting power, or faculties." Du Cange, *Glossarium Mediae et Infimae Latinitatis* (edition of 1840) quotes a passage where *absolutionem facere* evidently has this meaning. (Under *absolutionem facere*.) Several good manuscripts of the letter in fact have instead of, *quod et a nobis esset absolutus,* the words *quod et a nobis acciperet licentiam ut . . . diocesim obtineret.* (See Tangl.) Thus, the phrase would equal a strong papal recommendation for that episcopal see. It would not be an appointment, because this might still depend on others, above all the papal legate, and rightly or wrongly, the Duke of Bavaria. The purpose of Virgil's intrigue was evidently to eliminate the legate, and receive the bishopric from the duke with papal approbation granted over the head of St. Boniface.

This also implies that at the time of the writing of St. Boniface's report to the pope, this Virgil was certainly not Bishop of Salzburg, and moreover that the bishopric which he strove to obtain was still vacant, i. e., if the last incumbent had died three years before, in 745. (See on this point Appendices M and N.)

APPENDIX G—PAGE 280

But may not Virgil have thought of something like the inhabitants of Mars or some other planet? The idea that there should exist somewhere in the universe a race similar to us Adamites may be foolish and untenable scientifically—but is it necessarily heretical? However, such a theory, which has become possible only in consequence of an endless series of discoveries, was too strange to the minds of the eighth century. For them the earth was the center of the universe, cosmographically and theologically. It is therefore not surprising, if Virgil (to return to our document) fancies his "other world" in

close connection with the earth, since he says that it is below
the earth. Mars, or any other planet, is certainly not below
the earth. Evidently he does not conceive his "other world"
as a separate heavenly body, another planet, perhaps, entirely
independent of the earth. Finally that "other world" of his
had also another sun and moon. But Mars, or any other planet,
if he thought of one, has not another sun. And as to the moon,
the fact that eleven hundred years after his death several little
moons of Mars were discovered, could not influence Virgil in
the eighth century. We might as well presume him to have
communicated with his "other world and other men" by ra-
diography. As long as we hold to the information we can glean
from the letter of Pope St. Zachary, the theory of "Martians"
or other suchlike "men" offers no salvation for Virgil.

APPENDIX H—PAGE 283

Latin original of the letter of Pope St. Zachary to St.
Boniface concerning the repetition of baptism.

*Reverentissimo et sanctissimo fratri Bonifatio coepiscopo
Zacharias servus servorum Dei:*

*Virgilius et Sidonius religiosi viri apud Bajoariorum pro-
vinciam degentes suis apud nos literis usi sunt, per quas inti-
maverunt, quod tua reverenda fraternitas eis injungeret chris-
tianos denuo baptizare. Quod audientes nimis sumus conturbati
et in admirationem quandam incidimus, si habetur ut dictum
est. Retulerunt quippe, quod fuerit in eadem provincia sacerdos,
qui latinam linguam penitus ignorabat, et dum baptizaret,
nesciens Latini eloquii infringens linguam diceret: "Baptizo te
in nomine patria et filia et spiritus sancti." Ac per hoc tua
reverenda fraternitas consideravit rebaptizare. Sed, sanctissime
frater, si ille qui baptizavit, non errorem introducens aut here-
sim, sed pro sola ignorantia Romanae locutionis infringendo
linguam, ut supra fati sumus, baptizans dixisset, non possumus
consentire, ut denuo baptizentur; quia quod tua bene comper-
tum habet sancta fraternitas, quicumque baptizatus fuerit ab
hereticis in nomine patris et filii et spiritus sancti, nullo modo
rebaptizari debet, sed per sola manus impositione purgari de-
beatur. Nam, sanctissime frater, si ita est ut nobis relatum est,
non amplius a te illis predicetur hujusmodi, sed ut sancti patres
docent et predicant, tua sanctitas studeat conservare.*

Deus te incolumen custodiat, reverentissime frater.

Data Kalendis Julii, imperante domno pissimo augusto Constantino, a Deo coronato magno imperatore anno XXVI, post consulatum ejus anno IIII, indictione XIIII.

Tangl says in a note: The imperial year would be 745; the postconsulatum year 744; the indiction 746. He decides for the year suggested by the indiction. (See his note to this letter, and on page 18 to St. Gregory's letter of appointment.)

APPENDIX I—PAGES 270 AND 284

We called attention to the conditional form of the letter of St. Zachary, which indeed left no doubt that the Sovereign Pontiff was far from believing the charge of the "pious men." But does not the pope use the same form when speaking of Virgil the Pseudo-Astronomer? Does he not say, "As to his perverse and iniquitous doctrine . . . IF he is found to hold that there is below the earth. . . ?" (p. 270). This is true. But the whole tenor of the passage referring to the Pseudo-Astronomer clearly shows the Pope's conviction of the guilt of this Virgil. He had before him an official report of his legate, which was confirmed by the oral information of its bearer, Bishop Burchard. The matter was supposed to have been investigated. Hence there is no doubting, hesitating, or questioning any more. The Pope appears fully satisfied that the facts are as reported. But to act according to ecclesiastical usage the affair is to be laid before a Provincial Council, which will call for a new hearing of the case. After all Virgil may retract his error even at the last moment. The "pious men" on the contrary were in no official capacity. The matter was not supposed to have been investigated by any competent authority, and it was evident that St. Boniface was expected to say the last word himself.

APPENDIX J—PAGE 291

Juxta praedecessoris nostri bonae memoriae Gregorii papae et sanctorum cononum traditum tibi mandatum. It seems that the Gregory meant here is Gregory III. The reference to Gregory II given in the first section of this letter is more reverential, and there is not the question of some individual *mandatum,* but of a whole system of doctrine. The very word *mandatum* used in the passage here under consideration indicates that St. Zachary has in view the decision of Gregory III, which says: ". . . *Ut denuo baptizes in nomine Sanctae Trinitatis mandamus.*" (Tangl, p. 50.)

APPENDIX K—PAGES 270 AND 293

Latin original of the passages concerning Virgil the Pseudo-Astronomer (I), and Virgil the Baptizer with Sidonius (II) in Pope St. Zachary's long letter of A. D. 748.

(*I*) *Nam et hoc intimatum est a tua fraterna sanctitate, quod Virgilius ille—nescimus si dicatur presbyter—malignatur adversum te, pro eo quod confundebatur a te erroneum se esse a catholica doctrina, immissiones faciens Otiloni duci Bajubariorum, ut odium inter te et illum seminaret, aiens quod et a nobis esset absolutus unius defuncti ex quattuor illis episcopis, quos tua illic ordinavit fraternitas, diocesim obtinere. Quod nequaquam verum est, quia mentita est iniquitas sibi. De perversa autem et iniqua doctrina, quam contra Deum et animam suam locutus est, si clarificatum fuerit ita eum confiteri, quod alius mundus et alii homines sub terra sint, seu sol et luna, hunc habito concilio ab ecclesia pelle sacerdotii honore privatum. Adtamen et nos scribentes predicto duci evocatorias prenominato Virgilio mittimus litteras, ut nobis presentatus et subtili indagatione requisitus, si erroneus fuerit inventus, canonicis sanctionibus condempnetur. Qui enim seminant dolores, ipsi metunt eos. Sic enim scriptum est: Perversae cogitationes separant a Deo, probata autem virtus corripit insipientes.*

(*II*) *Pro Sidonio autem supradicto et Virgilio presbiteris, quod scripsit sanctitas tua agnovimus. Illis quidem, ut condecebat, comminando scripsimus; tuae qutem fraternitati plus credulitas quam illis admittetur. Si autem placuerit Deo, vita comite, sedi apostolicae eos missis apostolicis litteris, ut praelatum est evocabimus. Docuisti enim eos et non susceperunt. Et factum est in illis sicut scriptum est: Qui docet fatuum, quasi qui conglutinat testam; harenam et salem et massam ferri facilius est portare, quam hominem imprudentem et impium; quoniam qui minoratur corde, cogitat inania et vir imprudens et errans cogitat stulta. Non ergo ad iracundiam provocetur cor tuum, frater. Sed in patientia tua ubi tales reppereris, admone, obsecra, argue, increpa, ut convertantur ab errore ad*

*viam veritatis. Et si conversi fuerint, salvasti animam eorum;
si vero in duritia permanserint, mercedem ministerii tui non
perdes. Illos autem juxta apostoli vocem devita.*

APPENDIX L—PAGE 297

Although there can be no doubt as to the meaning of this
passage, its actual wording, or rather the form of the termi-
nations of its words, has been handed down differently. Thus
a part of the manuscripts has, *Per diversitate et declinatione
linguarum gentilitatis,* which in another class of manuscripts
is changed into *Pro diversitate,* etc., and in a third class, into
Per diversitatem et declinationem, etc. (See Tangle, page 73,
notes.)

APPENDIX M—PAGES 299 AND 302

Date of St. Virgil's accession to the episcopal see. There are
two reasons why I would prefer the year 765 as the date
when St. Virgil assumed the position of Abbot-Bishop of Salzburg. First—this date is expressly given in the *Conversio
Bajuariorum et Caranthianorum,* which is the chief if not the
only source for this part of St. Virgil's life. (It is reprinted in
the *Monumenta Germaniae Historica, Scriptores,* Vol. XI.)
Unfortunately this chief source is rather confused. The editor
of this part of the *Monumenta* thinks that those chapters are
much younger than the rest; that their original somehow perished, and the present text was compiled by ill-informed authors. But the year 765 is clearly stated. There is a contradiction between two items connected with this. It says that
St. Virgil was recommended by King Pepin to Duke Otilo.
Now Otilo died in 748, when Pepin was not king but only
mayor of the palace. On the other hand, in 765 Pepin was
indeed King of the Franks, but the Bavarian Duke of that
time was Thassilo. One of the two combinations must therefore be wrong. Since we have, however, one testimony for the
year 765, we may safely presume that the compiler mixed up
the names of the Dukes of Bavaria, and wrote Otilo when he
should have written Thassilo. So we may hold with a considerable degree of probability that St. Virgil became abbot-
bishop of Salzburg in 765. (See Appendix N.)

A second reason points in the same direction. It excludes the

year 757 or 758 assigned by some authors for that event. Of
course the names of the rulers, as amended before, will fit on
these dates also. But it is not likely that Virgil should have
postponed his consecration ten years. The institute of abbot-
bishops, that is, of abbots who were only priests but had permanent episcopal jurisdiction, while one of their monks, consecrated, of course, administered the sacraments of Confirmation
and Holy Orders, was indeed of frequent occurrence in the
Irish world, but was unheard of on the continent. To the
people it might seem very incongruous. The bishops might look
upon it as a lowering of the episcopal dignity. So we may
certainly presume that this period of St. Virgil's administration did not last long, that people and bishops would urge
the holy man to have himself consecrated. In fact, the *Conversio* says expressly that he finally did so on account of their
solicitations, *"populis petentibus et episcopis regionis."* It is
therefore more probable that St. Virgil remained only two
years without episcopal consecration; and that, as he was consecrated in 767, he took over the administration of the diocese
in 765. On the other hand, Mabillon in his *Analecta,* IV, 527
—decides for a pontificate of about forty years, basing this
statement upon a poetical work of the ninth century. (Quoted
from *Monumenta Germ. Hist., Scriptores,* Vol. XI, page 6.)
Yet a *Catalogue of the Bishops of Salzburg,* printed in *Scriptores,* Vol. XIII, page 353, gives Virgil 21 years, which
would bring his accession down to 763, more in harmony with
the text of the *Conversio* than any other. Pertz prizes this
catalogue very highly—because, though the manuscript does
not date farther back than the fourteenth century, this list
of bishops and archbishops is evidently compiled from excellent sources.

What reasons those have who assign 756 or any other year
in the fifties for St. Virgil's accession to the position of abbot-
bishop, I do not know. The matter is too far beyond the
scope of the present paper to be followed up any further.
Whatever the year in which the great Irish saint assumed the
duties of his office, the fact remains that he was a person
different from Virgil the Baptizer and from Virgil the Pseudo-
Astronomer. The writer would be happy if his remarks were
to suggest to somebody else the desirability of a more extensive

investigation, which, however, must be made according to Pope Leo XIII's direction, *adeundis rerum fontibus,* by going directly to the original documents. The study of modern writers will avail nothing.

A problem similar to that of the identity of the three Virgils is connected with the name of Sidonius. There were about this time a Bishop Sidonius of Passau and a Bishop Sidonius of Constance. Was either of them identical with the Sidonius who together with Virgil the Baptizer, reported St. Boniface to the Sovereign Pontiff?

APPENDIX N—PAGE 303

Friends have called my attention to the fact that the name of Virgil occurs very rarely in historical documents, and that consequently it is quite surprising that here we should have three persons of the name appearing at the same time in the little country of eighth century Bavaria. But if genuine and consistent investigations lead us to such a result, we shall have to put up with the fact. The identity of the name of three coexisting personages is no argument against their separate existence. If the sources show that there were here three Virgils instead of one, the number of men of this name occurring in historical documents is thereby increased by two, and that name has become a little less rare. The first to call attention to the triplicity of Virgils was Monsignor H. Mann, as stated above on p. 283.

APPENDIX O—PAGES 271 AND 302

There is another point not cleared up by the letter reprinted above. The Pope expressly states that one of the four Bavarian dioceses had become vacant by the death of its incumbent, but he does not say which. All the authors, whose works I have been able to consult, consider it a matter of course which it would be superfluous to doubt or to prove that this bishopric was Salzburg. In this supposition Bishop John, whom St. Boniface had appointed in 739, must have died before the year in which the letter was written, i.e., 748, or at least during the early part of that year.

In the present investigation the question of the succession

of the Salzburg bishops is a side issue, though it is likely to
throw light upon the question of the fictitious identity of Virgil
the Pseudo-Astronomer with St. Virgil of Salzburg. My own
view, as derived from the study of the documents at my disposal, is set forth in *Appendix M*. At that time I did not have
at hand the monumental edition of the great *Salzburg Ver-
brüderungsbuch* prepared by T. C. Karajan (Wien, 1852).
This *Confraternity Book* is a long list of persons recommended
to the prayers of the monks of the Abbey of St. Peter, Salzburg.
It was started about the year 780, and continued through about
five hundred years. It contains more than eight thousand
names. Dr. Karaja's edition, the first and most elaborate ever
issued, is valuable also on account of the copious notes with
which the editor prefaces the lists. (In G. F. Browne's *St.
Boniface of Crediton,* pp. 317 ff., there is a long description
and discussion of this and similar *Confraternity Books.*)

Dr. Karajan gives to Bishop John, the predecessor of St.
Virgilius, all the years from 739 to 764. After a vacancy of
one year he says the saint succeeded as Abbot-Bishop, and
was ordained in 767. Dr. Karajan refers to several ancient
documents and also to the *Germania Sacra* by M. Hansiz, S.J.,
a work of the eighteenth century. According to his view, therefore, Salzburg was not vacant in 748, and could not be referred to as vacant by Pope St. Zachary in that year. If this
view is correct, it will make the identity of Virgil the Pseudo-
Astronomer with the Irish Saint of Salzburg still more improbable. It will, moreover, remove the uncertainty as to
the incumbency of the Bishopric of Salzburg at the time of
the writing of the papal letter, and between that date and
the accession of St. Virgil to the bishopric in 765.

The bishopric vacant at that time was probably either Passau
or Freising. There are indications that the incumbents of
both of them died about 748. But neither the documents I
have at my disposal nor the notes of Dr. Karajan are sufficient
to warrant any definite statement.

APPENDIX P—PAGES 284 AND 303

The following list of modern works which identify either the
three Virgils or two of them, or express indefensible views
concerning these men or St. Boniface or the attitude of the

Popes towards the antipodian theory, is far from being complete. It goes without saying that if good writers have been mistaken in this one item, it will not disparage their otherwise well deserved reputation of reliability.

Encyclopedia Britannica, eleventh edition, under "Boniface," p. 206; and "Geography," p. 621.
HAUCK, *Kirchengeschichte Deutschlands* (Prot.) Vol. I, pp. 529-3.
HEFELE, *Conciliengeschichte.* German edition (1858), Vol. III, pp. 521 ff. French edition (1870), Vol. IV, pp. 462 ff.
Catholic Encyclopedia, under "Antipodes"; "Geography"; "Virgilius of Salzburg."
HERGENROETHER, *Kirchengeschichte,* Vol. II, p. 59, note.
D'ALTON, *History of Ireland,* Vol. I, p. 90.
McCAFFREY, *History of the Catholic Church,* pp. 56-59.
POHLE-PREUSS, *God the Author of Nature,* p. 136.
ZIMMER, *Die Romanischen Sprachen mit Einschluss des Keltischen,* p. 7.
MEYER, *Conversationslexicon,* under "Antipoden."
Kirchenlexicon, under "Virgil."
SMITH, *Dictionary of Christian Biography,* under "Virgilius of Salzburg."
BROWNE, G. F., *Boniface of Crediton and His Companions* (Prot.), pp. 104 ff.
CRABBO, H., *Bischof Virgil von Salzburg und Seine Kosmologischen Lehren.* An extensive article in *Mitteilungen des Instituts für Oesterreichische Geschichtsforschung,* Vol. XXIV (1903), pp. 1-28.

(All the modern lives of St. Boniface except that by Kurth-Day reproduce this error in one way or the other.)

We evidently have here one of the cases to which James Harvey Robinson refers in the introductory chapter of his *Readings in European History.* Even current statements, he says, which are making the rounds of historical literature, occasionally need revision. It may happen that when some truly great historian has made the mistake of misreading the sources the error is perpetuated, and commonly exaggerated with every further remove from the original documents. As an instance he mentions the assertion that about the year A. D. 1000 there reigned in Europe a terrible fear of the impending end of the world; whereas a close study of the sources of that time reveals the fact that there was no doomsday terror at all.

APPENDIX Q—PAGE 248

This paper on St. Boniface and St. Virgil appeared in pamphlet form as a publication of the Benedictine Foundation (St. Anselm's Priory), Washington, D. C. That pamphlet is out of print. It is made up of a number of articles and addresses, which, however, have been revised, differently arranged, and in some points augmented. Chapter II, *Early Knowledge of the Sphericity of the Earth,* was given at the Convention of the American Catholic Historical Association at New Haven, 1922, and printed in the *Catholic Historical Review,* New Series, Vol. III (1923-4), pp. 74 ff. Chapters III and V were delivered as one address at the convention of the same organization at Columbus, Ohio, in 1923, and printed in the *Catholic Historical Review,* Vol. IV (1924-5), pp. 187 ff. Chapter IV, also an address, appeared in the report of the Annual Convention of the Jesuit Educational Association of 1924.

INDEX

INDEX

Adamnan, Irish Saint, advocates
Roman Easter, 219-222
Aidan, St., and Irish missionaries
in Northumbria, 193-195
America, Ptolemy manuscripts in,
38
American Catholic Historical Association, aim of, 1
Anti-Catholic statements, correction of, 13
Antipodes, existence of, see same
references as for Sphericity of
the earth
Arabian science, not source of
our knowledge of the shape of
the earth, 309
Augsburg, religious peace of in
1555, 119; new struggle about
in 1566, 156-158; St. Pius V
and, 158
Augustine, St., Roman missionary to the Anglo-Saxons, 192
Baptism, errors about, at time of
St. Boniface, 288-295
Baronius, Cardinal, 159
Bede, Saint, the Venerable, Doctor of the Church, Historian,
185-209
Bede the Venerable, homeland
and early years, 185, 186; occupation, 186, 187; as historian,
197; his work De Tempore,
188; Bible studies, 189, 190;
his historical works, 190; his
Historia Ecclesiastica Gentis
Anglorum, see Church History
of the English Nation; other
historical writings, 200; "History of the Abbots," 201; "Letter to Bishop Egbert," 202; St.
Bede's service to the Church,
203-205; Bede compared with
other historians of Teutonic
nations, 206, 207; on the sphericity of the earth, 265, 266

Bellarmine, Cardinal, and the
Galileo Affair, 104-110.
Bellarmine, Cardinal, demands
proofs for heliocentric theory,
109, 110
Bohemia, activity of Jesuits in,
145, 146
Boniface, St., and St. Virgil, 242-
305
Boniface, St., homeland and first
years, 242-244; missionary life,
244-246; charges against him,
246, 247; plan of investigation,
247, 250; charge that he considered it a heresy to maintain
the existence of antipodes, 270-
282; the document relied on,
and discussion of it, 269-274;
character of information received by Pope St. Zachary,
274, 275; the teaching of St.
Boniface's adversary, 274-278;
knowledge of the facts by St.
Boniface and Pope St. Zachary,
278-280; charge against St.
Boniface needlessly to have ordered rebaptism, 282-299; the
document and discussion of it,
282-286; the Pope's decision, 286-
288; errors in Germany especially as to baptism, 288-295;
papal verdict on the accusers
of Boniface, 292-295; previous
papal utterances on baptisms
in Germany, 295-299
Books, desire for, in 15th century, 80; kinds of books desired
and printed, 80; book trade,
82
Britons, refuse to coöperate with
the Roman missionaries, 192,
193
Calixtus, Catacomb of, 23
Canisius, St. Peter, see Peter
Canisius

fluence of, 37; manuscripts of in America, 38
Reformation, Protestant, in Germany, 117-120
Research, importance of, 3-7
Ronan, champion of the Roman Easter, 233
Runes, 57
Santori, cardinal, in papal election, 93, 94
"Scoti," ancient meaning of, 211
Society of Jesus, and Germany, 119, 120
Sphericity of the earth, early knowledge of, 248-269; among Greeks, 249-250; among Romans, 250-254; among Christian authors, 254-269; Lactantius, 254-255; St. Hilary, 255; St. Ambrose, 256; St. Augustine (of Hippo), 256-259; (his "City of God," 257 ff.) Cassiodorus, 260, 261; St. Isidore, 261-264; St. Bede, 265, 266
Sussex, Earl of, commissioner of Elizabeth, executions by, 85-87
Thurston, Herbert, S.J., on adoption of Roman Easter, 230
Tongues, miracle of, on Pentecost Day, 16
Tonsure, Celtic, 228
Topcliffe, Richard, professional torturer under Elizabeth, 89, 90
Torture, use of, under Elizabeth, 89
Trent, Council of, Peter Canisius and, 130, 150-155; in danger of breaking up, 152, 153; de-

crees of taken to German princes by Peter Canisius, 154
Truchsess, Otto, Cardinal, friend of St. Peter Canisius, 130
Tudor Queens, The: A Comparison, 84-91
Turks, danger of, 147
Type, printing, diversity of, 75, 76
Vatican Library, treasures of, 33
Vienna, St. Peter Canisius at, 136-143
Viking Adventure, A Belated, 56-62
Virgil, St., Bishop of Salzburg, not identical with those who accused St. Boniface, 300-303; his character and activity, 305; date of his accession to Salzburg, 314-316
Virgil the Baptizer, his charge against St. Boniface to have needlessly ordered rebaptism, 282-299; not identical with St. Virgil the bishop, 300-303
Virgil the pseudo-astronomer, see under Boniface, charge, etc.; his character, 280; not identical with St. Virgil the bishop, 300-303
Whitby, The Meeting at, (664 A. D.) 232-240
Whitby, meeting at, 232-240; for what purpose summoned, 232-234; transactions, 235, 236; decision, 237; character of the meeting, 238-241
Wilfrid, St., champion of the Roman Easter, 233, 234, 236